Registration

of

Slaves *to* Work

in the

Great Dismal Swamp

Gates County
North Carolina
- 1847-1861 -

Compiled by:
Raymond Parker Fouts

Southern Historical Press, Inc.
Greenville, South Carolina

This volume was reproduced
from a personal copy located in
the Publishers private library

Please direct all correspondence and book orders to:
SOUTHERN HISTORICAL PRESS, Inc.
PO Box 1267
Greenville, SC   29602-1267

Originally Copyrighted 1995 by:
          Raymond Parker Fouts
Copyright Transferred 2023 to:
          Southern Historical Press, Inc.
ISBN #978-1-63914-247-7
Printed in the United States of America

The book in which these records are found is in the North Carolina State Archives, Stack File #C.R.041.928.1. Its initial purpose was to record the minutes of meetings of the Commissioners of the Town of Gatesville, beginning 11 June 1833. Those minutes fill pages one through five. The final meeting, on 30 June 1833, contains an order to the Clerk to "procure a suitable Book for the use of this Board and that he transcribe immediately to former proceedings of the Corporation." Pages six through eight are blank. This verbatim transcription was made from Microfilm Reel #C.041.90003, beginning with page nine.

The word "Slaves," in this title, is something of a misnomer. There are numerous free men and a number whose descriptions more closely fit those of Native-American than African-American ancestry. All are indexed under "WORKERS." Though these records were created in Gates County, North Carolina, the large majority of the workers, and their employers or owners, were residents of Nansemond County, Virginia. Their ages ranged from eight to 72 years. Physical descriptions include age, complexion, height, scars or other distinguishing marks, and, consistently through 14 April 1847, weight.

The Orapeake Canal and Turnpike Company was incorporated by act of the General Assembly of North Carolina, ratified 18 January 1847. These records begin 1 March 1847. Though this company is not mentioned by name in this registration book, it would appear that the workers most probably were hired for the purpose of cutting the Orapeake Canal from White Oak Spring Marsh, in Gates County, to the Dismal Swamp Canal in Camden County. The map on page 144 shows its location. Several members of this company employed workers registered herein.

It appears some pages were initially left blank, then used at later date, e.g. original page 283. Completely blank pages have been duly noted. Original page numbers were machine stamped. Page 366 was hand marked as "356." There were various formats used and they have been retained where practical. Surnames and single slave names are printed in bold capitals.

Each original page has been given an assigned number, printed in bold within parentheses, for indexing purposes. The original page number appears to the right of the assigned number. Registration numbers are underlined. Reissued registration numbers are not underlined, unless they appear so in the original. Ages and scars from various injuries are indexed. Free men are indexed with an asterisk by their given names. Age at registration is shown in brackets following each worker's name. Female given names and county officials are indexed under separate headings and under their surnames. Multiple occurrences of any one name on each original page are noted within parentheses.

Some pages appear rather faint and the numerous recorders present a significant challenge to the transcriber. Alternate spellings are provided within brackets, though the researcher is urged to consult the original record for confirmation.

Some look-alikes are: by=y; th=h; W=M; R=B; O=A; ST=H; o=e; a=o,u,r; r=n; i=e; stout=strat; JACK=JOSH. In the words "five" and "seven," the "v" and "e" are often blended into one stroke. "===" denotes words overwritten or crossed out and illegible. "Their" denotes a crossed-out word. "/which is/" denotes interlined words. "cole" emphasizes verbatim spelling. "ofhishands" indicates failure to lift the pen between words.

27 January 1995

CONTENTS

REGISTRATION OF SLAVES TO WORK

IN THE GREAT DISMAL SWAMP

GATES COUNTY, NORTH CAROLINA

1847-1861

Vol.: -   Years: 1847-1861   Pages: 9-374 [375]

(1) 9 State of No Carolina County Court Clerks office
                                 March 1/st/ 1847
                    1   EDMOND the property of Nathaniel BOOTH of · Nansemond
County Virginia hired the present year by Wm B WHITEHEAD of Suffolk and by him registered as one of his hands in the dismal swamp.
                         EDMOND appears to be about forty five years old, Black
good teeth, a little gray tolerable full beard with a scar on the Stomache, about 3
inches long and a scar on the out sid /of/ right Kne about and inch long ̄ and stands
without shoes, Five Feet eight & 1/2 inches high, and weghs one Hundred seventy Six
pounds

                    2   JACKSON the property of Javan R. FRANKLIN of Nansemond
County in the State of Virginia hired the present year by Wm BWHITEHEAD of Suffolk and
by him registered as one of his hands in the Dismal swamp. Reissued Jany 10/th/ 1849.
No. 30
                         JACKSON appears to bee about fifteen years old Black with
a small scar on the outer corner of the left eye and stands without shoes Four Feet
ten and a quarter inches high. [Margin:] 17 years old

3 No. 79.
Reissued 5/th/ Mach 1848   WESTWARD the property of Javan R FRANKLIN of Nansemond
County in the state of Virginia hired the present year, by Wm B WHITEHEAD of Suffolk
and by him registered as one of his hands in the Dismal Swamp, WESTWARD seems to be
about twenty two years old, with good teeth, Without beard and has a scar on the shin
bone of the left leg about six inches from the ancle stands badly, is Five feet Six
and a fourth inches high and weght [sic] one ̄Hundred, & forty eight pounds.
[Margin:] Reissued Jany 10 1849. No. 29

(2) 10 Reissued 8/th/ Mach 1848-82
4
                         DAVY the property of Daniel BRINKLEY Jr. of Nansemond
County Virginia hired the present year by Wm B WHITEHEAD of Suffolk as one of his
hands in the dismal swamp
                         DAVY seems to bee about twenty two years old with a sugar
loaf head remarkably sunken eyes no hair? good teeth with a vacancy between the upper
front teeth without without [sic] beared? s?ide mouth with a spot under the outer cor-

1

1 March 1847

(2) (Cont.)   ner of the left eye, stands wide upon his feet, and has a scar on the
shin bone of the the [sic] left leg and is five feet Six Inches high without shoes
[Margin:]   Reissued Jany 10 1849. No 38

5   JACK the property of Abram BRINKLY of Nansemond County in
the state of Virginia hred the present year by WmB. WHITEHEAD of Suffolk and by him
registered as one of his hands in the Dismal Swamp. JACK is thirty five years Old
Black with flat forehead without beard, with a circle of hair around the fore head
good front teeth bad jaw Teeth without scars of any kind, and ept? a fresh bruise upon
the Outside of the right foot. stands Five feet seven inches without shoes.

6   Reissued 8/th.. March 1848..80 WILLIS the property of Javan R FRANKLIN of Nansemond County Virginia and hired the present year by Wm. BWHITEHEAD of Suffolk and by
him registered as one of his hands in the dismal Swamp. WILLIS is about twenty five
years old light Complexion with a remarkable full fore head large flat nose large
nostrils, scattering beard good teeth and a small scar about the size of a fourpen? on
the inside of the left leg, about two inches above the ancle stands without shoes five
feet half inch, and weghs One hundred & twenty seven pounds.

(3) 11 Reissued 8/th/ March 1848-81.
7   Jack ANDERSON a free boy bound to Nathl BOOTH of nansemond County Vurginia and hired by Wm B WHITEHEAD the present year and by him
registered as one of his hands in the Dismal Swamp Jack ANDERSON is about Twelve
years old Bow legged Bow Backed aished? faced with a scar just at the edge of the
hair, with hair remarkable almost down to his eyes, and stands without shoes Four feet
five inches Reiss/d/ Jany 22/nd/ 1850 No. 31-15 yrs old [Margin:] Reissued Jan
10/th/? 1849? No 32

[No Reg. #.]   VIRGIL the property of admeral BRINKLEY and by him
registered as one of his hands in the dismal Swamp. VIRGIL is about 37 years Old
stick Black with large features large mouth and nose

8   Reissued M?arch 8t. 48. 94 PRENTIS the property of Jackson BRINKLY of Nansemond
County Vurginia and hired the present year by Will. B WHITEHEAD, of Suffolk and by him
registered as one of his hands in the dismal Swamp. PRENTICE is about thirty years
old, Black wide high forehead rather small nose and mouth tolerable broad draws his
mouth tiete? [tight?] when he smils and produces two uncomon wietes? [white?] rimbs at
the sides of his mouth a very small scratch on the forehead between the eyes a little
to the left side a scar on the ==== outside of the left knee and a Scar? on the inside
of the calf of the right leg stands without Shoes Five Feet Six and one fourth inches
and weighs one hundred and Sixty one pounds. Reissued January 10/th/ 1849. No. 26.
Reissued Jany 22nd 1850 No. 30-33 yrs. old.

(4) 12 Reissued 5/th/ March 1848-88.
9   ISAAC the property of Huldah KNIGHT of Nansemond County
virginia hired the present year by WmB WHITEHEAD of Suffolk and by him registered as
one of his hands in the Dismal Swamp. ISAAC is about Thirty years old of Dark brown
Complexion full forehead deep eyes a small Spot in the forehead a scar under the right
Corner of the mouth bad teeth and no toe on the nail [sic] on the left great Toe and
stands Five feet four inches without shoes and weighs one Hundred and fifty seven
pounds

10 Ressed? 5/th/ March 1848 /100/ NED the property of Wrispes =====LEY RABY senr, of
Nansemond County Virginia hired by Wm. B. WHITEHEAD of Suffolk and by him registered
by him as One of his hands in the Dismal Swamp. NED is about Fifty years Old dark

2

(4) (Cont.) brown complexion Sharp Features thin lips tolerably full beared with a faint Scar upon the forehead at the ege of the hair a small flesh mole between the left eye at the side of the nose tolerable teeth and a scar upon each shin bone stands five feet seven inches without Shoes and weight one Hundred and fifty five pounds. [Margin:] Reissued Jany 10/th/ 1849 No. 21

(5) 13 Reissued 8/th/ March 1848-85
11 JOHN the property of Benjamin RIDDICK of Nansemond County Vurginia hired the pesent year by Will B. WHITEHEAD and by him registered as one of his hands in the Dismal Swamp. JOHN is about Forty five years Old, wide forehead wide flat nose large mouth good teeth tolerably fool beard with a scare on the out Side of the right eye brow with several small black moles on the face two saw Cuts on the left wrightst and a large faint scar on the left wrist is Five feet four and a half inches high weight One Hundred & seventy Two pounds. Reissued January 10/th/ 1849. No. 24

12 Ressd 8/th/ Mach 48-87. SAWYER the property of James GOODMAN of Nansemond County Vurginia hired the pesent year by Will B WHITEHEAD of Suffolk and registered by him as one of his hands in the Dismal Swamp. SAWYER is about Thirty five years old of Dark brown Complexion, has a wild look full eyes, but thin beard around the mouth small mouth with a small scar in the Center of the forehead and a small scar in fronet of the right year and one on the back of the Cheek bone behind the left eye and a not [sic] on each nuckle bone of the Great toe and a large Scar on the right leg half way from the foot to the Knee stands five feet five & ahalf inch, and weghs one hundred and fifty five pounds [Margin:] Reissued January 10 1849. No. 20

13 Reissued 5/th/ Mach 1848 91 JACK the property of Ann BROWN of Nansemond County Vurginia hired the pesent year to Wm. B. WHITEHEAD and him [sic] registered as one of his hands in the Dismal Swamp, JACK is of a light brown Complexion about Fourty Five years old his runing [sic] down to a point in his forehead, small Thin beard a small scar on the forehead over the left eye a scar on the right & on the left leg, a small

(6) 14 scar on the back of the left hand stands Five feet aght [sic] inches high without shoes and weighs One Hundred and Fifty seven pounds.

14 Reissud 5/th/ Mach 1848 92 MOSES the property of Ann BROWN of Nansemond County Viginia & hired the present year by Will. B. WHITEHEAD /of Suffolk/ and by him registered as one of his hands in the Dismal Swamp, MOSES is of verry dark brown Complexion about Twenty seven years olld, bushy head high round forehead thin beard thick under lip a small scar across his nose a small scar on the upperjoint? of the forefiger of the right hand a bad forked Scarr on the leg or right shin bone six inches below the Knee stands five feeet six four and a half inches without Shoes & Weight One hundred and forty one pounds.

15 Reissud March 8/th/ 1848 96 WRIGHT The property of Tamer BROTHERS of Nansemond County Virginia hired the present year by Wm. B. WHITEHEAD of Suffolk and by him registered as one of his hands in the Dismal Swamp, WRIGHT is about twenty two years old Coal black Complexion with large years that stands well off from his head small eyes no beard except on the upper lip, good teeth with a considerable vacansy beetwen the four [sic] teeth both in the upper & under jaws a scar on the left side of the forehead under the hair three scars on the left wrist one just above the upper joint of the Thumb of the same hand scars on both the shoulder bones stands without Shoes Five feet ten & three fourth inches and Wgts one hunred & seventy five pounds.

16 Reissued 8/th/ March 1848 93. GEORGE the property of Josephus MEREDITH of Nansemond County Virginie hired for the present year by Will. B. WHITEHEAD of

3

(6) (Cont.) Reissued Jany. 10/th/ 1849 No. 22 [Written at the bottom of this page.]

(7) 15 Suffolk, and by him registered as one of his hands in the Dismal Swamp. GEORGE is Black about forty years Old heavy beard with a peak in his forehead as scar [sic] under the edge of the hair on the left side ofthe peak in the forehead good teeth, a scar runing across the upper joint of fore and seckond finger a scar on the left Knee and one on the right Knee and a Small scar on the low edge of the right brest. stands without shoes Five feu?t seven and a half inches and weghs one Hundred and Sixty five pounds

17 Reisseed 8/th/ March 1848 95. WILLIS the property of Edmond BROTHERS of Nansemond County Virginia hired the present year by Will BWHITEHEAD of Suffolk and by him registered as one of his hands in the Dismal Swamp, WILLIS about twenty two years Old of Dark brown complex [sic] Flat forehead sunk eyes A small scar on the left side of the forehead and a small Scar on the left side of the chin a scar on the left hand inside of the upper joint of thee little finger a large Scar running acrost the inside of the left foot two red scars on the inside of the right leg with a black scar between them each about the size of a five Cent pease [sic] stands without Shoes five feet Seven and a half inches and weight one hundred Fifty seven pounds and a half.

18 Reisd 8 March 48 106 CHARLES the property of James BRIN?KLY of Nansemond County Virginia hired the present year by Will B WHITEHEAD of Suffolk and by him registered as one of his hands in the Dismal swamp CHARLES is about Fifty years old a little gray Head thin upon the the [sic] top of the head left eye out a large scar across the left side of the forehead runing under the

(8) 16 hare A small scar between the eyes a scar upon the back of the left wrist and on the upper joint of the left thumb one on the upper joint of the left fore finger adeformg? scar on the right leg from the Kne down and sevral long? scars on the left leg an fresh ones and ajcent? left leg and several right breast and a small one on the right collar bone and badly marked upon the back

19 Reissued 8/th/ Mach 1848 97. JACK the property of Tamer BROTHERS of Nansemond County Virginia hired the present year /by/ WmBWHITEHEAD of Suffolk and registered as one of his hands emply/d/. in the Dismal Swamp. JACK is cold Black with small Eyes wide cheak bones tolerable good teeth a small scar upon the right cheek a scratch upon the the [sic] left cheek a scar between the little and Third finger of the right hand a small scar upon the upper joint of the thumb of the right hand just above the nuckle of the fore finger of the left hand and a scar on /the/ shin bone bone [sic] stands withot? Shoes Five feet Eight and a half inches high

20 Reissud 8 Mach 48 99 HENRY the property of Jethro FRANKLIN of Nansemond County Virginia hired the present year by Will. B. WHITEHEAD of Suffolk and by him registered as one of his hands in the Dismal Swamp. HENRY is Cold Black about Twenty five years old with asmall scar on the left Side of his forehead a scar under the left leg and one at the other corner of the same leg three small scars on the upper part of the right hand and a large scar on the inside of the leg stands without shoes Five feet six inches. [Margin:] Reissued Jany 26/th/ 1849 No 83 hired by W. S. RIDDICK

(9) 17 21 DICK the property of Abram BRINKLY of Nansemond County Vurginia hired the present year by Will. BWHITEHEAD of Suffolk and by him registered as one of his hands in the Dismal Swamp. DICK is about thirty years Old with sharp featers [sic] round head tolerable teeth rather a stupid look a scare on the right arme below the elbow on the Out side of the arm a small Scar just above the left Knee stands without shoees Five feet five inches and weighs one Hundred and thirty nine pounds

1 March 1847

(9) (Cont.) 22 WILLIS the property of Abram BRINKLEY of of Nansemond County Virginia hired the present year by Will B WHITEHEAD of suffolk and by him registertered [sic] as one of his hands in the Dismal Swamp, WILLIS is about Forty five years old dark brown complexion flat face tolerably large nose and mouth tolerable large, a large scar about Six inches long on the left shoulder runing under the arm and a large scare just between the left Kne on the inside, stands without shoes Five feet Six and a half inches high and weight One Hundred and thirty seven pounds

23 BURWELL The poperty of Samuel WILKINS of Nansemond County Virginia hrred [sic] the present year by Will B. WHITEHEAD of Suffolk and by him registered as one of his hands in the Dismal Swamp. BURWELL is a malatto about twenty two years old with streight hair and plump features has a number of pits on his face like the pitts? of the small Pox three of which are on his forehead a scar acrss the fore the [sic] forehead of the left hand [sic] with a sore on the shin of the right leg stands without shoes Five feet Eight and a half inches and weighs One hundred and fifty seven pounds.

(10) 18 24 WILLIS the poperty of Riddick JONES of Gates County N. C. hired the present year be? Will B WHITEHEAD of Suffolk and by him registered as one of his hands in the Dismal Swamp. WILLIS is Crow Black with - high forehead veery thin beard spare made - a small scar on the left side of the mouth and a scar upon each Shin bone stands 5 feet 7 1/2 Inches weight without Shoes 138 lbs. Reissud 10 Jany 1849 as the property of the heirs of R. JONES No. 31. [Margin:] p? X 14?

25 Reissued 17/th/ Aug. 1848 No 106 JIM a boy about 10 years old the prperty of Daniel BRINKLY of Nansemond County Virginii?a hired the present year by Will B. WHITEHEAD of Suffolk and by him registered as one of his hands in the Dismal Swamp JIM is Cold black has a scare on the left side of the neck, with a scare from a bruise upon the out side of his left leg

26 Reissued 8/th/ Mach 1848, 83 NED the property of Daniel BRINKLEY senr of Nansemond County Virginia hired by Will B. WHITEHEAD of Suffolk and by him registered as one of his hands in the Dismal Swamp. NED is about Fifty years old Dark Brown Complexion sharp Features thin lips, tolerable full beard with a faint scar about the forehead at the edge of the hair a small flesh mole between the left eye at the side of the nose tolerable teeth and ascar upon each shin bone Stands Five feet seven Inches without shoes and weght One hundred and fifty five pounds. [Margin:] Reissued 10 Jany: 1849 No 21

27 Reissud March 8/th/ 1848 98 WATSON the property of Jetho FRANKLIN of Nansemond County Vurginia hired the present year by Will BWHITEHEAD and by him registered as one of his hands in the Dismal Swamp. WATSON is about 50 years old Cole Black

(11) 19 flat face small eyes large nose and flat head a small scar on the left Temple a small scar on the left Side of the under lip stands with out shoes 5 feet 5 inches 155 1/2 lbs.

278 Reissud Mach 8/th/ 1848-90 STEPHEN the property of William S RIDDICK of Portsmouth Vurginia hired the present year by Will B WHITEHEAD of Suffolk and by him registered as one of his hands in the Dismal Swamp, STEPHEN is about Fifty years old Copper Collar flat featurs hair inclined to bee streight without scares on the face or hands Stands without shoes Five feet seven inches R I Jany 22 1850 53 yrs old No. 32 [Margin:] Reissued Jany 10/th/ 1849 as the property of the heirs of W S. RIDDICK No. 33

289 Reissud 8/th/ March 1848 84? SAM the property of Daniel BRINKLEY Snr. of Nan-

(11) (Cont.) semond county Virginia hired for the present year by Wm B WHITTHEAD of suff [sic] and by him registered as one of his hands in the Dismal Swamp. SAM is eighteen years old Cold Black with large flat features flat nose good teeth Has a spot under the left year and two Shot in the breast Stands without shoes Five feet two and a half inches and weght One Hundred and thirty two pounds.

30 Reissud Mach 48-86 LONG JACK the property of Benjamin RIDDICK of Nansemond county Virginia hired the present year by Will B WHITEHEAD and by him registered as one of his hands in the Dismal Swamp. JACK is about Sixty years old gray hare heay? gray beard good teeth and long features has a whillow on the thumb of the left hand which make it large and shrter that [sic] the other Stands without Shoes six feet four and a half inches and weght one hundred and eighty two pounds. Reissued Jany 10/th/ 1849. No 25. [Margin:] Reissued Jany 22/nd/ 1850 No 33-63 yrs. old as the prop. of E. W NORFLEET.

31 Reiss 8/th/ Mach 48-89 HENDERSON the property of Estate Mathew JOINER of south Hampton County

(12) 20 Virginia hired the present year by Will B. WHITEHEAD of Suffolk and by him registered as one of his hands in the Dismal Swamp. HENDERSON is about twenty seven years old of dark brown complex tolerable flat face tolerable rank? beard a little bow legged a snall scar on the left cheek a small scratch on the back of the left hand a scar across the right they about one and a half inches long a Black scare on the inside of the Ca?lf of the left leg Stands Five feet six and a half inches high and weght One Hundred and Seventy one pounds

32 SAM the property of Anny GRIFFIN of Nansemond Co?un?ty Vginia [sic] hired the present year by Wm.B. WHITEHEAD ofSuffo andby him rgisterd as one of his hands in the Dismal Swamp SAM is about 35yeas old light Brown complixon with lage features with flat broad nose broad mouth small beard, and that ony upon the upper lip a number of small pimples under each eye without scares of any Kind. Stands wthout shoes Five feet Nine inches and weghs One Hundred and fifty five pounds

(13) 21 33 LEWIS the property of Spencer GRIFFIN of Nansemond County Virginia hire the present year by WmBWHITEHEAD ofSuffolk by him rgisterd as one of his hands in the dismalSwamp
LEWIS is Crow black face a little inclined tobe one sided three? Scares just above the left eye near together and One of them on the same eye a little distance off a scare on the inside of the right Knee. Stands without shoes Five feet Six inches and a half and weighs One Hundred and fifty three pounds

34 JACOB the property of Henry GRIFFIN of Nansemond County Va hired the present year by Wm?. B WHITEHEAD of Suffolk and by him registered as one of his hands in the Dismal Swamp
JACOB is Black with small sharp features stiff right Knee with a bad scare on the inside of the Kne and the toe next to the great toe on the right foot off stands with out shoes Five feet six and a half inches high and weghs One Hundred and forty eight pounds.

(14) 22 State of No. Carolina} Clerks office County Court
Gates County} March 2nd 1847.
1 RUBIN the property of Edward RIDDICK Senr of Nansemond County Virginia and hired the present the present [sic] year by Jetho RIDDICK &Co of Nansemond Virginia and by them registered as one of their hands in the Dismal Swamp
RUBIN is about thirty years old dark brown Collor, large Features verry thick

(14) (Cont.) under lip, heavy beard, a scar just on the out side of the left Kne and a scar on the left arm just above the wrist stands without Shoes six feet and weght One Hundred and fifty nine and a half pound

2   JACOB the property of Hamellon L EPPS of Nansemond County Virginia hired the present year by Jethro RIDDICK &Co and by them registered as one of their hands in the Dismal Swamp.
    JACOB is a Cole black about twenty Five years old, high around forehead bad teeth a vacancy between the front teeth in the upper & lower jaw a scar on the right eye, a scar over the left eye a scar at the outside of the right eye, and one on the right side of the nose a scar on the right wrist stands without Shoes Five feet five inches and three quarters, and weght One Hundred and Sixty pounds

3   PAUL the property of Capt. Edward RIDDICK of Nansemond County Virginia hired the present year by Jetho RIDDICK &Co and by them registered as one of thir hands in the Dismal Swamp
    PAUL is about Forty five years old

(15)   23 light Brown complexion a scar on the right eye and one at the outer corner of the left eye, a large scar on the outside of the Kne and a swelling? of the left ancle stands wuthout shoes Five feet six inches and three quarters &? weght One Hundred and fifty Six pounds

4   JACOB the property of Capt. Edward RIDDICK of Nansemond County Virginia & hired the present year by Jethro RIDDICK &Co of Nansemond County and by them registered as one of their hands in the Dismal Swamp
    JACOB is remarkably black with full bushy? head verry large nose and thick lips a small scar on the right Collar bone, A large scar across the left foot and a scar on the right shin bone Stands without Shoes Five feet Six inches and thre quarters and weight One Hundred and fifty four pounds.

5   ISAAC the property of Will D. MC CLENNY of Suffolk and hired the present year by Jetho RIDDICK &Co and by them registered as one of their hands in the Dismal Swamp.
    ISAAC about Sixty years old dark brown Complexion gray beard Gray head a lump on the forehead tolerable teeth one on the upper jaw in front growing on the inside of the other and a little not on the right Collar bone stands without Shoes Five feet Six and a half inches & weght One hundred and seventy pounds.

6   SIMON the property of Archibald BRINKLY/s/. estate of Nansemond County Virginia hired the prsent year by Jethro RIDDICK &Co of nansemond and by them registered as one of their hands in the Dismal Swamp. SIMON is dark brown with larg_ [Fold in corner of page.]

(16)   24 Short features turkey head his hair on the left Side running down near to the eye brow and a scar under the left eye athe [sic] edge of the hair and a Scar on the left cheak a scar on the outside of the right leg and one on the rght [sic], stands without Shoes Five feet two inches & thro Quarters and weght One Hundred and fifty thre pounds and is twenty Three years Old.

7   SAM the property of Samuel BAKER of of Nansemond county Virginia & hired the present year by Jetho RIDDICK &Co of said County and by them registered as one of their hands in the Dismal Swamp. SAM is about Sixty five years Old Black, Gray hedded with full Gray beard good teeth both shin bones fire lict and without scars of any Kind stands without Shoes Five feet ten inches and a quarter and weght One hundred and

(16) (Cont.) seventy one pounds and a half.

<u>8</u> MILES the property of Andrew BRINKLY of Nansemond County Virginia and hired the present year by Jetho RIDDICK &Co. of said County and by them registered as one of their hands in the Dismal Swamp.

MILES is about Forty Years Old large face wild look slick? black narrow forehead without scars upon the face or breast and but little fire burnt upon the Shins, stands without Shoes Five feet seven and three quarter inches weght one hundred and eighty four pound

<u>9</u> ABRAM the property of H L EPPS of of Nansemond County Virginia hired the prsent year by Jethro RIDDICK ofSaid County

(17) 25 and by them registered as one of their hands in the Dismal Swamp. ABRAM is about Fifty years Old Dark brown conplexion rather full face that inclines to the right side a little gray a small scar on the forehead a scar on the rght side of the face immediately upon the under jaw Bone a Small Scar on the right wrist one on the same had [sic] just above the thumb and one runing across the left hand from the upper joint of the fore finger. Stands without shoes Five <u>Fet</u> seven and one fourth inches, and weght, One Hundred Sixty four pounds

<u>10</u> TOM the property of H. L. EPPS of Nansemond County Virginia and hired the present year by Jethro RIDDICK &Co of said County and by them registered as one of their hands in the Dismal swamp

TOM is about Fifty Seven years Old dark brown Complexion full broad <u>h</u>orehead large flat nose with? little gray one the head full beard gray very bad teeth three small black Spots on the upper lid of the right eye and one on the nose, a large Scar from a burn on the right hand and wrist. stands without Shoes <u>F</u>ve feet four inches and weight One Hundred and Sixty Eight pounds.

<u>11</u> BENJAMIN the property of James HAUTON decd. of Nansemond County Virginia and hired the present year by Jetho RIDDICK & Co. of said county and by him registered as one of his hands in the Dismal Swamp. BENJ is about Twenty years old dark brown complexion pointed face good tee<u>e</u>th, two small scars on the outside of the right eye. Stands Five feet Six and three quarter inches <u>h</u>ght and weght one Hundred fifty Six pounds.

(18) 26 <u>12</u> ISAAC the property of H. L EPPS of Nansemond County Virginia and hired the year by Jetho RIDDICK of said county and by them registered as one of their hands in the Dismal Swamp

ISAAC is about thirty years Old remarkably black red eyes large mouth with un-co<u>m</u>only thick under lip tolerable teeth unusueal large br<u>e</u>st particu<u>l</u>y the left one right shins long Scare?d stands without Shoes Five feet Eight inches and weight One Hundred and fifty nine pounds.

<u>13</u> BOB the property of Capt Edward RIDDICK of nansemond County Virgin<u>i</u>a and hired this year by Jetho RIDDICK &Co of said county and by them registered as one of their hands in the Dismal Swamp. BOB is Black rather a sharp nose plesing Counternance a whale near the Center of the brest and a snall scar on the left sid of the pit of the Stomache and ascar on the right side of the left leg just below the Kne and scar on the left Nee pan. stands without shoes Five feet Six & a half inches weght One hun?dred and fifty eght pounds.

<u>14</u> JIM the property of Nancy Ann GRIFFIN of Nansemond County Virginia and <u>hird</u> the present year by Jetho RIDDICK of said County and by them registered as one of their hands in the Dismal Swamp. JIM is thirty five years Old slick black round fore<u>hed</u>

(18) (Cont.) tolerable beard with a small scar over the left eye tolerable teeth a large dark scar under the right breast from a burn Stands without Shoes Five feet Six inches and weght One Hundred and forty eght pounds.

(19)   27   15 TONY the property of Jethro RIDDICK of Nansemond County Virginia and hired the present year by Jetho RIDDICK &Co, of said County by them registered as one of their hands in the Dismal Swamp TONY is about thirty years Old Black with a scar over? the right eye, a scar on the outer rim of the left year, and a deformity of the seckone? finger of the left hand stands without shoes Five feet six and a half inches and weight One hundred and thirty seven pounds and a half

16   NAT the property of Frak [sic] DUKES of Nansemond County Virginia and hired the year by Jetho RIDDICK &Co and by them registered as one of their hands in the Dismal Swamp.
     NAT is about Fifty years old. Black rather Sharp features suken eyes tolerable teeth with one of the front teeth in the under part out, a small scar on the inner Corner of the upper eye lid of the right eye a scar on the and [sic] ==== exetermity? of the left Knee Stands without shoes, Five feet Eight and a half inches and weght One Hundred and fifty pounds.

17   MOSES the property of Jethro RIDDICK of Nansemond County Virginia & hired the present year by Jethro RIDDICK &Co. and by them registered as one of his hands in the Dismal Swamp. MOSES is about seventy years old. Black with a scar on the right temple just below the poin? and one on the right side of the forehead a large scar on the out side of the left leg. stands with out shoes Five feet two inches and weght one Hundred & twenty two pounds.

(20)   28 18 BURWELL the property of Edward RIDDICK of Nansemond County Va. and the [sic] present year by Jethro RIDDICK &Co of said County and by them registered as one of their hands in the Dismal Swamp. BURWELL is about fiften years Old with full face flat nose thick lips no scar on the face a large scar runing acrost the shin bone and one up and down the same bone Stands without Shoes Five feet three and a half inches and weght One Hundred and ninteen pounds

19   LEVIS the property [sic] Edward RIDDICK of Nansemond County Virginia and hired the present year by Jetho RIDDICK &Co of said county and by him registerd as == One of their hands in the Dismal Swamp
     LEVIS is about thirteen years old & Stands wihout Shoes Four feet ten & 1/2 inches

[No Reg. #.] WILLIS the property of ==== ====== Capt RIDDICK estate of Nansemond County Virginia and hird the present year by Jethro H? RIDDICK ==== &Co and by him registered as one of his hands in the Dismal Swamp. WILLIS about Ten years old full eyes prodgius? mouth thick lips a small Scar on the left Shin, and stands Four? Five feet four Inches without Shoes

20? [partially obscured] ISAAC the property of the estat of Miles GRIFFIN of Nansemond County Va and hired the present year by Jethro RIDDICK &Co and by them registered as one of their hands in the Dismal Swamp. ISAAC is about Sixteen years old Black with full bluff face several small Specks of scars on the hands and stands without Shoes Five feet thre and a half inches and weght One Hundred twy? Six pounds.

(21) 29 [No Reg. #.] ISAAC the property of Jethro RIDDICK of Nansemond County Virginia and hired this present year by Jehro RIDDICK &Co of said County and by them registered as one of their hands in the Dismal Swamp.
     ISAAC is about fifteen years old of anuncomoon [sic] full face with ascar over

(21) (Cont.) the the [sic] left eye a scare on the out side of the left wrist and one on the inside left Kne and boot? shins all full of fire? Lick? has uncomonly thick lips stands without shoes Five feet two and a half inches Has a scar on the rght side of the head [Margin:] Reissued-See May 7/th/ 1849.

[No Reg. #.] WILLIS the property of John SAVAGE estate of Nansemond County Va and hired this year by Jetho RIDDICK &Co of said County and by them registered as one of thir hands in the Dismal Swamp. WILLIS about Tin years old full eyes prominents? mouth thin lips a small scar on the left cheek and stands Four feet four inches without Shoes

[No Reg. #.] DAVID the proper. of James ROGERS of Nansemond Virginia and by him as one of their hands [sic] in the Dismal Swamp DAVID is about seventy years Old flat forehed hair but little gray tolerable beard and mot. gray no scares on the face a scare on that out Side of the rght leg, stops a little his gat? stands without shoes Five? feet six and thre quarter inches and weight One Hudred and Sixty eght pounds.

[No Reg. #.] SAM the property of Janes ROGERS of Nansemond County Virginia and by registred [sic] as one of his hands in the Dismal Swamp SAM is about Forty five Black with flat head large prgecting forehead deep eyes small

(22) 30 beard with holes in his years renarkably Small with a scar on the outside of the right arm and a scar on the upper part of the calf of right leg. Stands without shoes Five feet three inches and weight one Hundred and thiry? five pounds.

State of No Carolina County Clerks office
Gates County March 2nd 1847.
1 SAM the property of the Estate of John R. KNGHT? of Nansemond County virginia and hired this year by Willis S. RIDDICK of said county and by him registered as one of his hands in the Dismal Swamp SAM is about tweny thre years old dark brown complexion full face with a scar on the forehead and cut on the end of the nose in the left nostril a black spot on the inside of the left leg Stands Five feet five inches and wegt One Hundred and Sixty nine pounds.

2 JERRY the property of the estate of John R. KNGHT of Nansemond County Virgini and hired the present year by Will. S. RIDDICK of said county and by him registered as one of his hands in the Dismal Swamp.
    JERRY is about twenty years old verry black full face has a scar in the forehead and on the left year a scar from a cut bow legged a scare upon the out side of the left leg Stands without shoes Five feet five inches and weight One hundred and Sixty pounds

3 HARRISON the property of John R KNIGHTs estate of Nansemond County Virginia and hired the present year by

(23) 31 Willis S RIDDICK of said County and by him registered as one of his hands in the Dismal Swamp HENDERSON [sic] is abought eighteen years old dark brown complexion flat made nose ascar on the Outside of the left wrist and a scar on the pan of the left Knee and one on the wright Knee stands without shoes five feet four inches and weigts One Hundred and six teen pounds

4 of Mills RIDD JACK the property of the estat Mills RIDDICH of Suffolk Va and hired the present year by Willis S RIDDICK of Nansemond County va and by him registered as one of his hands in the Dismal Swamp. JACK is about forty five years old dark brown color with high forehead projecting eye brow tolerabl beard a little gray a sar [sic]

2 March 1847

(23) (Cont.) on the head near the top under the hair asmall scar on the back of the left hand and a scar at the hand of the same one [sic] the inside a scar on the left Knee stands without Shoes Five feet six and a quarter inches and weght One hundred and thirty eght pounds.

5   HENRY the property of Daniel BRINKLY of the County of Nansemond in the State of Va and hired the present year by Willis S. RIDDICH of said county and by him regis-tered as one of his hands in the Dismal Swamp HENRY is about sixteen years old dark brown complexion Sharp forehead with scar on it from burn just at the edge remarkably small eyes has a scar on the right Kne stands without shoes Five feet five inches and weight One Hundred and seventeen pounds

(24) 32 6 DANIEL the property of Burwell RIDDICK of Nansemond County Virginia and hired the present year by Willis S RIDDICK ofsaid county and by him registered as one of his hands in the Dismal Swamp. DANIEL is about years [sic] old Brown Complexion Gray hare thin beard very bad teeth, without scars upon the face a dark spot or scratch just above the collar bone of the right side and a Small scar lower down of the breast on the same side A large scar just below the Knee on the left leg stands with out Shoes Five feet six and thre quarter inches and weght one hundred & forty Six 1/2 pounds.

7   MOSES the property of the Estate of Marmauke JONES of Nansemond Co Va. and hired this year by Willis S RIDDICH of sad County and by him registered as one of his hands in the Dismal Swamp. MOSES is about Sixty years Old dark brown Collor high retreeting from? head no teeth in the upper jaw in front a scar on the right side of the right e=lbow a scar on the left wrist both shins badly skined and stands without Shoes Five feet thre and 3/4 inches weight One hundred and thirty four pounds he is quite gray.

8   JIM the property of Albert SMITH of Nansemond county Virginia and hired the pesent year by Willis S RIDDICK of said County and by him registered as one of his hands in the Dismal Swamp. JIM is about Sixty years old brown complexion bad teeth a scar on the right eye and one at the outer _ims? of the eye a scar on the back of ithe rgh hand a scar on the outside of the rght leg and booth legs badly fire burnt.

(25) 33 Teeth more? and vacancy between the upper ones in front Stands without Shoes Five feet six inches and a quarter and weight one Hundred and fifty four pounds

9   ENOCH the property of Burwill RIDDICK of Nansemond County Virginia and hired the present year by Willis S RIDDICK of said county and by him registered as one of his hands in the Dismal swamp. ENOCH is about Forty years Old Brown Collor high forehead a large nose thin lips, only tolerable teeth a small scar on the chin a small scar on the left arm a scar under the left Kne stands without Shoes Five feet four and a half inches and stands without Shoes [sic] one Hundred and twenty five pounds

10   ISAAC the property of Mills RIDDICK decd. of Suffolk Virginia and hired the present year by Willis S RIDDICK of said County Nansem Va and by him Registered as one of his hands in the Dismal Swamp. ISAAC is about Ten years old without scars of any Kind Sh ws [sic] his teeth a little when when [sic] his mouth is shut is Four feet one inch high shoes off

[No Reg. #.] STEPHEN the property of Archibald BRINKLY of Nansemond County Va hired this year by Willis S RIDDICK of said county and by him registered as one of his hands in the Dismal swamp STEPHEN is dark brown about twelve years old high round forehead with a scar on the left side of the forehead and two scars on the right Kne Stands without his shoes Four Feet 3 1/4 inches

(26) 34 State of No Carolina} County Court Clerks office
                  Ga<u>ts</u> County }   March 5/th/ 1847.

<u>1</u> MOSES the property of WmB WHITEHEAD of Suffo Va and by him registered as one of his hands in the Dismal Swamp

MOSES has a scar on the left eye brow is of dark brown Complexion, about Forty years Old has a scar on the right arm, tolerable teeth, his great toe of the right foot has only one bone in the kncle [sic] and is shorter than the other toes and his left leg shorter than the other Stands without shoes Five feet five inches and weght One Hundred and fifty pounds.

<u>2</u> TOM the property of WmB. WHITEH<u>ED</u> and by him registered as one of his hands in the Dismal Swamp

TOM is about Forty years Old of Crow black Complexion plesent counternantce full beard with a large scar from a burn on the right side of the face a large scar from a cut on the inside of the left hand and two deform<u>it</u>ed f<u>ig</u>ers on the same hand stands Five feet Eight and a half inches and weight One Hundred and sixty seven? pounds

<u>3</u> ROLLEY the property of Will B. WHITEHEAD of Suffolk Va and by him registered as one of his hands in the Dismal Swa<u>n</u>p.

ROL<u>LY</u> is about Forty Five years Old, dark brown complexion full face, without teeth on the under Jaw & cept [sic] two Right fingers with a scar on left temple just at the ege of the hair, two scars near together on the right arm, and a scar on the out side of the left leg Stands without Shoes Five Fet Six and a half inches and weght One Hundred & fifty four pounds

(27) 35 <u>4</u> HARDY the property of Wm B WHITEHEAD of Suffolk and by him registered as one of his hands in the Dismal Swamp HARDY is coal black Forty five years Old with beard on the chin only with a scar on on [sic] right side of the nose a scar between the eye brows a scar on the outer angle of the left eye and a scar on the outer rim of the left ear a scar on the the the [sic] brest a scar on the back of the left hand & is unable to Shut the left hand stands without Shoes Five feet Six inches and a quarter and weght One Hundred and thirty seven pounds.

<u>5</u> WATKIN the property of Wm B WHITEHEAD of Suffolk Va. and by him registered as one of his hands in the Dismal Swamp WATKIN is crow Black about thirty years Old with Small features high forehead a remarkably small nose a small scar on the outside of the left elbow a scar on the left heel stands without Shoes Five feet Six inches and weight one Hundred and fifty four pounds.

<u>6</u> JIM the property of William B WHITEHEAD of Suffolk and by him registered as one his hands in the Dismal swamp.

JIM is about forty two years Old of brown complexion full face flat wide nose with se<u>a</u>ral small Scars on the outside of left eye a scar on left Jaw bone three s<u>n</u>all scars on the left arm a scar on the tip of the left foot. Stands Five feet Six and 1/4 inches without Shoes and weight One Hun- [sic] and seventy five pounds.

<u>7</u> ALBERT the property of WmB. WHITEHEAD of Suffolk & by him registered as one of his hands in the dismal swamp

ALBERT is crow Black with pointed? features large nostr<u>u</u>ls rather small eyes a s<u>n</u>all scar on the

(28) 36 right eye brow, a very small eye a small Scar on the right eye brow a very small eye a small Scar on the right eye brow [sic] a very small scar on the breast a small scar on the left arm, the mi<u>d</u>le finger on the left hand shought and a scar on the inside of the third finger. stands without Shoes Five feet three inches & thr<u>e</u>

(28) (Cont.) quarter and weight One Hundred and thirty five pounds-is aboutthirty years old.

<u>8</u>   CORNELIUS the property of Will BWHITEHEAD of Suffolk and by him registered as one of his hands in the Dismal Swamp. CORNELIUS is about Fifteen years Old, light complexion, a scar upon the nose with the left eye mark [sic] thick full lips two scar upon the back of the left hand a scar on the right leg onethe [sic] out side Stands without Shoes Four feet nine and a half inches and weight Eighty two pounds

<u>9</u>   ADMERAL the property of William B WHITEHEAD of Suffolk and by him registered as one of his hands in the dismal Swamp.   ADMERAL is about Thirteen years Old rusty Black Snall eyes pouted? lips shoes his teeth a little when his mouth is shut a scar on the inside of the right Knee and a scar on the left instep Stands without Shoes Four feet Eight and a quarter inches and weight Eight [sic] two pounds

<u>10</u>   Reissd March 8 1848 101 Henry REID a free boy of Collor son of Julia REID and hired the present year by Will B. WHITEHEAD of Suffolk and by him registered as one of his hands in th Dismal Swamp. Henry is of Copper Collor full face prominet eyes thick lips a large scar upon right Shin bone and one upon the left
Reissued Janry: 10/th/ 1849 No. 36

(29) 37 shin bone stands without shoes Five feet one inch fifteen years Old & weght one Hundred pounds

<u>11</u>   Reissd 8 March 1848 112 Mills a free boy of the Son of Julia REID hired the present year by Wm B WHITEHEAD and by him registered as one of his hands in the Dismal Swamp
    Mills REID has a small Scar on the back of his right hand near the wrist, and another on the front of the right leg, is of brown conplexion about Seventeen year of age, has good teeth Stands without shoes four feet five? inches & a half and weight One hundred and twenty two pounds. [Margin:] Reissued Jany 10 1849. No. 37

<u>12</u>   OSBORNE the property of William B WHITEHEAD of Suffolk Va and by him registered as one of his hands in the Dismal swamp. ORSBORN [sic] has a small Scar on the left cheeck, a Scar in the front of the right leg a scar on the left Kne?, & one also in the plenen?, about Twenty eght years old has god teeth stands without shoes, five feet three Inches &3 fourths high & weight one Hundred &fifty pounds.

[No Reg. #.]   NELSON the property of Wm B WHITEHEAD of Suffolk Va, and by him registered as one of his boys in the Dismall Swamp.
    NELSON has a small scar over thee right lege, also a small scar on the breast, a burn on the right leg and a scar on the bon [sic] of the left leg is of a copper Colour about 14 year of age has god teeth with thick lips stands without Shoes 4 feet 9 inches & weghs 90 lbs.

(30) 38 State of No Carolina, County Court Clerks office
                    Gates County March 20/th/ 1847.
[No Reg. #.] DAVID the property of Elizabeth GRAMBERY of Perquimons County No Carolina, hired the present year by Ro R? HILL of Gates County and by him registered as one of [sic] hands enployed in the Dismal swamp.
    DAVID is about seventy years old With remarkable broad high forehead. Gray beard and Gray head, a broad pinted nose, little finger of the right hand crooked from having been fish poisoned a scar across the breast Stands without Shoes Five feet four inches and weight One Hundred & sixty Two 1/2 pounds [Margin:] Reisd RRHILLs property 19/th/ March 48 No 111

(30) (Cont.) [No Reg. #.] Reissud 19 March 1848 110
   DEMPSEY the property of the estate of Jesse WIGGINS of Gates County, and hired the
present year by Ro. R. HILL of Gates County and by him registered as one of his hands
employed in the dismal swamp.
   DEMPSEY is about Sixty year old dark brown conplexion, high forehead with a potion
of hair runing down the middle, but little Gray, tolerable Teeth a small scar on the
left hand and some stiffness in the middle finger of the same hand ruptured and wears
a true?ss a scar across the instep of the left foot and a small piecen? of the great
toe on the same foot off. stands without shoes Five feet Four Inches and weight One
Hundred & Sixty one pounds.

(31) 39 [No Reg. #.] Reissud 19/h/ March 1848 No 109
   DRED the property of Charles BARNS of Gates County No Carolina hired the present
year by Ro R. HILL and by him registered as one of his hands employed in the Dismal
Swamp.
   DREAD is about Fifty years Old light Copper collor streight hair small beard,
sharp nose, thin v?issaged a scar on the left under jaw a scar on the left thunb a
scar on the inside of the right arm about two and a half inches from the hand and
several bae?d scars on the right leg: Stands without shoes Five feet nine inches and a
half has very bad teeth and weight one Hundred and fifty Nine pounds.

[No Reg. #.] Reissud 19 March 1848 J R HUNTERs property No 108
   GRANVILLE the property of Mrs Mary GOODMAN of the County of Gates hired the presnt
year by Ro R HILL of said county and by him registered as one of his hands in the Dismal Swamp.
   GRANVILL [sic] is about thirty six years old renarkably Black, high Square
forehead almost without beard flat nose wide mouth, the left leg is much larger than
the right, linps a little in his gait. Stands without Shoes Five feet Eight and a
half inches and weght One hundred and sixty three pounds

(32) 40 [No Reg. #.] ISAAC the property of Mary GOODMAN of Gates County and hired
the present year by Ro R HILL and by him registered as one of his hands in the Dismal
swamp.
   ISAAC is about thirty three years Old, black with high sharp forehead wide nose, a
Scar on the forehead, a scar on the left cheek verry bad teeth a scar on the left
breast about two inches a [sic] half long. Stands without Shoes Five feet Six 1/2
inches high and weight One Hundred and sixty four 1/2 pounds.

[No Reg. #.] RUBIN the property of the estate of Jesse WIGGINS decd. of Gates County
and hired the present year by Ro R HILL and by him registered as one of his hands in
the Dismal Swamp.
   RUBIN is about twenty Five years Old dark brown Complexion, small eyes, small
beard, a scar on the left wrist a small scar on the middle finger of the right hand
and a slick scar on the inside of the left Shin and Stands without shoes Five feet six
inches and wieght One hundred & sixty nine pounds and a half.

(33) 41 State of North Carolina County Court Clerks off
                  Gates County April 3/rd/ 1847.
[No Reg. #.] JACK the property of Albert BRINKLY of the County of Nansemond Virginia
hired the present year by Wm B. WHITEHEAD of Suffolk and by him registered as one of
his hands employed in the Dismal Swamp
   JACK is about twenty years old verry black, right wide nostrils, thick lips, good
teeth without beard, a small scar on the left breast a verry small white Scar on the
right thumb, and a small scar on the right shin bone, weight One Hundred and thirty
two pounds and stands without shoes Five feett seven and a half inches

3 April 1847

(33) (Cont.) [Remainder of this page is blank.]

(34) 42 State of No Carolina County Court Clerks office
Gates County April 14/th/ 1847.

1 Owin HOPPER the property of James S SEGUINE of Deep Creek Norfolk County in the state of Virginia and employed by him as one of his hands in the Dismal Swamp.
   Owin HOPPER is about Forty two years old Copper Complexion sharp features, Small eyes bad teeth, having lost a number of Jaw Teee?th one tooth in front and has the appearance of having lost more, high forehead – a little Gray tolerable full beard, a small Scar on the Right breast, a large Scar on the upper part of the right fore arm from a burn; and a scar on the midle finger of the same hand, a scar across the top of the left foot Stands without shoes Five fo?et seven & a half Inches & weight One hundred & sixty Two pounds.

2 George GRIMES the property of James S SEGUINE of Deep Creek in Nofolk County Va and by him registered as one of his hands in the Dismal Swamp
   George is about Fifty years old, dark brown Complexion flat Rinkled Face short teeth full beard quite gray, full eyes, the fore finger of the left hand a little stiff a large deep scar upon the left leg just above the Knee and two large flat scars on the right leg on the Out side, the first joint of the litte toee of [sic] on the left foot. stands without shoes Five Feet Eight & 1/2 inches Weight one Hundred & sixty /70-/ pounds

(35) 43 3 Jo [sic] WEBB the property of James S SEGUINE of DeepCreek Nofolk County Virginia and by him registered as one of his hands employed in the Dismal Swamp.
   Joe is about thirty seven years old, light brown complexion sharp features, with high forehead, wide nostrils bad teeth tolerable bard, a small scar on the breast a Scar on the left hand betwen the thumb and fore finger a scar on the out side of the right Knee and a bad scar across the top of the right foot and and [sic] on the instep of the left foot stands without shoes Five feet Seven and a half inches weght One Hundred and Sixty five pounds.

4 Robert WILLIAMS the poperty of Francis WILLIAMS estate of Minno Creek Nofolk County Virginia and hired the present yearby James S SEGUINE of Deep Creek in said county and state and by him registered as one of his hands in the Dismal Swamp.
   Robert is about Thirty Two years Old. Black Complexion dished Face with a large Yellow splotch on the right side of his face has the first joint of the forefinger of the the [sic] left hand stiff-and a desperate scar on thee left Kene [sic] from a burn stands without shoes /5 feet one?/ one Hundred & fifty six Pounds weght.

(36) 44 5 Isaac SAUNDERS the prperty of James SAUNDERS of Norfolk Virginia and hired the present year by ==James S SEGUINE of Deep Creek Norfolk County Va and by him registered as one of his hands in the Dismal Swamp.
   Isaac is about Fifteen years Old, mulatto full lips and eyes with pleasant counternance, rather streght hair, without scars on the face, has red scars on the right Knee pan and one on thee left Knee just above the joint in front stands without shoes Five Feet Six inches and weght One Hundred thirty one pounds

[No Reg. #.] Isaac BROWN the prperty of George BROWN of Deep Creek Norfolk County Va and ==== hired the present year by James S SEGUINE of the aforesaid place in Virginia and by him registered as one of his hands in the Dismal Swamp.
   Isaac is about Forty years old, dark brown complexion sharp Features, pinted nose large nostrils rather wild look Good teeth large beard, two scars on the right breast one about the sise of ten cents piece the other not half so large a small scar on the inside of the left arm two verry small scars on the back of the lef hand and a scar on

15

(36) (Cont.) the right fore arm a scar on the shin bone of left lee?g & a small scar on the rigt sid [sic] of the left Knee Stands without Shoes Five feet nine inches & weight One Hunderd and sixty Five Pounds.

(37) 45 State of North Carolina County Court Clerks office
                    Gates County. May 1/st/ 1847.
[No Reg. #.] FOSTER the property of the Estate of Col Josiah RIDDICK decd late of Nansemond County Virginia & hired by WmB WHITEHEAD of Suffolk Va and by him registered as one of his hands imployed in the Dismal swamp.

   FOSTER is about twenty three years of age of a copper complexion hair inclined to be straight, has bad teeth having lost two teeth in front, has the appearance of being cross eyed with a down look has two scars on the outside of the right leg one about the sise of ten cent peace, two scars on the front of the left leg and one on the inside of the foot on the same side from a burn Stands without shoes Five feet Eight & 3/4 inches

[No Reg. #.] Jacob YOUNG a free man of Color of Nansemond County Virginia hired by Wm B WHITEHEAD as one of his hands in the Dismal Swamp.

   Jacob YOUNG is of a dark brown complexion about Sixty Six years old, streght hair quite Gray small beard a scar on the right Side of the neck, the seckond finger on the right hand Crooked, the great toe on the right foot larger than the one on the other foot with a scar a cross the top of it, a scar on the inside of the ancle, & two Scars on the top ofthe same foot. stands without Shoes Five Foot six & aquarter inches.

(38) 46 State of North Carolina County Court Of___?
                    Gates County May 3rd 1847.
1 BOB th [sic] property of Owen R FLYNN of Suffolk Va and by him registered as one of his hands enployed in the Dismal Swamp.

   BOB is about Forty years old, verry black verry hairy? head, a Scar scar [sic] near the Center of the forehead and one on the inner angle of each eye brow one on the == right cheek bone & a large not on the ancle of the right leg. Stands withoutShoes Five feet 9 inches & 1/2

2 _AVY [damaged] the property of Owen R FLYNN of Suffo. Va and by him registered as one of his hands employed in the Dismal Swamp

   DAVY is of a Dark brown complexion snall features. has? long lips a Scar on the forehead a little to the right of the Center, remarkable furrows rings from the nose the face to the outer angles of the mouth, with eyes inclind to be closed? ther? forefinger of the rght hand crooked fron a cut on the first? joint quite gray has but five teeth aft is about seventy year old. Stands without Shoes Six inches [sic]

(39) 47 [No Reg. #.] PHIL the property of Joseph D HANDLEN of Richmond /City/ Va and by him hired the present year OR FLYNN of Suffolk Va and by him registered as one of his hands in the Dismal Swamp.

   PHIL is about Seventy years old Crow black, very gray, has but four? teeth small features thin lips with furrows from the nose to the Cheek a small scar on the right arm, a scar on the shin bone and on the inside of the right foot stands without Shoes Five feet five inches and a half

[No Reg. #.] Dempsey REED a free man of Clor of Suffolk Virginia, hired the present year by OR FLYNN of Suffolk and by him registered as one of his hands employed in the Dismal swamp.

   Dempsey REED is about twenty years old, has the appearance of being White, with gray eyes stregh [sic] hair, has a bad scar on the outside of the left arm stands without shoes Six feet one inch

(39) (Cont.) [No Reg. #.] STEPHEN the property of Abram MILTEIR? decd. late of Nansemond County Va, hired the present year by OR FLYNN of Suffolk Va and by him registered as one of his hands employed in the Dismal Swamp.

STEPHEN is about forty years old Black small features rather full cheek smal̲ eyes has a small black mole on the arm has a scar on the great toe of the rght foot and a large hind? on the top of

(40) 48 the same foot a little one the [sic] face and a fresh skined place on each shin bone stands without Shoes Fivefeet Eght ___ 1/2 inch̲s̲.

State of North Carolina County Court Clerk/s/ offic_
   Gate [sic] County.   May 15/th/ 1847.
[No Reg. #.] GLASCOW the property of the Estate of Whitmel JONES decd. late of S Cates County; hired the present year by Ro R HILL of == Cates County and by him registered as one of his hands in the Great Dismal Swamp.

GLASCOW is about Sixty years old, ver̲r̲y Gray with full beard, one front tooth out in the upper jaw with flat features, open nostrils, a scar on the inner angle of the left eye & one on the outer corner of the mouth on the right Side & a scar from a burm̲ on the top of the rght hand Stand [sic] without Shoes Five feet 7 1/2 inches

[No Reg. #.] ISAAC the property of the estate Jesse WIGGINS decd late of Gates County hired the present year by Ro R HILL of Gates County and by him employed as one of his hands in the Great Dismal Swamp.

ISAAC is about forty five years old of a dark brown compl̲xion heavy eye brow small nose, a scar on the forehead a little to the left of the center, a little pusofle? just below the right breast small Scar on the left hand from a hurt with a saw Stands without Shoes Five feet 4 1/2 inch̲i̲s & has a scar on the right begingat [sic] the upr [sic] join? of th midle toe

(41) 49 State of No Carolina} Gates County Court
                Gates County } Clerks office May 17/th/ 1847
[No Reg. #.] SAM the property of Jacob RICHARDSON of Pasqu̲tank County North Carolina and hired the present year by Ro R HILL of Gates County and by him registered as one of his hand [sic] enployed in the Dismal Swamp.

SAM is about fifty Three years old quite black Good teeth large features a small scar on the out side of the left fore arm, a small scar on the inside of the right Knee and two scars on the shin bone, stands without Shoes Five feet sev̲i̲n and & [sic] 1/2 inches.

State of North Carolina Gates County Clks off
Reissued 8 March 48-103   May 18/th/ 1847.
[No Reg. #.] ISOM the property of Jackson BRINKLY hired of Nansemond County Va & hired the present year by William B WHITEHEAD of Suffolk & by him employed as one of his hand in the Dismal Swamp.

ISOM is about 35 years old Black, has a one sided face large lips & nose & a scar on the right cheek very bad teeth a scar across the left Shin, a scar upon the great toe of the left foot the nail on the same foot of the toe [sic] rather Shorter a scar on the inside of the right Knee stands without Shoes Five feet 3 inches   [Margin:] Reissued January 10/th/ 1849. No. 27.

(42) 50 [Entire page is blank.]

(43) 51 State N Carolina} Gate County Court Clks office
             Gates County}   May 19/th/ 1847.
[No Reg. #.] NAT the property of Richd BROTHERS of Gates Co N. C & employed by

(43) (Cont.) Burwell BROTHERS as one of his hands employed in the great dismal swamp

NAT is about fif<u>y</u> five years old black rather Sharp Featurs Bad teeth, the front the front [sic] or midle teeth<u>e</u> gone in the uper Jaw has as [sic] Scar on the inner angle of the right eye, has varycos vains on the Calf of the left leg Stands without Shoes Five feet 7 1/4 inches.

R K SPEED.

May 19/th/ 1847.

[No Reg. #.] HARMON the property of Thomas BARNES of Gates County N. C. and by him hired the present year by him to Ro R HILL of said County and by Said HILL employed as one of his hands in the Great Dismal Swanp.

HARMON is about thirty ===== years old Black has a small scar in the forehead on the left side full features round forehead a plesant counternance a small scar on the left Knee Stands without Shoes 5 feet 6 1/8 inches.

[No Reg. #.] WILLIS the property of Thomas BARNES of Gates Country North Carolina and hired by him to Ro R HILL of said county and by him enployed as one of his as one of his [sic] hands employed in the Great Dismal Swamp

WILLIS is about twenty three years old light mula<u>to</u> complexion, has a number of whitish looking Spots on his face has a scar on the outside of the right wrist several small Scars on the on the [sic] inside of the

(44) 52 arm & has fire h<u>uts</u> on on [sic] both Shins Stands without Shoes 5 feet 5 1/2 inc<u>hs</u>.

State of No Carolina}   County Court Clerks office

     Gates County}   May 29/th/ 1847.

[No Reg. #.] LETTETON? the property of Miss May C SUMNER of Gates County NC, and hired for the present year by Marmaduke BAKER of said county and by him hired to WmB WHITEHEAD of Suffolk Virginia and by Said WHITEHEAD employed as one of his hands in the Great Dismal Swamp

LETTETON is about thirty five years old Black with full features & very large lips has a scar on the left side of the forehead his hands are un<u>s</u>ual small for one of his si<u>se</u> & a small not on the right ham string stands without sh<u>o</u>es Five feet 9 inchs

(45) 53 State of North Carolina   County Court Clerks office

     Gates County . . . June 19/th/ 1847

[No Reg. #.] CHARLES the property of the estate of John SAVAGE decd of Nansemond County Va. hired the present year by Edward RIDDICK &Co. of said County & state and by them employed as one of their hands in the Great Dismal swamp &? by them registered

CHARLES is about fourteen years old of Copper Collor features full a small scar on the left Side of chin and a small scar on the uppr. joint of the little finger of the left hand stands without shoes Five Feet s<u>i</u>ven inches

State of North Carolina}   County Court Clerks Office

     Gates County }   June 25/th/ 1847.

[No Reg. #.] HARRY the property of Admeral BRINKLY of Nansemond County Virginia and by him registered as one of his hands enployed in the Great Dismal Swamp.

HARRY is about twenty three years old Quite Black, with rather large features has agap in the upper teeth in front & one very defective tooth has a deformity in the lower part of the chst? & a very large Scar on the Stomache & abdomen from a burn, has som [sic] small Scars on the left hand, has a sore? on the left leg & a large ancle & scars on both Shin bo<u>ns</u>. Stands without Shoes Five feet four and three quarter inches

[No Reg. #.] MURPHRY the property of Admeral BRINKLY of Nansemond County Virginia and by him registered as one of his hands enployed in the Dismal Swamp.

(45) (Cont.) MURPHRY is about Thirty Two years, old, guite black with small features
& prominet mouth fine full feetures forehead? has two small scars on the outer angle
of the left leg has a small scar on the back of the right hand, two small scars on the
left wrist a mole on

(46) 54 the right Side of the stomache, just below the wribs. Stands without Shoes
5 feet 4 inchs.

State of North Carolina}   County Court Clerks office
      Gates County }   June 28/th/ 1847
[No Reg. #.] BEN the property of WmB. WHITEHEAD of Suffolk Virgina and by him
registered asone of his hands Inployed in the Great Dismal Swamp.
      BEN is about Sixty five years old, brown Complexion, flat features flat nose with
large nostrils, bad teeth, uncomonly large and Some longer than others but little
Gray, for aman of his age Several scars on the wrist arm snall & white most of them
seem to be from bleading. Stands without shoes Five Feet two Inches and a half

[No Reg. #.] SAM the property of Wm B. WHITEHEAD of Suffo Va and by him registered as
one of his hands employed in the Great Dismal Swamp.
      SAM is about Fifty five years old, brown complexion full broad forehead, bad teeth
in frone?t quitegray with a scar on the right collar bone, just at the junction with
the right left? a scar on the right wrist the scar finger next to the litle finger on
the right hand off at the Seckond joint a Scar on the left ancle on the inside Stands
without Shoes Five feet five and a half Inches and Stoops Considerably.

(47) 55 [No Reg. #.] Eason BRIGGS Son of Denniss BRIGS a free man of Collor of
Nansemond County Virginia and hired by him to Col WHITEHEAD of Suffo. Va and by him
imployed as one of his hands in the Great Dismal Swamp & and [sic] by him registered
      Eason is about seventeen years old quite Black with full rather pontry [sic]
featurd? two small scars on the the [sic] inside of the left arm below the elbow a
large scar runing down on the right ancle on the outside from the instep Stands
without Shoes Five feet four and a half inches

[No Reg. #.] Lemus [or LOMUS] SOWERY a free man of Color of Nansemond County Vurginia
& employed by Wm B WHITEHEAD of Suffolk as one of his hands in the Great Dismal Swamp
and by him registered.
      Lemus is about twenty two years old, brown Complexion large mouth and nose, a scar
on the forehead abov the outer angle of the right eye and two small scars near the
center of the forehead and larg scar across the back of the right foot and a scar on
the inside of the left instep Stands without Shoes Five feet 9 inches.

[No Reg. #.] Israel BRIGGS son of Dennis BRIGGS afree man f [sic] Collor of Nansemond
County Virginia & hired by WmB WHITEHEAD of Suffolk and by him registered as one of
his hands in the Great Dismal Swamp
      Israel BRIGGS is about nineteen years old dark brown Complexion pointed nose and
lips, has a scar on the under lip from a cut a scar on the outside of the right arm, a
scar just below the Knee of

(48) 56 of the left leg and a scar on the inside of the right foot. Stands without
Shoes Five feet five + a half inches.

[No Reg. #.] Ben WIGGINS of Nansemond County Virginia of Peny WIGGINS a free woman of
Color hired the present year by William BWHITEHEAD of Suffolk Va & by him registered
as one of his hands in the Dismal Swamp
      Ben is Eighteen years old very Black with full features large flat nose small

(48) (Cont.) eyes, a verry heavy deform rim to the left year, a scar on the left arm & one across the thum of the same hand, a scar on the inside of the right foot Stands without shoes Five Feet three Inches, has a small not under the lid of right eye

State of North Carolina   County Court Clerks offic_
     Gates County   July 5/th/ 1847.

[No Reg. #.] JIM the property of Elisha BRINKLY of Nansemond County Virginia hired the present year by Wm B WHITEHEAD of Suffolk Va & by him registered as one of his hands imployed in the Great Dismal swam [sic].

   JIM is about fifteen years old, Dark Brown complexion, long face with large features flat broad nose, large teeth, has a very large Scar on the left leg, above the ancle from a burn. Stands without Shoes Four feet 11 1/2 inch [Margin:] Reissued January 10/th/ 1849. No. 35.

(49) 57 State of North Carolina County Court Clerks
     Gates County   office July 12/th/ 1847

[No Reg. #.] ABRAM the property of the Estate of Jno KNGHT decd of Nansemond County va and hired the present year by Willis S RIDDICK of Suffolk and by him Registered & by him inployed as one of his hands in the Great Dismal swamp

   ABRAM is about fifty three years Old, has Good teeth for his age with one upper one out quite black sharp Cheek bons has a mole on the left side of the Chin Stands without Shoes Five feet 6 1/4 inchs

State of North Carolina County Court Clerks office
     Gates County   July 19/th/ 1847.

[No Reg. #.] RUBIN the property of Edward RIDDICK Junr. of Nansemond County virginia and hired the present year by Jetho RIDDICK &Co and by them Registered as one of their hands in the Great Dismal swamp

   REUBIN is about Forty five years old, sharp features with a face a little one sided. Has lost his upper teeth in front on the upper jaw, has a small scar on the forehead. Has a deformity of the breast, the left one much the largest, has a scar on the rght shin stands without shoes Five feet Six and three Quarter inches

(50) 58 [No Reg. #.] JACK the property of Edward RIDDICK Jun of Nansemond County Va, and hired the present year by Jethro RIDDICK &Co and by them inployed as one of their hands in the Great Dismal Swamp and by them Registered

   JACK is about Forty Years Old, has a large full forehead deep eyes, large lips has a long scar on the right leg at the Kne & several smaller ones around and about it stands without Shoes Five feet seven and a half inchs

   July 16/th/ 1847

[No Reg. #.] Dick JONES a free man of Color of Nansemond County Va, and imployed by Wm B WHITEHEAD of Suffolk Va as one of his hands in the Great Dismal swamp, & by him Registered.

   Dick is about twenty one Years old lite brown Complexion has tolerable sharp featurs, a very bushy head of hare & very Quick spoken, one small scar on the Rii?ght great toe, with one small scar on the same shin, one scar on the instep of the left foot, also one on the Great toe of the same foot, and has a large scar on the right arm, about six inches from the elbow Caused by a scald, stands without Shoes five feet eght inchs & a half   Kufus Kng SPEED [Rufus King SPEED]

(51) 59 State of North Carolina County Court Clerks office
     Gates County   July 21/st/ 1847

[No Reg. #.] JEROM the property of Daniel BRINKLEY Sen of Nansemond county Va and hired by WmB WHITEHEAD of Suffolk and by him imployed as one of his hands in the Great

21 July 1847

(51) (Cont.) Dismal Swam [sic]
JEROM is about forty three years old has small features, a wild look, has a small scar in the forehead, a scar on the Right breast two scars on the Out side of the left arm a scar on the out side of the left leg Stands without shoes Five feet five and a half inches [Margin:] Reissued June 14/th/ 1848 Reissud July 14 1851

[No Reg. #.] JOHN the property of Daniel BRINKLY Senr of Nansemond County Va hired the present year by W BWHITEHEAD of Suffolk and by him register [sic] as one of his hands in the Great Dismal Swamp
JNO is about twenty yeas old, has a blount [blunt] nose, deep eyes prominest mouth hight? round forehead with a scare just between the eye brows, without scars or marks on the arms, legs or breast Stands without shoes Five feet nine inches (Burn?) [sic] [Margin:] Reissued June 14/th/ 1848 [Overwritten vertically across the text:] Issud the 14 July 1851.

(52) 60 Gates County   July 26?/th/ 1847
[No Reg. #.] BOB the property of James MILLER of Nansemond County Va and hired by Wm B WHITEHEAD of Suffolk and by him Registered as one of his hands in the Great Dismal Swamp.
BOB is about twenty four years old, has rather a bushy head has a scar on the outer angle of the left eye has a large scar on the left hand just above the thumb, and one on the wrist of the same hand, has a scar on the inside of the Right arm a scar on the shin bone of the Right leg and one on the ancle of the same leg &ascar on the out side of the lef [sic] shin stands without shos Five feet 9 1/2 inchs

State of No Caro.
[No Reg. #.] MIKE the property of James MILLER of Nansemond County Va and hired by Wm B WHITEHEAD of suffolk and by him Registered as one of his hands in the Great Dismal swamp
MIKE is about Twenty three years old has full features, large mouth small eyes has a vacancy betwen his upper front tooth [sic] has a small scar ==== ==== ==== ==== between the eye brows has a large scar on the outside of the Right arm & a smaller one on the oute? side of the wrist of the same arm, has a small faint scar on the left arm a small scar on the right leg just above the ancle Stands without shoes five feet 4? 1/2 inches

R. H. B.

(53) 61 State of North Caro. County Court Clerks office
                Gates   July 26/th/ 1847.
[No Reg. #.] BEN the property of Abram BRINKLEY Jr of Nansemond County Va - hired by Wm B WHITEHEAD of Suffolk Va and by him Registered as one of his hands in the Great Dismal swamp
BEN is about sixteen years old flat features large nose and lips has a scar on the outside of the Right eye has a scar on the inside of the right arm near the elbow has a scar on the outside of the left foot Stands without shoes Five feet two inchs [Margin:] Reissued 17/th/ Aug. 1848 No 107

State of No Caro   County Court Clerks office
   Gates County   July 26/th/ 1847.
[No Reg. #.] HENRY the property of Mills C. DAUGHTREY of Nansemond County Va hired the present year by WmB WHITEHEAD of Suffolk and by him regisered as one of his hands in the Great Dismal swamp.
HENY is about Twenty years old is Cross eyed, has a number of small bumps on the face, has a small scar on the left wrist has three small scars on the /left leg/ on the Right leg [sic] Stands without shoes Five feet 6 inchs

21

(53) (Cont.) [No Reg. #.] EVERIT the property of Solomon CARR of Nansemond County Va and hired by WmBWHITHEAD of Suffolk & byhim Registered as one of his hands imployed in the Great Dismal swamp. EVERITT is about Twenty yeas old has a very small fore-head has a very large scar on the left arm abovthe [sic] elbow has a scar from a burn on the left thy [sic] and a scar on the left /righ/ foot Stands without shoes five feet 4 1/2 inches

(54) 62 State of North Carolina}   County Court Clerks
           Gates County}   office August 26th/th/ 1847.
1   GEORGE the property of Edward C MILLER of Nansemond Norfolk County Virginia hired by John & Nathl GAINES? and by them registered as one of thir hands in the Great Dismal Swamp.

GEORGE is about twenty five years old Quite black, has small featurs the rght eye smaller than the left has a number of small pimples on his face has a small scar on the rght elbow, a small scar on the rght lg [sic] and a scar on the left lg on the inside of the on the inside of the [sic] Calf of the leg stands without shoes Five feet six inches and 1?/4.

2   MATHEW the property of the Estate of Josiah MILLER decd. of Norfolk County Virginia and hired the present year by John and Nathl GAINES and by them imployed as one of their hands in the Great Dismal Swamp.

MATHEW is about forty yeas old quite Black has a pinted nose with Large nostrils small mouth, hghte? forehead, a small scar on the inside of the Right Leg and one on the upper jou?nt of the great toe of the same foot. Stands without shoes Five feet 8 inchs

3   FLENERY? the property of James FLENERY of Norfolk County Va and hired the present year by John & Nathanil GAINES and by them imploy [sic] as one of their hands in the Great Dismal Swamp

FLENERY is about Twenty two years old quite Black has a very large flat nose full round forehead thick Lips no beard a small scar under the inter angle of the left eye, a small scar on the left arm

(55)   63 above the elbow a large flat scar on the outside of the rght leg above the Knee a scar on the shin bone of the same leg and one on the upper joint of the Great toe of the rght foot stands without shoes Six feet.

4   DENIS the property of Mary WESTON of Nansemond /Norfolk/ County Virgim?ia hired the present year by John & Nathl GAINES and by them registered as one of their hands in the Great Dismal Swamp.

DENIS the? is about thirty six years old Copper Complexion flat features, flat nose two of his upper teeth out in front, has a large Scar across his breast a small Scar on the upper joint of the thumb of the r/i/ght hand several small scars on the left arm both on the out & inside a small Scar on the shin bone and one on the outside of the right leg stands without shoes Five feet nine and three quarter inches

5   JOHN the property of Josiah MILLER of Norfolk County And. and [sic] hired the present year by John & Nathl GARNES & by them registered as one of ther hands in the Great Dismal Swamp.

JOHN is about Twenty four years old, Quite black large full face, large thick lips, small eyes has a number of small lumps upon the face, has a large scar across the inside of the rght wrist and one upon the bale of the thumb, a scar on the Right shine bone and several faint scars on the left leg Stands without shoes Five Feet Five Inches.

(56) 64 6 LEMUL [sic] the property of Edward C MILLER of Norfolk County Vig and hired the present year by Jno & Nathl GAINS [or GARNS] and by them inployed as one of their hands in the Great Dismal Swamp

SEMUEL is about Twenty five years old Copper Complexion remarkably long forehead with a rather down? face full beard a small scar on the inside of the rght arm just above the rist a small Scar on the Shin bone of the right leg and a small scar on the Shin bone of the left leg. [End of entry.]

7 ALEXANDER the property of the estate of JeSe BOTT [or BOLT] decd. of Norfolk County Virginia and hired the present year by John & Nathl GUARNS [sic]; and by them Registered as one of their hands emplyed in the Great Dismal

ALEXANDER is about nine years old, quite black with flat features without marks or scars of any Knd and has remarkable wide nose and the eyes lids seem to run under the nose. Stands without Shoes Three feet elevin inches.

State of North [sic]   County Court Clerks offce
    Gates County   Septemb 3rd. 1847,
[No Reg. #.] Justin a free boy of Col, Son of Ede FOLK S of Nansemond county va hired the present Year by Wm B WHITEHEAD by == of Suffo Va. and by him registered as one of his hands imployed in the Great Disnal Swamp.

Justin FOLK is about Sixteen yeas old dark brown complexion hevy eye brow large nose, scar on the right side of the forehead a large scar on the wrist of the right arm and a large scar on the outside of the left leg and a small one on the outside of the foot of th [sic]

(57) 65 Same Side Stands without Shoes Five feet 2 inchs

[Remainder of page is blank.]

(58) 66 State of North Carolina County Court Clerk's office
      Gates County   January 11/th/ 1848
No1 Peter EDWARDS, the property of Allen EDWARDS ofSouthampton County Virginia and hired the present year by William B WHITEHEAD ofSuffolk Virginia and by him registered as one of his hands inployed in the Great Dismal Swanp

Peter is about Fifty years old, quite bald, with a patch of hair on the brim ofthe forehead with bad teeth, particularly in the under jaw, & a scar from a burn on the top of his head. Stands with out Shoes Five feet, five and three quarter inches

State of North Carolina County Court Clerks office
    Gates County   Jan 11/th/. 1848
No 2. Warich FRANKLIN, the property of Jethro R FRANKLIN of Nansemond County Virginia hired the present year by William B WHITEHEAD of Suffolk Virginia, and by him registered as one of his hands, inployed in the Great Dismal Swamp.

Warich is about Thirty foar years old, sharp features, sunken eyes, with two small scars on the ======== right? eye, and some small scars on the left hand Stands without shoes Five? feet five & a half inches

(59) 67 State of North Carolina County Court Clerks office
      Gates County   January 11/th/ 1848
No 3. Peter SAUNDERS the property of James SAUNDERS of Nansemond County Virginia, and hired the present year by Wm. B WHITEHEAD of Suffolk Virginia and by him enployed in the Great Dismal Swamp.

Peter is about twenty one years old, dark Copper Complexion, has a scar in the under lip, thick lips, some small scars on the breast, Stands with out shoes five feet, seven inches.

11 January 1848

(59) (Cont.) State of North Carolina County Court Clerk's office
            Gates County   January 11/th/ 1848
No. 4. EMMOND? the property of Nathaniel BOOTHE of Nansemond County Virginia and
hired the present by [sic] Wm.B WHITEHEAD of Suffolk Va. and by him registered as one
of his hands employed in the Great Dismal Swamp.
    EMMOND is about FSixty? five years old, has a scar on the stomach about three
inches long, a scar on the outside of the right Knee, and stands with out shoes Five
feet Eight and a half inches.

(60) 68 State of Noth Carolina County Court CLerks office
            Gates County   January 15/th/. 1848
5 WILLIS, the property of Jasn BRINKLY of Nansemond County Virginia, and hired the
present year by Wm.illiamB WHITEHEAD of Suffolk Va, and by him employed as one of his
hands in the great Disnal Swamp.
    WILLIS about twenty years old, light brown Conplexion retreating forehead, full
mouth, a bump on the forehead, and stands with out shoes Five feet three inches.

State of North Carolina County Court Clerks office
  Gates County   January 15/th/. 1848
6 WILLS, the property of Isajah LANGSTON of Nansemond County Virginia, hired the
present year by Wn. B WHITEHEAD of Suffolk and ⁀ him registered as one of his hands,
inployed in the great Dismal swamp
    WILLS, is about twenty three years old, light brown complexion, with a scar on the
left side ofthe spine, and stands without shoes Five feet five inches [Margin:] Reissued January 10/th/ 1849. WILLS No. 23

(61) 69 State of North Carolina County Court Clerk's office
            Gates County   January 15/th/. 1848
7 SOLOMON, the property of Jason BRINKLY of Nansemond County Va, & him hired the
present year by Wm. BWHITEHEAD of Suffolk Va, and by him imployed as one of his hands
in the Great dismal Swamp.
    SOLOMON is about thirty one years old, quite black, very flat broad nose has lost
two teeth one in each jaw one just above the other; has a bad scar on the right foot
at the top ofthe middle toe. Reissued Jany 22nd 1850-33yrs. old No 34

State of North Carolina County Court Clerk's office
  Gates County   January 15/th/. 1848
8 JACKSON, the property of Javan R FRANKLIN of Nansemond County va. and him hired the
present year by Wm.B WHITEHEAD of Suffolk va and by him registered as one of his hands
inployed in the great Dismal Swamp
    JACKSON is about Fifteen years old, with a small scar on the outer angle of the
left eye, and stands without shoes five feet half one inch. Reissued Jany. 22 /nd/.
1850 No. 29-17 yrs. old.

(62) 70 State of NCarolina County Court Cerks [sic] office
            Gates County   Januay 18/th/ 1848
9 ALFRED the property of the estate of William HINTON dec_ of Gates County and hired
the present year by Isaac S HARRELL &co and by them employed to work in the Great
dismal Swamp
    ALFRED is about Twenty years old very black remarkley [sic] wide mouth and thick
lips has a Scar on the fore head a little to the left of the Middle Line a large Scar
on the out Side of the /right/ arm about the elbow, and Stand without Shoes Five feet
three Inches and a quater Inches

State of North Carolina County Court Clerk's office

(62) (Cont.)   Gates County   January 18/th/ 1848

<u>10</u> PHILIP the property of Isaac S HARRELL? of Gates County No. Ca, and him registered as one of his hands enployed in the great Dismal Swamp as one of Isaac S HARRELL &co.

     PHILIP is about fifty two year old, light brown conplexion remarkably flat face & nose, bad teeth scars on the forehead, has the index of finger nail of the left hand Split a small scar on the breast, Stands with out shoes five feet ten inches

(63)   71 State of North Carolina County Court Clerks office
        Gates County   January 18/th/ 1848.

<u>11</u> WASHINGTON, the property of William HINTON deceased, of Gates County and hired the present year by Isaac S HARRELL&co of said County and by them enployed in the Great Dismal Swanp & by them registered.

     WASHINGTON, is about twenty two years old, small eyes and features, with good teeth, a scar on the left === ==== == ==== side of the forehead, just above the edge of the hair, has a scar above the bend ofthe arm on the left side, & has no nail upon the great toe, of the right foot. Stands with out Shoes five feet eleven inches.

State of North Carolina County Court Clerks office
        Gates County   January, 1848

<u>12</u>   Charles JONES a free man of Color resident of Gates County registers himself as imployed == to work in the Great dismal Swamp by WOODWARD &PARKER & any one else who will imploy him

     C. JONES is about thirty-six years old, quite a bright mulatto has a scar on the outer side of the left arm and a scar across the inside of the right foot and stands without shoes five feet Six inches.

(64)   72 State of North Carolina County Court Clerk's office
        Gates County   January 18/th/. 1848

<u>13</u>   NOLAND, the property of John MORGAN ofGates County, hired the present year by Isaac S HARRELL &co of Said County and by them employed in the Great Dismal Swamp, and by them registered

     NOLAND is about twenty five years old, very black, has a large scar on the right side of the face above the eye, and a bad scar on the inside of the right foot, and Stands without shoes Five feet eight inches. [Margin:] 15

State of North Carolina County Court Clerk's office
        Gates County   January 21/st/. 1848

<u>14</u>   ENOCH, the property of Burell? RIDDICK of Nansemond County virginia and hired the present year by Willis S RIDDICK of Suffolk, and by him inployed as one of his hands in the Great Dismal swamp.

     ENOCH is about Forty one years old, brown conplexion high fore head; a large nose thin lips a small scar on the chin, a small scar on the left arm, a scar on the left Knee, Stands without shoes Five feet four and a half inches.

(65)   73 State of North Carolina County Court Clerk's office
        Gates County   January 21/st/. 1848

<u>15</u>   DANIEL the property ofBurwell RIDDICK, of Nansemond County Va, and hired the present year by Willis S RIDDICK of Suffolk, and by him registered as one of his hands inployed in the Great Dismal Swamp

     DANIEL is Sixty one years old, brown conplexion, Gray head, thin beard, very bad teeth, a dark spot or scar just above the collar bone ofthe right side, a small scar runs down the breast on the same side, a large scar just below the Knee on the left leg; & stands with out shoes five feet six & three quarter inches.

State ofNorth Carolina County Court Clerk's office

(65) (Cont.)   Gates County   January 21/st/. 1848

16   JOE the property of the estate of Marmaduke JONES decd. of Nansemond County Virginia and hired the present year by Willis S RIDDICK and by him registered as one of his hands employed in the Great Dismal Swamp

JOE is about fifteen years old, quite black, has a scar on the left arm just at the joint, near the sisze of ten cent piece, two scars just above the Knee of the left leg, & stands with out shoes four feet ten inches.

(66) 74 State of North Carolina County Court Clerk's office
                Gates County   January 21 /st/. 1848

17 MOSES, the property of the estate of Marmaduke JONES deceased, of Nansemond County Va, and hired the present year by Willis S. RIDDICK of Suffolk and by him registered as one of his hands inployed in the great Dismal Swamp

MOSES is about sixty years old, has some defect of the left eye, very thin hair and nearly bald in the crown of the head, no teeth but stumps in the upper jaw in front, & has a deformity of the left thumb, and stands with out shoes Five feet four & a quarter inches.

State of North Carolina County Court Clerks office
                Gates County   January 21 /st/. 1848

18 SAM the property of Nancy GRIFFIN of Nansemond County Virginia hired the present year by Willis S. RIDDICK of Suffolk and by him registered as one ofhis hands employed in the Great Dismal Swamp.

SAM is about Twenty four years old large features, with flat broad ==== nose, broad mouth, small ==== beard principally upon the upper lip, a number small pinples under each eye. [End of entry.]

(67) 75 State of North Carolina County Court Clerk's office
                Gates County   January 21/st/. 1848

19 ARMSTEAD the property of Daniel BRINKLY of Nansemond County Va and hired the present year by Willis S. RIDDICK of Suffolk and by him registered as one of his hands in the great Dismal Swamp

ARMSTEAD is about Twelve years old, has a bad scar on all the right side of the face, and a peculiar suppression of the right eye produced from the burn, and a small scar on the right Knee pan, and stands without shoes four feet one inch.

State of North Carolina County Court Clerk's office
                Gates County   January 21/st/. 1848

20 HENRY, the property of Daniel BRINKLY of Nansemond County Va hired the present year by Willis S. RIDDICK of Suffolk & by him registered as one of his hands in the Great Dismal Swamp.

HENRY is seventeen years old, sharp forehead, ====== ==== === with a small? scar just at the point ofthe forehead, small deep eyes & remarkably small eye brows, a small scar on the middle joint of the fore finger & === mid?dle finger, and a scar on the right Knee Stands with out shoes five feet Six inches

(68) 76 State of North Carolina County Court Clerk's office
                Gates County   January 21/st/. 1848

21 JACK the property ofthe estate of Wills [or Mills] RIDDICK of Suffolk va, hired the present year by Willis S. RIDDICK, of Suffolk and him registered as one of his hands in the Great Dismal Swamp.

JACK is Forty Six years old Dark brown Color, high forehead prominent eye-brows, a little gray, a scar on the head near the top, a small scar on the back ofthe left hand and a scar on the hand of the same arm on the inside of the thumb on the left hand and stands with out shoes Five feet six inches? and & [sic] a quarter inches.

(68) (Cont.) State of North Carolina County Court Clerks office
    Gates County   January 21/st/. 1848

22 JIM the property of Daniel BRINKLY of Nansemond County Va, hired the present year by Willis S. RIDDICK of Suffolk, and by him registered as one of his hand [sic] in the great Dismal Swamp.

 JIM is about Eight years old, quite black fierce look, wth? teeth very wide in the upper jaw, and wide apart. Stands with out shoes four feet three inches.

(69) 77 State of North Carolina County Court Clerk office
    Gates County   January 21/st/. 1848

23. WRIGHT the property of Nelly BRINKLEY of Nansemond County Va., hired the present year by Willis S. RIDDICK of Suffolk == and by him registered as one of his hands in the Great Dismal Swamp.

 WRIGHT is Fourteen years old, dark yellow complexion, flat nose, a scar on the forehead, a scar on the right cheek, a red spot on the right side of the left elbow, stands with out shoes five feet six inches. Reissued Apl. 11/th/ 1850, sixteen years of age hired by WmB. WHITEHEAD-No 52. [Margin:] Reissued Jany 28/th/ 1849. No 55.

State of North Carolina County Court Clerk's office
Gates County   January 21/st/. 1848

24 SAM, the property ofthe estate of John R KNIGHT of Nansemond County Va. and hired the present year by Willis S. RIDDICK of Suffolk, and by him registered as one of his hands in the Great Dismal swanp.

 SAM is Twenty four years old, full face with a scar on the forehead and a cut on the nose on the left nostril, a black spot on the outside of the left leg. Stands with out shoes five feet five inches.

(70) 78 State of North Carolina County Court Clerks office
    Gates County   January 21/st/. 1848

25 HANCE the property of Gilley BROWN of Nansemond County Va, hired the present year by Willis S. RIDDICK of Suffolk and by him registered as one ofhis hands in the Great Dismal swanp.

 HANCE is about Fifty years old, small deep eyes, very wide nose, a scar on the in out side ofthe left eyebrow, very bad teeth, has two small naked places of the right side of the head. Stands with out shoes five feet six inches.

State of North Carolina County Court Clerk's office
Gates County.   January 21/st/. 1848

26 HARRISON, the property of John R KNIGHT of Nansemond County Va. and hired the present year by Willis S. RIDDICK of Suffolk and by him registered as one [sic] his hands in the Great Dismal swanp

 HARRISON is Nineteen years old, flat wide nose, a scar on the outer side ofthe left wrist, a scar on the left Knee pan and one on the right Knee, Stands with out shoes five feet six? inches. [Margin:] Reissued January 21/st/ 1849 No 56

(71) 79 State of North Carolina County Court Clerk's office
    Gates County   January 24/th/. 1848

27 ADDER the property of Elisha EASON, of Perquimans County, hired the present year by Robt R HILL of Gates County and by him employed as one of his hands in the Great Dismal swanp

 ADDER is about forty years old, un Commonly [sic] large features, nose and mouth, with bad teeth, a small scar on the forehead and very thin hair on the forehead === and a large scar on the right shoulder; and stands without shoes six feet two inches.

(71) (Cont.)   State of NoCarolina   County Court Clerks Office
                Gates County   January 24/th/. 1848

<u>28</u> PETER the property of Solomon EASON of Perquimins Co hired the present yearby RoRHILL ofGates Co andby him rgisterd [sic] as one ofhis hands intheGreat Dismal Swamp

PETER is about Forty year old, lage flat nose wide mouth open teeth a scar on the left side ofthe forehead, a scar on the left breast appears to have no nails on the midd?1e toe or the one next the Great toe stands without shoes Six feet half an inch.

(72) 80   State ofNoCarolina   County Court Clerks Office
                Gates County   January 24/th/. 1848

<u>29</u> JOHNthe property of William BEEMAN of Gates County and hired the presentyear by Israel BEEMAN andbyhim hired to RoRHILL &byhim rgisterd as one of his hands emplyed in the GreatDismal Swamp

JOHN is about sevety? twoyers [sic] old ha a pleasant counternance, some snall scares onthe forehead, has breast quite large, has a scar on the left thunb some scars on the right leg in front an just below the Knee. Stands without shoes Five feet four inches.

State of NoCarolina County Court Clerks office
                Gates County   January 25/th/. 1848

<u>30</u> RUBEN the property of Edward RIDDICK Senr of Nansemond va hired the present year by Jethro RIDDICK &Co &by them registerd employed in the Great Dismal swamp

RUBEN is Forty six years old, sharp features has lost the upper teeth in front has a deformity ofthe breast the left one much the largest a small scar on the forehead a small scar on the right shin. Stands without shoes Five feet Six and three quarter inches.

State of NoCarolina County CourtClerks office
                Gates County   January 25/th/. 1848

<u>31</u> RUBEN the property of Edward RIDDICK Sen of Nansemond va hired the present year by Jethro RIDDICK &Co ofsaid Couny? an by them registerd as oneoftheir hands

(73) 81 in the Great Dismal Swamp

RUBEN is about thirty one years old large features verry thick under lip a scar on the pit ofthe stomach, a scar on the outer side ofthe left Knee a scar on the left side of the head and a scar on the left arm justabove the wrist. Stands without shoes 3ix feet

State of NoCarolina County CourtClerks office
                Gates County   January 25/th/. 1848

<u>32</u> EVERETTE the property of Eve?rette CARR of Suffolk hired the presentyear by Jetho RIDDICK &Co of Nansemond Va and by them registerd as one oftheir hands in the Great Dismal Swamp

EVERETTE is about Twenty? years old, full featurs a black [sic] on the left cheek bone a lage scar onthe left armjust above the elbow a lage scar on the left leg just above the Knee Stands withoutshoes Five feet five inches

State of North Carolina County Court Clerk's office
                Gates County   January 25/th/. 1848

<u>33</u> JIM the property of Nancy GRIFFIN of Nansemond Va., hired the present year by Jethro RIDDICK &co of said county and them [sic] registered as one of their hands in the Great Dismal swamp

JIM is about Thirty five years old broad high forehead, a small scar over the left eye, a large dark scar under the right breast from a burn, stands with out shoes five feet six inches.

(74) 82 State of North Carolina County Court Clerk's office
        Gates County   January 25/th/ 1848
34 JACIT the property of Henry GRIFFIN, of Nansemond County Va. hired the present
year by Jethro RIDDICK &co of said County, andby them? registered as one oftheir hands
in the Great Dismal swamp.
            ==== JACIT, is thirty years old, stiff right Knee, a bad scar on the inside
of the right Knee, and the toe next the great toe ofthe right foot off, stands with
out shoes five feet six & a half inches

State of North Carolina County Court Clerk's office
Gates County   January 25/th/ 1848
35 ISAAC the property of the estate of Miles GRIFFIN decd. of Nansemond Va. hired the
present year by Jethro RIDDICK & co of said County and by them registered as one of
their hands in the Great Dismal swamp.
      ISAAC is about seven teen years old, full bluff face, several small scar specks or
scars on the hands & stands with out shoes Five feet five & a half inches.

State of North Carolina County Court Clerks office
        Gates County   January 25/th/ 1848
36 LEWIS, the property of Isaac R. HUNTER of Gates County, hired the present year by
Jethro RIDDICK & co of Nansemond Va. and by them registered as one of their hands in
the

(75) 83 Great Dismal Swamp
      LEWIS, is about Forty years old, remarkably full high forehead peculiarly shap
[sic], two scars on the breast, a scar on the right arm just above the elbow, a scar
on the left arm on the outside at the elbow, a scar on the out side of the rigt leg.
Stands with out shoes five feet seven inches. [Overwritten vertically on the text:]
Duplicate issued 13 April 1854

State of North Carolina County Court Clerks office
Gates County   January 25/th/ 1848.
37 ROLAND, the property of Eulenia? EPPS of Nansemond County Va., hired the present
year by Jethro RIDDICK & co. of said County, and by them registered as one of their
hands in the Great Dismal swamp.
      ROLAND is about twenty four years old, large features, two scars on the left hand,
and one on the fore arm of the same side, a small scar on the rigt fore arm & four
large scars from a burn on the outside ofthe rigt leg. Stands with out shoes five
feet ten & three quarter inches.

State of North Carolina County Court Clerks office
Gates County   January 25/th/ 1848
38 MOSES, the property of the estate of Col. Jn. RIDDICK decd. of Nansemond. hired
the present year by Jethro RIDDICK &co of said county, and by them registered as one
of their hands in the Great Dismal swamp.
      MOSES is about Forty years old, quite bright, rather small features, a small scar
on the left eye, a small scar on the pit of the stomach, a large scar

(76) 84 on the inside of the left fore arm and a cut across the inside of the two
middle fingers, a scar on the left instep. Stands without Shoes Six feet

State of North Carolina County Court Clerks offic_
Gates County   January 25/th/ 1848
39 JOE, the property of Israel BEAMAN of Gates County, hired the present year by
Jethro RIDDICK & co of ======Nansemond County Va. and by them registered as one of

(76) (Cont.) their hands in The Great Dismal swamp.

JOE, is about fifty years old, with a pouting mouth, & pop eyes, two small scars on the left eye, large veins in the left breast, some deformity of both thumbs from sprains, and a very large scar on the right shin, and one on the left shin, stands without shoes Five feet six inches.

State of North Carolina County Court Clerks office
Gates County   January 25/th/ 1848
40 DAVY, the property of Nancy STREPSON? of Nancysemond co Va, hired the present year by Jethro RIDDICK &co of said County, and by then registered as one of his their hands in the Great Dismal Swamp

DAVY is about twenty years old a large scar on the nose between of the eyes, a scar on the outside of the right fore arm, stands with out shoes Five feet nine inches, and his hair very low on his forehead.

(77) 85 State of North Carolina County Court Clerks office
        Gates County   January 25/th/ 1848.
41 WILLIS, the property of Andrew M/C/ ALLISTER of Suffolk, hired the present year by Jethro RIDDICK & co of Nansemond Va and by them registered as one of their hands in the Great Dismal swanp

WILLIS is about Eighteen years old, quite bright, has two teeth from his under jaw in front. Stands with out shoes five feet.

State of North Carolina County Court Clerks office
Gates County   January 25/th/ 1848
42 JIM the property of Edwin SMITH of Somerton Va. hired the present year by Jethro RIDDICK &co of Nansemond County, &by then registered as one of === their hands in the Great Dismal Swamp.

JIM is about Fifteen years old, round shoulders with out [sic] a long faint scar on the left side of the breast, two small scars on the left freheadore arm. Stands with out Shoes Five feet & ten? inches.

State of North Carolia County Court Clerks office
Gates County   January 25/th/ 1848
43 SAM, the property of Samuel BAKER of Nansemond County Va, hired the present year by Jethro RIDDICK &co of said County, and by them registered as one of their hands in the Great Dismal swanp.

SAM, is about Sixty five years old, with out particular scars, and very good teeth for one so old. Stands with out shoes Five feet ten inches and a quarter inches.

(78) 86 State of North Carolina County Court Clerks office
        Gates County   January 25/th/ 1848
44 LEWIS, the property of Israel BEAMAN of Gates County, hired the present year by Jethro RIDDICK &co of Nansemond and by them registered as one of their hands of in the Great Dismal Swamp

LEWIS, is about nine years old small sparkling eyes, and a small black spot on the outer angle ofthe right eye. Stands without Shoes Four feet four and a half inches.

State of North Carolina County Court Clerks office
Gates County   January 25/th/ 1848
45 ISAAC, the property of William D MC CLENNY of Suffolk, hired the present year by Jethro RIDDICK and by him registered as one of his ==== hands in the Great Dismal swamp.

ISAAC is about Sixty years old, has a bump on the forehead, good teeth for one of his age, and [sic] of the teeth in the upper jaw growing on the inside ofthe others,

(78) (Cont.) and a little == Knot on the right Collar bone. Stands without shoes Five feet, Six and a half inches.

State of North Carolina County Court Clerks office
Gates County   January 25/th/ 1848
46 SIMON, the property of Archibald BRINKLEY deceased, hired the present year by Jethro

(79) 87 RIDDICK &co, and by them registered as one of his their hands in the Great Dismal Swamp.
      SIMON, is about thirty? four years old, large Short features, has hair on the left side running down nearly to the eye-brow, a scar on the left eye-brow, two scars on the Outside of the right leg. Stands without shoes Five feet three and a half inches.

State of North Carolina County Court Clerks office
Gates County   January 25/th/ 1848
47 STEPHEN the property of the estate of Archibald BRINKLEY of Nansemond County, and hired the present year by Jethro RIDDICK & co of said county, and by them employed as one of their hands in the Great Dismal swamp.
      STEPHEN is about twelve years old, high round forehead, very small eyes with a scar on the left hand? side? of the forehead, two scars on the right knee, a scar on the upper joint ofthe forefinger of the left hand. Stands with out Shoes four feet five & a half inches.

State of North Carolina County Court Clerks /office/
Gates County   January 25/th/ 1148 [sic]
48 WILLIS, the property of the estate of John SAVAGE decd. of Nansemond Va. hired the present year by Jethro RIDDICK &co of said County, and by them registered as one of his their hands in the Great

(80) 88 Dismal Swamp.
      WILLIS is about Eleven years, full eyes, prominent mouth, thick lips, a small scar on the left cheeck. Stands without Shoes Four feet six inches.

State of NoCarolina CoCo Clks office
Gates County   January 29/th/ 1848
49 HENY? the property of Josiah BALLARD of Nansemond CoVa hired the present year by Admeral BINKLY ofsaid Couty &by him rigistered as one ofhis hands intheGreat Dismal Swamp.
      HENYis about Thirty two yeas old, very black, lage features, a scar on the left fore arm a wort on the back ofthe left hand a large number of small warts on the right hand a scar on the outside ofthe right foot a scar on the outside ofthe left Stands without shoes Five feet Six and ahalf inches.

State of NoC. CoCoCleks office
          Jay 29/th/ 1848
50 TURNER the property of Saml WILKINS? of NansenondVa hire the prsent year by WmBWHITEHEAD ofSuffolk &byhim rgister as one ofhis hands in the Grat DismalSwamp
      TURNE [sic] is about twety three yeas ole quite Black flat features a small scar on the rght side ofthe forhad stands without shoes 5feet 9 Inches

(81) 89 StateofNoCa CoCoClks office
          Gates Co.   Jay 29/th/ 1848.
51 PETER thepropertyof James JOHNSON ofNansemondVahired thepresentyear byWBWHITEHEAD ofSuffolk&byhim registeredasone ofhis hands in thGreatDismal Swamp

29 January 1848

(81) (Cont.) PETERis about 2=2? yers old, Black flatfeaturs, small eyes a scar across the rght arm, partofmiddle finger? ofthe rght?hand off, sevral small Scars about the left Knee and sevral small Scarsonthe outside ofthe rght Knee stands without shoes 5feet9 Inches

StateofNoCa CoCoClksoffice
            Jay 29/th/ 1848
52   JIM the propety of Elisha BRINKLY ofNansemondVa hire [sic] the present year byWBWHITEHEAD ofSuffolk byhimregister as oneofhis hands in the Great Dismal Swamp
     JIMis about Sixteenyears old, boy? faced, bad teeth, a a [sic] scaronthe little figer & one on the forefiger of the left hand and a very bad Scar on the left leg Stands without shoes 5feet 1 inch.

(82) 90 StateofNoCa CoCoClksoffice
            Gats [sic] Cout?y Jny 29/th/ 1848
53   BURWELL the property of Samuel WILKIN? of NansemondCoVa hire the presentyear by WBWHITEHEAD ofSuffolkand byhim register as Oneofhis hands in the Grat Dismal Swamp
     BURWELLis about a mull?atto about Twty three yeas old, stregit hair a nunberofsmall pits upon theface a scar across the forefigerofthe lefthand and asca [sic] onthe right shin Stands without shoes 5feet 8 1/2 inches

State of North Carolina County Court Clerks office
Gates County   February 1/st/. 1848
54   WILLIS, the property of John V? FRANKLIN of Gates County, hired the present year by Burwell BROTHERS of said County, and by him registered as one of his the hands employed /by himself and James A SMALL?/ in the Great Dismal Swamp
     WILLIS is about twenty-seven years old, black, has a scar on the left Cheeck, a scar across the nose and one on the right side of the neck and breast, from a burn, a scar on the left fore arm, a scar on the outside ofthe right leg. Stands with out shoes five feet five & a half inches.

(83) 91 State of North Carolina County Court Clerks office
            Gates County   February 1/st/. 1848
55   LEMUEL, the property of the estate of Thomas SAUNDERS deceased, of Gates County hired the present year by Burwell BROTHERS, of said County and by him registered as one ofhis hands imployed by himself and Janes A SMALL in the Great Dismal Swanp.
     LAM [sic], is about twenty eight years old, mulatto, has two light spots on the right Cheeck, has a scar on the apple of the neck, a scar on the right collar bone, a small scar on the inside ofthe right fore arm, a scar on the back ofthe left hand, a scar on the left Knee, and one just before the Knee, a scar on the inside of the right leg-Stands with out shoes five feet six inches.

State of North Carolina County Court Clerks office
Gates County   February 1/st/. 1848
56   PHILIP, the property ofBurwell BROTHERS ofGates County and by him registered as one ofhis hands imployed by himself & Janes A SMALL in the Great Dismalswanp
     PHILIP is about thirty years old, full round forehead flat nose, deep eyes, has a scar on the upper lip, a scar on the pit of the stomach, three scars on the right fore arm, a scar on the back ofthe right hand, two scars on the left leg, and a scar from a burn of? right leg. Stands with out shoes ==== Five? feet nine & a half inches.

(84) 92 State of North Carolina County Court Clerks office
            Gates County   February 1/st/. 1848.
57   LEWIS, the property ofBurwell BROTHERS ofGates County and registered by him as one ofthe hands imployed by him ==== self and one of the hands Janes A SMALL in the Great

1 February 1848

(84) (Cont.) Dismal Swamp.

LEWIS is about Sixty years old, quite gray, has bad teeth, has a number of small warts upon the hands, has a scar on the left instep. Stands without Shoes five feet Six inches.

State of North Carolina County Court Clerks office
Gates County   February 1/st/. 1848
58 NOAH, the property of Mrs. Elizabeth RIDDICK, of Gates County hired the present year by Andrew VOIGHT of said [sic] and by him registered as one of his hands employed in the Great Dismal Swanp.

NOAH is about fifty five years old, brown Color, sharp mouth, deep eyes no upper teeth in front, a scar on the left Cheek, a scar on the left inside of the left forearm, and a white spot on the right shin bone. Stands with out shoes five feet six and a half inches

(85) 93 State of North Carolina County Court Clerks office
         Gates County   February 1/st/. 1848
59 STEPHEN, the property of the estate of James BAKER decd. of Gates County, hired the present year by Burwell BROTHERS and by him registered as one of his hands employed in the Great Dismal Swanp by himself and James A SMALL.

STEPHEN is about thirty seven years old, Copper Color, large flat forehead, has a scar on the right Cheeck==, has some defect of the right eye-lid. Stands with-out shoes, five feet nine & a half inches.

State of North Carolina County Court Clerks office
Gates County   February 1/st/. 1848
60 KEDAH, the property of the estate of James BAKER decd. hired the present year by John LASSITER & by him registered as one of his a hand employed in the Great Dismal Swamp by Burwell BROTHERS and James A SMALL-of said County.

KEDAR is about thirty five years old, black, round features, a small scar on the upper of the stomach, asmall scar on the inside of the right fore arm, a scar from a burn on the left elbow, scar on the right knee, little inclined to be bald on the top of the head, & stands with-out shoes Five feet five inches.

(86) 94 State of North Carolina County Court Clerks office
         Gates County   February 1/st/. 1848
61 JIM, the property of Albert SMITH of Nansemond County, Va. hired the present year by WmB WHITEHEAD, of Suffolk, va and by him registered as one of his hands in the Great Dismal Swamp

JIM is fifty nine years old, Black, flat face, small eyes, gray head and beard, a scar on the right eye, and on the outer angle of the left eye, a scar on the back of the left hand, a scar on the outside of the left right leg, teeth worn, and a vacancy between the upper ones in front - Stands with out shoes five feet Six inches. [Margin:] Reissued January 10th 15th 1849 Reissued 22nd Jany 1850 No. 21 - 61 yrs old

State of North Carolina - County Court clerks office
Gates [sic]   February 5/th/. 1848
62 GEOGE the property of /the estate of/ James COSTEN decd. of Gates County, hired the present year by GATLING & COSTEN of said county and by them employed as one of their hands in the Grat Dismal swamp

GEORGE is about twenty three years old, Copper Color, very large mouth has a scar on the left cheek one on the outside of the face forehead, a scar on the inside of the left arm, and on the outside of the same arm, some scars on the left knee, Stands with out shoes five feet Seven inches

5 February 1848

(87) 95 State of North Carolina County Court clerks office
Gates County   February 5/th/. 1848
<u>63</u> JIM, the property of John **GATLING** of Gates County, and by him registered as one of the hands employed by **GATLING &COSTEN** in the Great Dismal Swamp.

JIM is about fifty five yeas old, brown color, has a small wart, on the nose, a small scar on the left breast, a scar across the left arm, a large scar on the left elbow-joint and some small scars on the same arm, from a burn, and a small scar on the inside ofthe right Knee - Stands with out shoes five feet six inches.

State of North Carolina County court clerks office
Gates County   February 5/th/. 1848
<u>64</u> **REUBEN** the property ofthe estate of James **COSTEN** decd hired the present year by **GATLING &COSTEN** all of Gates County and by them registered as one oftheir hands enployed in the Great Dismal swamp.

REUBEN is about thirty years old, Copper color, flat face, small eyes, has a scar on the outside ofthe right arm, Stands with out shoes five feet seven and a half inches. [Margin:] Re registered the 3/rd/ Jany 1852 [A very faint "1851" is beneath "1852," and may have been erased.]

(88) 96 State of North Carolina County Court Clerks office
        Gates County   February 5/th/ 1848
<u>65</u> LUKE, the property of John **GATLING** of Gates County and by him registered as one of h̶i̶s̶ the hands enployed by **GATLING & COSTAN** of said County, in the Great Dismal swamp

LUKE is Fifty four years old, Copper Color, has a black scar on the left side of the nose, a scar on the forehead a scar on the upper part of the breast, two small scars on the outside of the right arm, two scars on the right Knee, one of? on the left Knee, and has been body shot in the legs behind. stands with out shoes Five feet four inches.

State of North Carolina County Court Clerks office
Gates County   February 5/th/. 1848
<u>66</u> NED, the property ofthe estate of Jesse **WIGGINS** decd. of Gates County, hired the present year by **GATLING &COSTEN** of said County and by them registered as one of their hands employed in the Great Dismal swamp.

NED is about Forty years old mulatto, remarkably sunken eyes, a scar on the left Cheek, a small scar on the outside of the right arm, and a scar on the back-side of the left leg & Stands with out Shoes Five feet Eight inches. Reissued March 15/50-42 yrs old & No. 47

(89) 97 State of North Carolina County Court Clerks office
        Gates County   February 5/th/. 1848
<u>67</u> DAVID the property of the estate of Jesse **WIGGINS** decd. of Gates County hired the present year by **GATLING &COSTEN** of said county and by them registered as one of their hands employed in the Great Dismal swamp

DAVID is about Twenty two years old, quite black, sharp features, a small scar on the right arm, a large scar on the outside of the right leg, and three large scars on the right leg-(read left on the first leg) - Stands with out shoes five feet seven & ahalf inches.

State of North Carolina County Court Clerks office
Gates County   February 5/th/. 1848
<u>68</u> ISAAC, the property of the estate of James **COSTEN** decd. of Gates County hired the present year by **GATLING &COSTEN** and by then registered as one of their hands in the Great Dismal swamp

ISAAC is about Forty two years old, dark brown Color, a small scar under the left

(89) (Cont.) eye, a scar on the stomach to the left side, a scar on the in outside of the left arm, a long scar on the inside of the left foot, and ascar on the right foot and a scar from a == burn on the back of the head. Stands without shoes Five feet Six inches and a half inches.

(90) 98 State of North Carolina County Court Clerks office
        Gates County   February 5/th/. 1848
69 DAVY the property of George COSTEN of Gates County and by him registered as one of their? his hands employed by GATLING &COSTEN in the Great Dismal Swamp
    DAVY is about fifty years old, rusty black Color, very large wide forehead, a scar on the left Cheek, a large scar on the outside of the right arm, two scars on the back of the left hand, and a scar on the inside of the left wrist, a scar from a cut on the left Great toe, and scar on the shin bone of the right leg. Stands with out shoes five feet six inches.

State of North Carolina County Court Clerks office
Gates County   February 5/th/. 1848
70 BEN, the property of George COSTEN of Gates County, & by him registered as one of the hands employed by GATLING &COSTEN in the Great Dismal Swamp
    BEN is about thirty seven years old, brown color, a scar on the right eye-lid, two small scars on the left wrist, a small scar on the inside of the right arm, a scar across the inside of both Great Toes Stands with out shoes five feet eleven inches.

(91) 99 State of NoCarolina County Court Clerk's office
        Gates County   Feby 5/th/. 1848.
71 RUBEN the property of the estate of Jesse WIGGINS decd of Gates County hired the present year by Charles J BARNES and by him registered as one ofhis hands in the Great Dismal Swamp
    RUBEN is about Twenty three years old, black, a scar under the left eye, a long scar onthe left thumb a scar on the inside ofthe right arm, stands without shoes Five feet Eight inches

State of NoCarolina County CourtClerks office
Gates County   February 7/th/. 1848
72 STORY? theproperty ofthe estate of James COSTEN decd ofGates County hired the present year by GATLING &COSTEN and bythem registered as one of their hands intheGreatDismalSwamp
    STORY is about twety? years Old Copper Color lage mouth and nose, the middle figen? ofthe left hand offatthe first joint Stands without shoes Five feetEight and ahalfinches

StateofNoCarolina County Court Clerks office
Gates County   Feby 7/th/. 1848
73 EDMOND the property ofthe estate of Washigton [sic] SMITH decd of Somerton Va hired the present year by Jethro RIDDICK&Co of Nansemond & by them registerd as oneoftheirhand in the GreatDismal Swamp
    EDMOND is about Fifteen years old Brown Color, two small scars on the back of the left hand has apleseant [sic] /open/ Countenance. Stands without Shoes Five feet nine inches

(92) 100 Stateof NoCarolina County Court Clerks office
        Gates County   Feby 7/th/. 1847 [sic]
74 RANDOLPH the property ofthe Estate of John LANGE [or LARGE] decdof Nansemond Va hird thepresent year by Jethro RIDDICK&Co &bythemregisterd as one of their hands em-

7 February 1848

(92) (Cont.) ployedintheGreat DismalSwamp
     RANDOLPH is about Fifty five yearsold quite black has a scar ontheleft cheek, teeth open in front ascaron the Outside ofthe ~~left~~ /right/ leg. Stands without shoes Five feetEightinches and is quite gray. [Margin:] X R B. W.?

State ofNoCarolina County Court Clerks office
Gates County   Feby 16/th/. 1848
75 NUSOM the property ofthe estate of Heony? KEOUGES? decd of Nansemond Couty?Va hired thepresent year by James B NORFLEET of Suffolk and byhim registerd as one of his hands emplyed inthe Great Dismal Swamp
     NUSOMis about Thirty five yeas old, Cellter color, has a scar in the forehead ascar in the breast and a number of white spots inthe breast Stands without shoes Five feet Eight inches

Stateof NoCa Conty CourtClerk?s office
Gates County   [No date.]
76 WILLIS the property ofthe estate of Archibald BRINKLEY of Nansemond CountyVa hired the present year

(93) 101 by James BNORFLEET ofSuffolkandby him registerd as oneofhis hands inthe GreatDismalSwamp
     WILLIS is about Twenty five? years old, light brown Color, remarkably lage mouth and thick lips, two scars uponthe right side ofthe neck, a lage scaron the right fore arm andoneon the backofthe righthand ascaronthe left elbow and one on the inside of the left forearm a scar onthe calfofthe left leg and stands without shoes Five feet six inches

State of NoCarolina County Court Clerks office
     Gates County   Febry 21/st/. 1848.
77 MILES the property of Joseph EASON ofGates County and by him registerd as one of the hands employed by Andrew VOIGHT in the Great Dismal Swamp
     MOSES [sic] is about Forty five years old, light brown color, full features, bad teeth with a scar across the great toe ofthe left foot stands without shoes Five feet Seven and a half inches

State of North Carolina Co. Co. Clerks office
Gates County   March 25/th/. 1848
[No Reg. #.] GILBERT the property of the estate of Joseph RIDDICK's estate of [sic] Nansemond County Va. hired the present year by Andrew VOIGHT of Gates County, and by him registered as one ofhis hands employed in the great Dismal
     See beyond [End of entry.]

(94) 102 State of NoCarolina CoCo Clerks office
          Gates County   March 7/th/ 1848
78 PETER the property of Nathl? BERRBE? of Nansemond CoVa hired the present year by WmB. WHITEHEAD ofSuffolk &by him registered as oneof his hands imployed in the great Dismal Swamp
     PETERis about Twety Eight years old, brown complexion broad forehead, pleasant counternance, a small scar ~~in~~ on the forehead, has lost two teeth in front one in each jaw immediately opposite each other, several small scars on the breast, a small scar on the right arm just above the wrist and one on the left arm just above the elbow joint on the ~~right side~~ outside and a scar on the left leg just on the front side of the shin bone. Stands withhout out [sic] shoes five feet five & a quarter inches. [Remainder of page is blank.]

25 March 1848

(95) 103 State of North Carolina Co. Co. Clerk's office
         Gates County   March 25/th/1848
79 GILBERT, the property of the estate of Joseph RIDDICK decd. of Nansemond
County Va. hired the present year by Andrew VOIGHT of Gates County, and by him
registered as one ofhis hands, enployed in the Great Dismal Swamp.
    GILBERT is about Sixty four years old, of black conplexion with eyes wide apat a
prominent forehead, has a scar across the nose extending to the corner ofthe right
eye, a wen on the right arm, and a nunber of scars on both legs from sores, and stands
with out shoes five feet eight inches

State of North Carolina Co. Co. Clerk's office
Gates County   March 31/st/. 1848
80 CHARLES the property of James SCOTT of Smithfield in Virginia, hired the present
year by John GAINES /of Camden County/ and Nathaniel GAINES, and by then registered as
one of their hands employed in the Great Dismal Swamp.
    CHARLES is about forty one years old, black conplexion, with a scar over the right
eye, and just above the elbow on both arms, and stands with out shoes five feet and
three & a half inches.

(96) 104 State of Noth Carolina Co. Co. Clerks office
         Gates County   March 31/st/. 1848
81 STEPHEN the property of Anisey WILSON of Norfolk County Va. hired the present
year by John GAINES and Nathaniel GAINES /of Camden County/ and by them registered as
one of their hands employed in the Great Dismal Swamp.
    STEPHEN is about seventeen years of age, of a dark complixion, with a broad flat
nose, with a nunber of scars on both legs, and a small scar between the points of the
eye-brows. and stands without shoes five feet four inches.

State of NoCarolina CoCoClurks office
Gates County   [No date.]
82 TURNER the property of Daniel BRINKLEY of Nansemond County Va hired the present
year by H. L. EPPES of Said County andby him registered as one of his hands employed
in the Great Dismill [sic] Swamp
    TURNER is a bout thirteen years old of black complixion with a large full face and
vary thick lips he has a number of small scars on both legs from burnes & skins and
Stands without Shoes four feet eight Inches.

(97) 105 State of North Carolina Co. Co. Clerk's office
         Gates County   [No date.]
83 TURNER the property of = Daniel BRINKLY of Nansemond County Va, hired the present
yea by H L EPPES of said County and by him registered as one of his hands employed in
the Great Dismal swamp.
    TURNER is about ====== thirteen years old of black conplexion with a large full
face and very thick lips he has a nunber of small scars on both legs from burns and
skins and stands without shoes four feet eight inches. [Margin:] Error - Error -

State of North Carolina Co. Co. Clerk's office
Gates County   [No date.]
83 LEWIS the property of Thos. SPENCER of Gates County hired the present year by H L
EPPES of Nansemond Va, and by him registered as one of his hands employed in the Great
Dismill [sic] swanp.
    LEWIS is about Fourty? five years old of brown conplexion has one tooth missing
in? the upper Jaw in front with the right leg shorter than the left. he has a scar on
the knee-pan of the right leg and stands without shoes five feet eight inches.

18 April 1848

(98) 106 State of North Carolina} Co: Co: Clerks offi__
             Gates County   }   April 18/th/.. 184_
84   WILLIAM - The property of Richard EPPES of Nansemond County Virginia, and the present year hired by Jethro RIDDICK &c Co: and by him ==== regirstered as one of his hands - to work in the Desemel [sic] Swamp
     WILLIAM is about 25 years old with black Complection with a high forehea_ with a rasbury mark (so called) on == the left side of his neck - & stands withou_ shoes five feet high.

State of North Carolina Co. Co. Clerk's office
  Gates County   April 23/d/.1848
85 DICK the property of J===== Charles WALTERS of Suffolk Va, and hired the present year by Willis S. RIDDICK of said place & by him registered as one of his hands employed in the Great Dismal swamp.
     DICK is about Forty five years of age old, of black Complexion === with a ==== tolerably large nose, has a considerable in dentation [sic] on the fore head just above the nose, & a scar over the left eye, with He has also a great protuberance == === === ofthe Knee-pan of the left leg. He stands with out shoes five? feet nine inches.

(99) 107 State of North Carolina} County court clerk's office
             Gates County   }   May 10/th/ 1848.
86 DAVY, the property of James CARR, orphan of James CARR dec/d/, of Norfolk County, hired the present year by James S?. SEGUINE of said place and by him registered as one of his hands employed in the Great Dismal Swamp.
     DAVY, is about fourteen years of age, of light black complexion, with a scar upon the external part of the left leg just below the Knee of the same from a burn & one just above the Knee of the same leg from a cut, and stands without shoes four feet nine inches high

North Carolina County Court Clerk's office
Gates County   May 10/th/ 1848.
87 LEWIS, the property of John MOORE of Norfolk County Va., hired the present year by James S. SEGUINE of said County of Norfolk, and by him registered as one of his hands employed in the Great Dismal Swamp
     LEWIS is about seventeen years of age, of a black complexion with a scar on the heel-string of the right leg, and one across the instep of the left foot, and stands without shoes five feet and four and a half inches high. . . . . .

(100) 108 North Carolina} County Court Clerk's office
             Gates County }   May 10/th/ 1848.
88. DAVY, the property of James S. SEGUINE of Norfolk County Va., and by him regis-tered as one of his hands employed in the Great Dismal swamp.
     DAVY, is about seventeen years of age, of black Complexion, with a large mouth & nose, & white teeth. He has a scar about three inches long upon the outside of the left leg, a small scar on the back of the left hand, and one just above the wrist of the same arm, and stands without shoes five feet two inches high.

North Carolina} County Court Clerk's office
Gates County }   May 10/th/ 1848.
89 CARY said to be a free boy of Colour hired by James S. SEGUINE as one of his hands employed in the great Dismal Swamp.
     CARY is about seventeen years Old, of a brown complexion, with a protuberance upon the top of the right ear, with a hole by the side of it, and stands without shoes five feet one inch and a half high.

10 May 1848

(101) 109 North Carolina} County Court Clerk's office
            Gates County }   May 10/th/ 1848.
90 JOHN, the property of James S SEGUINE of Norfolk County Virginia, and by him registered as one of his hands employed in the Great Dismal Swamp.

JOHN is about fifty eight years old of dark complexion, with a small mole under the left breast, and a small scar on the outside of the left leg, and also a small scar on the front part of the left thigh below the groins, and stands without shoes five feet eight inches high.

North Carolina} County Court Clerk's office
Gates County }   May 10/th/ 1848.
91 Robert COWPER, the property of James S. SEGUINE of Norfolk County Va., and by him registered as one of his hands employed in the great Dismal Swamp.

Robert is about seventeen years of age, of yellow complexion, with bushy hair. He has a purple mark on the right shoulder, and a tumour on the right Collar bone, and stands without shoes four feet eleven inches high.

(102) 110 North Carolina} County Court Clerk's office
            Gates County }   May 10/th/ 1848.
92 DANIEL, the property of James S SEGUINE MOORE? of Norfolk City, and hired by James S. SEGUINE of Norfolk County the present year and by him registered as one of his hands employed in the great Dismal Swamp.

DANIEL is about six teen years old, of a black Complexion, with two scars on the right thigh from the bite of a dog and one just below the Knee of the same leg, and also one on his thumb and wrist of the left arm, and stands without shoes five feet.

State of North Carolina} County Court Clerk's office
            Gates County}   May 10/th/ 1848.
93. AMOS, the property of James S. SEGUINE of Norfolk County Va., and by him registered as one of his hands employed in the Great Dismal Swamp.

AMOS is about fifteen years of age, of black complexion, with a scar on his left arm above the elbow, a scar on the left Knee, one [sic] the great toe with with [sic] the nail off, and a scar on his tongue from a bite, and stands without shoes four feet ten and a half inches.

(103) 111 State of NoCarolina County Court Clerks office
            Gates County   May 15/th/ 1848
94 JOthe property of Jackson BRINKLEY of Nansemond County, va hired the present year by WmBWHITEHEAD of Suffolk and by him registerd as one of his hands employed in the Great Dismal Swamp

JOis about Twenty five yeas old quite black, large nose and mouth, without beard, has a scar on the right cheek, a lage scar on the right wrist, and stands without shoes Five feet five inches. Reissued Jany: 22nd 1850 No 21-27 vrs old. [Margin:] Reissued Jany 10/th/ 1849 No. 28.

State of No.Carolina CoCoClerks office
            Gates County   May 15 th 1848
95 SAM the property of Jacob RICHARDSON of Pasquatank County County NoC and hired the present year by R R HILL of Gates County and by him employed as one of his hands in the Great Dismill Swamp

SAM is a bout fifty three years old quite black Good thick large fetures a small scar on the out side of the left arm a small scar on the inside side of the right Knee and two scars on the left shin bone /&/ Stands with out Shoes five feet sevin and a half /Inches/ high

39

(104) 112 State ofNoCarolina CoCoClerks office
                    Gates County } May 15th 1848
96 HARMUN the property of Tho/s/ BARNES of Gates County NoCarolina and by him hired
the present year by ===== R. R. HILL of Said County and by Said HILL employed as one
ofhis hands in the Great Dismill Swamp
     HARMAN is about Thirty years old Black has a Small Scar on the forehead on the
left Side full featurs, round fore head aplesent countenance a Small Scar on the left
Knee Stands without Shoes five feet Six Inches and one eight high

State of North Carolin_ County Court Clerk's offic_
Gates County   May 26/th/ 1848
97 DANIEL, the property of William BEEMAN of Gates County hired the present year by
Robert R HILL of said County and by him registered as one of his hands enployed in the
Great Dismal Swamp
     DANIEL, is about twenty four years old of black complexion, with a small scar on
the elbow ofthe right arm, and a scar from a blow on the front of the right leg.
     DANIEL Stands with out Shoes Five feet eight inches.

(105) 113 State of North Carolina County Court clerk's office
                 Gates County   May 26/th/ 18468
98 WILLIS the property of Thos. BARNES of Gates County, hired the present year by
Robert R HILL and by him registered as one of his hands enployed in the Great Dismal
Swamp
     WILLIS a bright mulatto, is about twenty two years old, with a ==== scar on the
right leg from a burn, one on the left arm ==== near the elbow, and also one on the
forefinger of the left hand.
     WILLIS has a large mouth, long upper lip and Stands with out Shoes five feet four
inches.

State of North Carolina} County Court Clerk's Office
         Gates County}   june 3rd 1848.
99 HENRY the property of Col. Jesse WIGGINS decd. and hired the present year by
Tho/s/. BARNS and registered by Ro. R. HILL as one of his hands to work in the Great
Dismal Swamp
     HENRY is about twenty four years of age, of black complexion with projecting lips
and flat Nose, with a scar on the left leg upon the Shin bone, also a small Scar upon
the right leg and a small scar upon the middle toe of the right foot, and Stands
without Shoes five feet and Seven inches high.

(106) 114 State of NCarolina} County Court Clerk's office
                Gates County   }   June 7?/th/ 1848
100 SAM the property of John RIDDICK of Nansemond County Va. and hired thepresent
year by Wm B. WHITEHEAD of Suffolk and by him registered as one of his hands to work
in the Great Dismal Swamp.
     SAM is about forty years of age of black Complexion with thick lips and flat nose
and has a scar in the palm of his left hand, and stands without shoes five feet nine
and a half inches high.

State of North Carolina County Court Clerk's office
Gates County   June 13/th/ 1848
101 JAMES, the property of Marmaduke JONES of Nansemond County Virginia, hired the
present year by William A JONES of said County, and by him registered to work upon the
land of William B WHITEHEAD in the Great Dismal Swamp.
     JAMES is about twenty eight years of age, of dark brown complexion. He has a bald
place on the back of the head, a number of large scars on the right thigh from a

(106) (Cont.) severe whipping has two scars on the right shoulder from a gun-shot wound, and many scars on the back, from whippings [End of entry.]

(107) 115 State of N.Carolina} County Court Clerk's Office
             Gates County   }   July 28/th/ 1848.
<u>102.</u> Hardy REID a free boy of Colour, a resident of Nansemond County Va and employed by Willis S. RIDDICK as one of his hands in the Great Dismal Swamp.

Hardy is about twenty one years of age, very fair for a person of Colour, and has blue eyes, Straight hair and a large prominent nose. He has no Scars about his person, and stands without shoes five feet two and a quarter inches.

State of N.Carolina} County Court Clerk's Office
Gates County   }   August 11/th/. 1848.
<u>103</u> PRENTICE, the property of Jesse R SAVAGE of Nansemond County Va., hired the present year by Wm. B. WHITEHEAD of Suffolk, and by him registered as one of his hands employed in the Great Dismal Swamp

PRENTICE is about thirty one years of age, brown complexion has a large mouth, flat nose and prominent eyes. He has two raised Scars on the bend of the left leg. His legs are a little bowed. And stands without shoes five feet seven inches.

(108) 116 State of N.Carolina} County Court Clerk's Office
             Gates County   }   August 11/th/. 1848.
<u>104</u> BURWELL, the property of Margaret BYRD of Nansemond County Va, hired the present year by Wm.B. WHITEHEAD of Suffolk an_ by him registered as one of his hands employed in the Great Dismal Swamp.

BURWELL is about twenty fou_ years of age, dark yellow complexion, has a large mouth, a flat pointed nose and holes for earrings in both ears. He has a scar on the front part of the left leg, and one on the instep of the right foot. He stands without shoes five feet seven & a half inches. <u>Reissued Jany 10/th/ 1849. No. 34.</u> Reiss/d/ 25 yrs oldJany 22/nd/ 1850 No. 19.

State of N. Carolina} County Court Clerk's office
Gates County   }   August 11/th/ 1848.
<u>105</u> MILES, the property of Willis WIGGINS of Nansemond County Va., hired the present year by Wm.B. WHITEHEAD of Suffolk and by him registered as one of his hands employed in the Great Dismal Swamp.

MILES is about twenty two years of age, has a light black Complexion, large sleepy eyes and high cheek bones He has a scar just perceptable over the right eye, and one also in /the/ hollow of the right foot. He stands without shoes five feet seven and a half inches. Reissued Janry 22/nd/ 1850 as the property of the estate of Willis WIGGINS 23years old No. 35

(109) 117 State of N. Carolina} County Court Clerk's Office
             Gates County   }   August 31/st/ 1848.
<u>106</u> LEWIS HENRY, the property of Archibald RIDDICK of Suffolk Virginia, hired the present year by Willis S. RIDDICK of Nansemond County Va. and by him registered as one of his hands employed in the Great Dismal Swamp.

LEWIS HENRY, a boy about twelve years old, has a brown complexion, good teeth, flat nose and large nostrils. He has a small scar on the front part of his left leg; also another small scar upon the instep of the right leg. And stands with out shoes four feet four inches.

State of N. Carolina} County Court Clerk's office
Gates County   }   August 31/st/ 1848.
<u>107.</u> WASHINGTON, the property of the heirs of John KNIGHT Dec/d/. of Nansemond

(109) (Cont.) County Virginia, hired the present year by Willis S. RIDDICK of Nansemond County Va, and by him registered as one of his hands employed in the Great Dismal Swamp.

WASHINGTON, a boy about Eleven years old, has a black complexion, good teeth and a ring worm upon his forehead. He has two small scars upon the left wrist, with several small scars on his legs, occasioned probably by burns. And stands with out shoes four feet two inches.

(110) 118 State of North Carolina} County Court Clerk's Office
        Gates County   }   November 1/st/ 1848.
108 WILSON the property of James R. [or B.] SPENCE of Camden County N Carolin_ hired the present /year/ by James S. SEGUINE of Norfolk County Virginia and by him registered as one of his hands employed in the Great Dismal Swamp lying in this County.

WILSON is about twenty three years old, of yellow Complexion with a large Scar across the instep of the left foot, from a burn and Stands without Shoes five feet nine inches.

State of North Carolina} County Court Clerk's office
Gates County   }   November 1/st/. 1848.
109 EDMOND, the property of James R. SPENCE of Camden County N. Carolina, hired the present year by James S. SEQUINE of Norfolk County Virginia, and by him registered as one of his hands employed in the GreatDismal Swamp in this County.

EDMOND is about twenty Six years old, of brown complexion, == no scars about his person, but has a black Splotch about the size of a half dollar upon the left breast. And stands without shoes five feet five and a half inches.

(111) 119 State of North Carolina} County court Clerks office
        Gates County   }   November 25th 1848.
110 JETHRO the property of A.R. HARRELL of Gates County N.C andby him registered as one ofhis hands employed in the Great Dismill Swamp. JETHRO the property of A

JETHRO is about Twenty three years of age of, black complexion with a scar on the in side of the left Knee from a burn, & stands with out shoes fivefeet five Inches

State of North Carolina} County Court Clerk's office
Gates County   }   December 4/th/ 1848
111 BOB, the property of Willis W. HARRELL of Gates County. hired the present year by Isaac S. HARRELL &Co of said County, and by them registered as one of their hands employed in the Great Dismal Swamp in Gates County

BOB is about twenty eight years of age, of black complexion, and has a large Scar on the outside of his right leg; and also another Scar near the left eye, and stands without shoes Six feet high.

(112) 120 State of North Carolina} County Court Clerk's office
        Gates County   }   December 26/th/. 1848.
112 JACK, the property of Isaac S. HARRELL of Gates County N.C and by him registered as one of his hands employed in the Great Dismal Swamp in said County.

JACK is about twenty Six years of age of dark complexion and has a small scar about one inch long immediately above the right eye, also a large scar on the front part of his left leg, with /and/ several scars on, above and below both knees occasioned probably by a burn. He has a very large scar on his right shoulder blade and several smaller ones on his back occasioned by whipping - also a large scar or mark on the outside of his left leg near the Knee; and stands without shoes five feet one and a half inches.

30 December 1848

(112) (Cont.) State of North Carolina} County Court Clerks Office
                 Gates County   }   Decr.. 30/th/ 1848
113.   JOHN the property of Henry COSTON decd. of Gates County, North Carolina, and
hired for the ensui_ [torn] year by Andrew WHITE, and by him registered as one of his
hands, employed in the Great Dismal Swamp in said county.
     JOHN is about Forty years of age of brown complexion, with two scars on the
outside of the left leg, with a scar on the right big toe, occasioned by being frost
bitten, with a low forehead and thin

(113) 121 visage, with a few scars on the back occasioned by the whip: Stands
without shoes, five feet one and one half Inches in heighth.

State of North Carolina} County Court Clerk's office
Gates County   }   January 2nd 1849.
114 No 1 ABRAM the property of Isajah LANGSTON of Nansemond County Virginia, hired
the present year by William B. WHITEHEAD of Suffolk and by him registered as one of
his hands employed in the Great Dismal Swamp.
     ABRAM is about twenty four years of age of black complexion and with thick lips.
He has no /and a good set/ of teeth. He has no scars about his person except a small
one upon the left hand above the thumb; and stands with out shoes five feet one and a
half inches. Reissued 25 yrs old. Janry 22/nd/ 1850 No. 23

State of North Carolina} County Court Clerk's office
Gates County   }   January 2nd 1849.
2   PAYTON the property of James RIDDICK of Nansemond County Virginia, hired the
present year by W. B. WHITEHEAD of Suffolk and by him registered as one of his hands
employed in the Great Dismal Swamp. R. I. 23 yrs. old Janry 22 1850 No 24
     PAYTON is about twenty two years of age of dark Complexion with large nostrils
good teeth and thick lips. He has Several Scars upon each hand and stands without
Shoes five feet five inches high.

(114) 122 State of North Carolina} County Court Clerk's Office
                 Gates County   }   January 2nd 1849.
114 3 HARVEY, the property of the heirs of Riddick JONES decd of Gates County, hired
the present year by William B. WHITEHEAD of Suffolk Virginia, and by him registered as
one of his hands employ_ in the Great Dismal Swamp.
     HARVEY is about twenty one years, of age of black Complexion with a flat nose,
tolerable thick lips and a good set of teeth. He has a small scar upon his nose and a
number of scars upon his knees and back; and stands without shoes five feet two
inches. Reissd 22 yrs old Janry. 22nd 1850 No. 20 five feet 3 Inches [Margin:]
Registered the 5 Jany 1852

State of North Carolina} County Court Clerk's Office
Gates County   }   January 2nd 1849.
4   SIMON, the property of the heirs of Riddick JONES, dec/d/. of Gates County, hired
the present year by William B. WHITEHEAD of Suffolk Virginia, and by him registered as
one of his hands employed in the Great Dismal Swamp.
     SIMON is about nineteen years of age, of black Complexion with /has/ a large mouth
and good teeth. He has no scars about his person and stands without shoes five feet
two inches. Reissd 20yrs old. Jany 22nd 1850. No 21.

(115) 123 State of North Carolina} County Court Clerk's office
                 Gates County   }   January 2nd 1849.
5   NELSON the property of the heirs of Riddick JONES, decd. of Gates County, hired
the present year by William B. WHITEHEAD of Suffolk Virginia and by him registered as

(115) (Cont.) one of his hands employed in the Great Dismal Swamp.

NELSON is about twenty three years of age, of light Complexion ~~with~~ /has/ large eyes, good teeth and a high forehead. He has a large scar upon the outside of the left leg; also one upon the right leg above the instep, and ==== one upon the left hand, and stands without shoes five feet three and a half inches.

State of North Carolina} County Court Clerk's office
Gates County   }   January 2nd 1849.
6   TURNER the property of Luke RABY J/r/. of Nansemond County Virginia, hired the present year by William B. WHITEHEAD of Suffolk, and by him registered as one of his hands employed in the Great Dismal Swamp.

TURNER, is about twenty one years of age, of dark of [sic] Complexion, ~~with~~ /has/ a wide mouth and a good set of teeth. He has a large Scar upon his left leg, also one upon his back – one upon the left arm and Several upon each hand, and stands without shoes five feet one and a half inches.

(116) 124 State of NorthCarolina} County Court Clerk's office
            Gates County   } January 2nd 1849.
7   ELI the property of the heirs of Robert R. SMITH ~~deceased~~ of Nansemond County Virginia, hired the present year by William B. WHITEHEAD of Suffolk, and by him registered as one of his hands employed in the Great Dismal Swamp.

ELI is about twenty eight years of age, of black Complexion, has good front teeth and a small /scar/ on the back of his left hand. He has a scar on his left arm below the elbow and a number of scars on his back from whipping; and stands without shoes five feet four inches.

State of North Carolina} County Court Clerk's office
Gates County   }   January 2nd 1849.
8. JACK, the property of James RIDDICK of Nansemond County Virginia hired the present year by William B. WHITEHEAD of Suffolk and by him registered as one of his hands employed in the Great Dismal Swamp.

JACK is about twenty one years of age, of brown Complexio_ has good teeth and thick lips. He has a small scar upon the left leg just below the knee; also a large sca_ upon his right knee – One upon the right hand and two small scars upon his right arm, and stands without shoes five feet five inches. Reissd 1 yr. older Jany 22nd 1850 No. 16

(117) 125 State of NorthCarolina} County Court Clerk's office
            Gates County   } January 8/th/ 1849.
9   SOLOMON, the property of Mary Ann HILL of Gates County, hired the present year by RobertR. HILL of said County and by him registered as one of his hands employed in the Great Dismal Swamp.

SOLOMON is about thirty two years of age, of black complexion, has good teeth, and large nostrills. He has two large Scars upon the right leg, and a bruise on the left leg; and a large Scar upon the elbow of his right arm; also a small scar upon his right hand and stands with out shoes four feet eleven and a half inches

State of North Carolina} County Court Clerk's office;
Gates County   }   January 8/th/ 1849.
10 KEDAR, the property of the heirs of Henry COSTEN deceased of Gates County, hired the present year by Robert R. HILL of said County, and by him registered as one of his hands employed in the Great Dismal Swamp.

KEDAR is about twenty five years of age, of black Complexion, has a flat nose and thick lips. He has a large scar upon the back part of his head and several scars upon his back and left arm. He has a very large scar === ==== upon his left arm about four

(117) (Cont.) inches from the top of his shoulder and a small /scar/ upon his right hand, and stands without shoes five feet four inches.

(118) 126 State of NorthCarolina}   County Court Clerk's offic_
             Gates County   }   January 8/th/ 1849.

JOHN, the property of the heirs of Henry COSTEN deceased, ofGates County, hired the present year by Andrew VOIGHT of Said County and by him registered as one _f his hands employed in the Great Dismal Swamp. (11)

JOHN is about forty years of age, of brown Complexion, with two scars on the outside of the left leg, & one on the right big toe occasioned by being frostbitten; he has a low forehead and thin visage and a few scars on his back occasioned by whipping, and stands without shoes five feet one and a half inches.

State of NorthCarolina}   County Court Clerk's office;
Gates County   }   January 9/th/ 1849.

12 PETER, the property of the heirs of Riddick JONES deceased ofGates County, hired the present year by William B. WHITEHEAD of Suffolk Virginia, and by him registered as one of his hands employed in the Great Dismal Swamp in Gates County.

PETER is about thirty five years of age, of dark Complexion, hasgood front teeth, and a full under lip. He has two large scars upon his right leg; and the end of his toe, next to the great toe, has been cut off; and a number of small scars upon his left leg. He has a small scar near the left eye, and three small scars upon his left hand, and stands without shoes five feet five inches high. Reissd. 36 yrs old, Jany 22 1850 No. 22 [Margin:] registered this 3/rd/ Jany 1852

(119) 127 State of North Carolina}   County Court Clerk's office;
             Gates County   }   January 10/th/ 1849.

13. GEORGE, the property of the heirs of John SAVAGE deceased of Nansemond County Virginia, hired the present year by William B. WHITEHEAD of Suffolk and by him registered as on_ of his hands employed in the Great Dismal Swamp. GEORGE is about twenty eight years of age, of dark complexion, ==== has good teeth and a scar in the corner of his left eye. He has several scars on the right leg and stands without shoes five feet eight and a half inches.

State of North Carolina}   County Court Clerk's office;
Gates County   }   January 10/th/ 1849.

14 WILLIS, the property of Javan R. FRANKLIN of Nansemond County Virginia and hired the present year by William B WHITEHEAD of Suffolk, and by him registered as one of his hands in the Dismal Swamp.

WILLIS is about twenty six years old, light complexion, with a remarkable full fore head; large flat nose, large nostrills, scattering beard, good teeth and a small scar, about the size of a four pence on the outside of the left leg about two inches above the ankle; stands without shoes five feet and a half inch. X Reissued Jany 22 nd 1850, 27 yrs. old No. 25

(120) 128 State of North Carolina}   County Court Clerk's office
             Gates County   }   January 10/th/ 1849.

No. 15   NOLAND, the property of Jno. MORGAN of Gates County, hired the present year by Wm.B.WHITEHEAD of Suffolk Virginia and by him registered as one of his hands _mployed in the Great Dismal Swamp.

NOLAND is about twenty six years of age, very black, has a long scar on the right side of the face above the eye, and a bad scar on the outside of the right foot, and stands without shoes five feet eight inches.

State of North Carolina}   County Court Clerk's office

10 January 1849

(120) (Cont.) Gates County   } January 10/th/ 1849.
No 16.   PETER, the property of James SAUNDERS of Nansemond County Virginia, and hired the present year by William B. WHITEHEAD of Suffolk and by him employed in the Great Dismal Swamp.

PETER is about twenty two years old, dark copper complexion, has a scar on the under lip, thick lips, some small scars on the breast, Stands without shoes five feet, seven inches. X. Reissued 1 year older Janry 22 nd 1850 No. 15.

(121) 129 State of North Carolina} County Court Clerk's office,
              Gates County   } January 10/th/ 1849.
No. 17   Peter EDWARDS, the property of Allen EDWARDS of Southampton County Virginia and hired the present year by WilliamB. WHITEHEAD of Suffolk Virginia and by him registered as one of his hands employed in the Great Dismal Swamp

Peter is about fifty one years old, quite bald, with a patch of hair on the brim of the forehead, with bad teeth, particularly on the under jaw, and a scar from a burn on the top of his head. Stands without shoes five feet five and three quarter inches. X. Reiss/d/ 52 yrs old Jany 22 1850 No. 17

State of North Carolina} County Court Clerk's office
Gates County   }   January 10/th/ 1849
No. 18   HENDERSON, the property of the heirs of Mathew JOINER of Southampton County Virginia, hired the present year by William B. WHITEHEAD of Suffolk, and by him registered as one of his hands in the Great Dismal Swamp.

HENDERSON is about twenty eight years old, of dark brown complexion, tolerable flat face, tolerable rank beard, a little bow legged, a small scar on the left cheek, a small scratch on the back of the left hand, a scar across the right thigh, about one and a half inches long; a black scar on the inside of the calf of the left leg, Stands five feet six and a half inches. Reissd 29 yrs. old Jany 22 1850 No. 18.
X.   Marked reissued from No 18 to No 39

(122) 130 State of North Carolina} County Court Clerk's office
              Gates County   } January 10/th/.. 1848 [sic].
No. 39 [sic] EDMOND the property of William B. WHITEHEAD of Suffolk and by him registered as one of his hands in the? Dismal Swamp.

EDMOND appears to be about forty six years old, black, good teeth, a little gray, tolerable full beard, with a scar on the stomach about three inches long and a scar on the right knee about an inch long and stands without shoes five feet eight and a half inches high. Reissued 27 [sic] yrs. old Jany 22nd 1850 No. 26.

State of North Carolina} County Court Clerk's office;
Gates County   }   January 10/th/ 1849.
No. 40   CHARLES, the property of Wm. B. WHITEHEAD of Suffolk Virginia and by him registered as one of his hands in the Dismal Swamp.

CHARLES is about fifty one years old, a little gray head, thin upon the top of the head; left eye out, a large scar across the left side of the fore head; running under the hair, a small scar between the eyes, a scar upon the back of the left wrist and on the upper joint of the left thumb, one on the upper joint of the left fore finger; a long scar on the right leg from the knee down and several scars on the left leg; and a small one on the right collar bone and badly marked upon the back. X. [End of entry.]

(123) 131 State of North Carolina} County Court Clerk's office
              Gates County   } January 10/th/ 1849.
No. 41.   RANDOLPH the property of the heirs of John SAVAGE dec/d/. of Nansemond Virginia, hired the present year by Wm. B. WHITEHEAD of Suffolk and by him registered as one of his hands employed in the Great Dismal Swamp.

(123) (Cont.) RANDOLPH is about fifty six years old, quite black, has a scar on the left cheek, teeth open in front, a scar on the outside of the right leg, Stands without shoes five feet eight inches and is quite gray. Reissued Jany 22nd 1850 No. 36 - 57 years old.

State of North Carolina} County Court Clerk's office
Gates County   } January 26/th/ 1849.
No 42   REUBEN the property of the estate of R. R. SMITH of Nansemond County Virginia, hired the present year by Willis S. RIDDICK of Suffolk & by him registered as one of his hands employed in the Great Dismal Swamp.

REUBEN is about twenty four years of age, of dark complexion, has good front teeth and a large scar upon his breast and stands without shoes five feet five and a half inches.

(124) 132 State of North Carolina} County Court Clerk's office
         Gates County   } January 26/th/. 1849.
No 43.   JOE the property of Johnathan RODGERS of Nansemond County Virginia, hired the present year by Willis S. RIDDICK of Suffolk and by him registered as one of his hands employed in the GreatDismal Swamp.

JOE is about twenty four years of age, of black complexion has a good set of teeth and two large scars upon his left leg and a small one /upon/ his right leg. He has a small scar upon the thumb of his right hand, and stands without shoes five feet three inches.

State of North Carolina} County Court Clerk's office
Gates County   } January 26/th/ 1849.
No 44   TOM the property of Elwin SMITH of Nansemond County Virginia, hired the present year by Willis S. RIDDICK of Suffolk and by him registered as one of his hands employed in the Great Dismal Swamp.

TOM is about sixteen years of age, of dark complexion, has thick lips and a small scar upon the left side of his face. And several scars upon his hands and legs and stands without shoes four feet six and a half inches.

(125) 133 State of North Carolina} County Court Clerk's office;
         Gates County   } January 26/th/ 1849.
No 45.   WASHINGTON the property of the estate of JnoR. KNIGHT of Nansemond County Virginia hired the present year by W. S. RIDDICK of Suffolk and by him registered as one of his hands employed in the GreatDismal Swamp.

WASHINGTON is about thirteen years of age, of dark complexion, has good teeth and a small /scar/ upon the back of his left leg and several small scars upon both knees and stands without shoes four feet two and a half inches.

State of NorthCarolina} County Court Clerk's office
Gates County   } January 26/th/ 1849.
No 46.   TURNER the property of Daniel BRINKLEY of Nansemond County Virginia, hired the present year by Willis S. RIDDICK of Suffolk, and by him registered asone of his hands employed in the Great Dismal swamp.

TURNER is about seventeen years of age, of black complexion, has good teeth, alarge mouth and a scar upon the left side of his neck from a burn. He has a /several/ large scars upon his left knee and several upon his right leg & knee and one upon his right hand; and stands without shoes four ==== feet 8 1/2 inches

(126) 134 State of North Carolina} County Court Clerk's office
         Gates County   } January 26/th/ 1849.
No 47.   MOSES the property ofthe estate of RoRSMITH of Nansemond Cty Virginia hired

(126) (Cont.) the present year by Willis S. RIDDICK of Suffolk, and by him registered as one of his hands employed in the Great Dismal Swamp.

MOSES is about twelve years of age, of brown conplexion, has thick lips and good teeth. He has several small scars upon his hands and legs and stands without shoes four feet six inches, nearly.

State of North Carolina}   County Court Clerk's office
  Gates County   }   January 26/th/ 1849.
No 48.   BOB the property of Sophia DUKES of Nansemond County Virginia, hired the present year by Willis S. RIDDICK of Suffolk, and by him registered as one of his hands employed in the Great Dismal Swamp.

BOB seems to be about fifteen years of age, of dark complexion, tolerable large eyes, thick lips and good teeth. He has a small scar at the corner of the right eye and one just below the same eye, and a small scar on the right side of his head just below the edge of the hair, and stands without shoes four feet seven & a half inches.

(127) 135 State of North Carolina} County Court Clerk's office,
            Gates County   } January 26/th/ 1849.
No. 49.   JERRY, the property of the estate of JnoR. KNIGHT of Nansemond County Virginia, hired the present by [sic] year by Willis S. RIDDICK of Suffolk and by him registered as one of his hands employed in the Great Dismal Swamp.

JERRY is about twenty two years of age, of black complexion /has a/ large full face, and good teeth. He has a small scar upon the left side of his face, one upon his left hand and a large one upon the right leg, and one upon the outside of the left leg and stands without shoes five feet four and a half inches.

State of No.Ca.} County Court Clerk's office
Gates County   } January 26/th/ 1849.
No 50.   LEWIS, the property ofthe estate of Robt.R. SMITH of Nansemond County Virginia, hired the present year by Willis S. RIDDICK of Suffolk and by him registered as one of his hands employed in the Great Dismal Swamp.

LEWIS is about twenty one years of age, of dark complexion, flat nose and large nostrills. He has a small scar upon the forehead one upon the right knee - one upon the left knee and several upon his hands - and stands with out shoes five feet four inches

(128) 136 State of North Carolina} County Court Clk's offic_
            Gates County   } January 26 1849
No. 51.   SAM, the property of Nancy GRIFFIN of Nansemond County Virginia, hired the present year by Willis S. RIDDICK of Suffolk and by him registered as one of his hands employed in the Great Dismal Swamp.

SAM is about twenty six years old, large features with flat broad nose, broad mouth, small beard principally upon the upper lip a number of small pimples under each eye. X.

State of North Carolina} County Court Clerk's office
Gates County   } January 26/th/ 1849.
No 52.   ENOCH, the property of Burwell RIDDICK of Nansemond County Virginia and hired the present year by Willis S. RIDDICK of Suffolk and by him employed as one of his hands in the Great Dismal Swamp.

ENOCH is about forty two years old, brown complexion, high fore head, a large nose, thin lips, a small scar on the chin, a small scar on the left arm a scar under the left knee. Stands with out shoes five feet four and a half inches X.

(129) 137 No. 53 marked reissued.

(129) (Cont.) State of North Carolina} County Court Clerk's office
                    Gates County   } January 26/th/ 1849.
<u>No. 54</u>   SAM, the property of the estate of Jno R KNIGHT of Nansemond Va and hired the
present year by Willis S. RIDDICK of Suffolk and by him registered as one of his
hands employed in the Great Dismal Swamp.
   SAM is twenty five years old, full face, with a scar on the fore head and a cut on
the nose on the left nostrill; a black spot on the outside of the left leg.   Stands
without shoes five feet five inches: X.

Number 55 marked reissued.
   Number 56 marked reissued
State of North Carolina} County Court Clerk's office
Gates County   } January 26/th/ 1849.
<u>No. 57.</u>   JACK, the property of the estate of Mills RIDDICK dec/d/. of SuffolkVa,
hired the present year by Willis S. RIDDICK of Suffolk and by him registered as one of
his hands employed in the Great Dismal swamp.
   JACK is forty seven years old, dark brown colour, high fore head prominent eye
brows - a little gray - a scar on the head near the top a small scar on the back of
the left hand and a scar on the bend of the same arm on the inside, a scar on the left
knee, and a scar on the inside of the thumb on the left hand and stands with out shoes
five feet six and a quarter inches.

(130) 138 State of North Carolina} County Court Clerk's office
                    Gates County   } January 26/th/ 1849.
<u>No 58.</u>   HENRY the property of Daniel BRINKLEY of Nansemond County Va. hired the
present year by W. S. RIDDICK of Suffolk and by him registered as one of his hands in
the Great Dismal Swamp.
   HENRY is eighteen years old, sharp forehead, with a small scar just at the front
of the forehead; small deep eyes and remarkably small eye brows, a small scar on
middle joint of the fore finger and little finger and a scar on the right knee stands
without shoes five feet six inches. X

State of North Carolina} County Court Clerk's office
Gates County   } January 26/th/ 1849.
<u>No 59.</u>   JIM, the property of Daniel BRINKLEY of Nansemond County Virginia, hired the
present year by Willis S. RIDDICK of Suffolk and by him registered as one of his hands
in the Great Dismal Swamp.
   JIM is about nine years old, quite black, fierce look, teeth very wide in the
upper jaw and wide apart: Stands without shoes four feet three inches. X

(131) 139 State of North Carolina} County C_urt Clerk's office
                    Gates County   } January 30/th/ 1849.
<u>No. 60.</u>   PHILLIP, the property of Isaac R. HUNTER of Gates County, hired the present
year by James B NORFLEET of Suffolk Virginia and by him registered as one of his hands
employed in the Great Dismal Swamp.
   PHILLIP is about thirty years of age, of dark complexion, has a large mouth, thick
lips and a tolerable stiff beard. He has two large scars upon his right leg and a
large knot upon the same leg just below the knee; and stands without shoes five feet
seven inches.

State of North Carolina} County Court Clerk's office;
Gates County   } January 30/th/ 1849.
<u>No. 61</u>   JACK, the property of H L EPPS of Nansemond County Virginia, and by him
registered as one of his hands employed in the Great Dismal Swamp.   JACK is about
forty years of age, of black complexion, has a tolerable high forehead, stiff beard,

(131) (Cont.) good front teeth and is cross eyed. He has a number of scars upon his back, from whipping and two large /scars/ on the front part of the right leg above the ankle and two scars upon the left leg, and stands without shoes five feet eight and three fourth inches.

(132) 140 State of North Carolina} County Court Clerk's offic_
     Gates County   } January 30/th/ 1849.
No. 62 JOE, the property of /the heirs of Abram SKINNER, hired the present year by/ H. L. EPPS of Nansemond County Va. and by him registered as one of his hands employed in the Great Dismal Swamp.

   JOE is about fifteen years of age, of dark complexion, prominent forehead and good teeth. He has several large /scars/ upon the back of his head and neck from a burn - a small scar below the left eye - several small scars upon his hands - a large scar upon the front part of the left leg and the same upon his right leg; a small scar on the right foot and stands without shoes four feet nine inches.

State of North Carolina} County Court Clerk's office
Gates County   } January 30/th/ 1849.
No. 63 FRANK, a free boy of colour hired the present year by James B. NORFLEET and by him registered as one of his hands employed in the Great Dismal Swamp.

   FRANK is about seventeen years of age, of dark complexion, has a full forehead and thick lips. He has several small scars upon his left wrist and arm - a small scar upon the back of his right hand near the thumb and stands with out shoes four feet eight and a half inches.

(133) 141 State of North Carolina} County Court Clerk's office,
      Gates County   } January 30/th/ 1849.
No. 64 JOHN, the property of James B NORFLEET of Suffolk Va. and by him registered as one of his hands employed in the Great Dismal Swamp.

   JOHN is about forty six years old, has a wide fore head, a wide flat nose, a large mouth, good teeth, tolerable full beard with a scar on the outside of the right eye brow, with several small black moles on the face, two saw cuts on the left wrist and a large faint scar upon the left wrist, is five feet four and a half inches high.

State of North Carolina} County Court Clerk's office
Gates County   } February 3/rd/ 1849.
65 DICK, the property of James S. SEGUINE of Deep Creek Virginia and by him registered as one of his hands employed in the Great Dismal Swamp.

   DICK is about forty nine years old, of dark complexion, has large nostrills and is quite bald. He has a /small/ scar on the left breast also a small scar on the fore finger of his left hand; and stands without shoes five feet nine and a half inches.

(134) 142 State of North Carolina} County Court Clk's off__
      Gates County   } February 3rd 1849.
66 JIM, the property of Daniel CULPEPPER of Norfolk County Virginia, hired the present year by Jas? S. SEGUINE of Deep Creek and by him registered as one of his hands employed in the Great Dismal Swamp.

   JIM is about thirty seven years of age, of black complexion, has a high forehead and a stout beard. He has no scars about his person, and stands without shoes five feet two inches.

State of North Carolina} County Court Clerk's office
Gates County   } February 3/rd/ 1849.
67. WILLIAM, the property of James FLEMING of Deep Creek Virginia, hired the present year by James S. SEGUINE of Deep Creek Norfolk County Virginia, and by him

(134) (Cont.) registered as one of his hands employed in the Great Dismal Swamp.

WILLIAM is about four teen years of age, of brown complexion, has a flat nose, high fore head, good countenance and a good set of teeth. He has a small scar on the right leg just above the knee, and a small /one/ on the right hand, and stands without shoes four feet six inches.

(135) 143 State of North Carolina} County Court Clerk's office
           Gates County   } February 10/th/ 1849.
No. 68. JACK, the property of Abram BRINKLEY of Nansemond County Virginia and by him registered as one of his hands employed in the Great Dismal Swamp.

JACK is about thirty seven years old, of black complexion, has a flat fore head and but little beard. He has good front teeth and a circle of hair around the forehead. He has no scars about his person and stands without shoes five feet seven inches.

State of North Carolina} County Court Clerk's office
Gates County   } February 10/th/ 1849.
No 69. DICK, the property of Abram BRINKLEY of Nansemond County Virginia, and by him registered as one of his hands employed in the Great Dismal Swamp.

DICK is about thirty two years of age, has sharp features, a round head, tolerable good teeth and rather a sleepy look. He has a scar on the right arm below the elbow, on the out side, a small scar just above the left knee and stands without shoes five feet five inches.

(136) 144 State of North Carolina} County Court Clerk's office
           Gates County   } February 10/th/ 1849.
No. 70. WILLIS, the property of Abram BRINKLEY of Nansemond County Virginia and by him registered as one of his hands employed in the Great Dismal Swamp.

WILLIS is about forty seven years of age, of dark brown complexion has a flat face, a tolerably large nose and mouth, a large scar about six inches long on the left shoulder running under the arm, a large scar on the inside of the left Knee, and stands without shoes five feet six and a half inches. Reissued Oct.. 1/st/. 1849. No. 87.

State of North Carolina} County Court Clerk's office
Gates County   } February 10/th/ 1849.
No 71. WILLIE, the property of the estate of Archibald BRINKLEY of Nansemond County Virginia, hired the present year by Abram BRINKLEY of said County and by him registered as one of his hands employed in the Great Dismal Swamp.

WILLIE is about twenty six years of age, of light brown Complexion, has a large mouth and thick lips. He has two scars upon the right side of his neck; a large scar on the right arm; one on the back of his right hand; a scar on the left elbow; one on the inside of the left arm and one on the calf of his lef_ leg and stands without shoes five feet six inches.

(137) 145 State of North Carolina} County Court Clerk's office
           Gates County   } February 13/th/ 1849.
No 72. SOLOMON, the property of Huldy KNIGHT of Nansemond County Virginia, hired the present year by Wm. B. WHITEHEAD of Suffolk and by him registered as one of his hands employed in the Great Dismal Swamp.

SOLOMON is about Sixty years of age, of black complexion, has a tolerably high fore head, bad teeth and is quite gray. He has several scars upon his left leg; a very large scar upon the right leg, from a burn, and a number of smaller ones upon the same leg; and stands without shoes five feet four and a half inches. Reissued January 30/th/ 1850. No. 40.

(137) (Cont.) State of North Carolina} County Court Clerk's office
              Gates County   } February 28/th/ 1849.
No. 73 NED, the property of the heirs of Henry COSTEN dec/d/. of Gates County hired
the present year by BROTHERS &SMALL of said county, and by them registered as one of
their hands employed in the Great Dismal Swamp.

NED is about thirty two years of age, of dark complexion, has large nostrills,
thick lips and Sorry teeth. He has a scar upon his left arm just above the elbow; a
scar on each foot, and several scars upon both legs, and stands without shoes five
feet nine and a half inches.

(138) 146 State of North Carolina} County Court Clerk's office
              Gates County   } March 12/th/ 1849
No. 74. JOE, the property of Daniel BRINKLEY of Nansemond County Virginia, hired the
present year by Willis S. RIDDICK of Said County, and by him registered as one of his
hands employed in the Great Dismal Swamp.

JOE is about twelve years of age, of dark complexion, has good teeth /tolerably?/
large nostrils and thick lips. He has a small scar upon his right cheek from a burn,
one on the under part of his left arm and several small scars upon each Kee [sic]
produced also from burns, and stands without shoes four feet six and a half inches.

State of North Carolina} County Court Clerk's office
Gates County.   } March 24/th/ 1849.
No. 75. NATHAN, the property of John C. GORDON of Gates County, hired the present
year by Mills ROGERS of said County and by him registered as one of his hands employed
in the Great Dismal Swamp.

NATHAN is about twenty five years of age, of black complexion, has a flat nose, a
wide mouth and a very low forehead. He has a scar, about one inch long, upon the
right side of his face near the corner of his mouth; Several scars upon both legs,
occasioned by the fire, and the little toe of the left foot has been burnt off: - And
stands without shoes five feet three inches.

(139) 147 State of North Carolina} County Court Clerk's office
              Gates County   } May 7/th/ 1849.
No. 76. ISAAC, the property of Jethro RIDDICK of Nansemond County Virginia, and by
him registered as one of his hands employed in the great Dismal Swamp.

ISAAC is about Seventeen years of age, has an uncommon full face, a scar over the
left eye, a scar on the outside of the left wrist, a scar on the inside of the left
knee, a scar on the right side of his head, has thick lips and stands with out shoes
five feet three inches.

State of North Carolina} County Court Clerk's office
Gates County   } May 7/th/ 1849.
No. 77. MILES, the property of the estate of John BYRD of Nansemond County Virginia,
hired the present year by Jethro RIDDICK of said County, and by him registered as one
of his hands employed in the Great Dismal Swamp.

MILES is about twenty years of age, of black complexion, has a low fore head, a
good set of teeth and thick lips. - He has a faint scar upon his right arm and two
small black spots upon the same arm, and a small scar upon the left wrist; and stands
without shoes five feet two and a half inches. He has a long scar upon his right foot
and a small one on the left foot.

(140) 148 State of North Carolina} County Court Clerk's office
              Gates County.   } May 19/th/ 1849.
No. 78. NOAH, the property of Abram BRINKLEY of Nansemond County Virginia, and by
him registered as one of his hands employed in the Great Dismal Swamp

(140) (Cont.) NOAH is about Ten years of age, of ~~black~~ /dark brown/ complexion has ·
good teeth, a high forehead and a flat nose. He has a scar a bout [sic] one inch long
on the top ~~ef~~ of his left foot, and stands without shoes four feet half inch

State of North Carolina} County Court Clerk's office
Gates County.   } May (blank) 1849.
No. 80. [sic] SAM the property of Jacob RICHARDSON of Pasquotank County N.C. and
hired the present year by Mills ROGERS of Gates County, and by him employed as one of
his hands in the Great Dismal Swamp:
SAM is about fifty three years old, quite black, good teeth, large features, a
small scar on the outside of the left fore arm, a small scar on the inside of the
right knee and === two scars on the left shin bone; - stands without shoes five feet
seven and a half inches high

(141) 149 State of North Carolina} County Court Clerk's Office,
         Gates County.   } May June 2nd 1849.
No 80. [sic] JACOB, the property of the heirs of Joseph FREEMAN deceased of Gates
County hired the present year by Willis R. HAYS of said County and by him hired to
Burwell BROTHERS and by said BROTHERS /registered/ as one of his hands employed in the
Great Dismal Swamp.
JACOB is about twenty nine years of age, has a light complexion, a good set of
teeth and large nostrills. - He has a small scar upon his right shoulder and a small
one upon his left hand, and stands without shoes five feet five and a half inches.

State of North Carolina} County Court Clerk's Office
Gates County.   } June 16?/th/ 1849.
No. 81   JIM, the property of John GATLING of Gates County, and by him registered as
One of the hands employed, by GATLING & COSTEN, in the Great Dismal Swamp.
JIM is about fifty four years old, brown color, has a small wart on the nose, a
small scar on the left breast, a scar across the left arm, a large scar on the right
elbow joint and some small scars on the same arm, from a burn; and a small scar on the
inside of the right knee;- Stands without shoes five feet five inches, nearly.

(142) 150 State of North Carolina} County Court Clk's office
         Gates County.   } September 1/st/ 1849.
No. 82   BEN, the property of Abram BRINKLEY of Nansemond County Virginia, and by him
registered as one of his hands employed in the Great Dismal Swamp in Gates County.
BEN is about eighteen years of age, has a light complexion, flat features large
nose, wide mouth, thick lips and a low forehead. He has a scar on the inside of the
right arm, near the elbow, and one on the inside of the left foot. Stands without
shoes five feet four inches.

State of North Carolina} County Court Clk's office
Gates County.   } September 10/th/ 1849.
No. 83.   SAM the property of James N. HARRELL of Gates County, hired the present year
by Isaac S. HARRELL &Co of said county and by them registered as oneoftheir hands
employed in the Great Dismal swamp.
SAM is about fifty six years of age, has a black complexion a tolerably large
mouth, flat nose, low fore head and sorry teeth. He has a scar on the left arm above
the elbow, a small scar just above the elbow on the same arm, and one upon his right
leg - stands without shoes five feet six inches.

(143) 151 State of North Carolina} County Court Clk's office,
         Gates County   } September 10/th/ 1849.
No. 84   JACK the property of Saml. R. HARRELL of Gates County, registered and

(143) (Cont.) employed the present year by HARRELL&Co of said County as one of their hands in the Great Dismal swamp.

JACK is about forty years of age, has a black complexion, flat nose, thick lips, large nostrils and a stout beard. He has a scar near his right eye; a scar upon his right leg, and a large sore on his left leg. He has a scar upon the back of his neck, one on the right side, And stands without shoes five feet six and a half inches.

State of North Carolina} County Court Clk's Office
Gates County.   } September 10/th/ 1849.
No. 85   LEWIS the property of Wm. B. WHITEHEAD of Suffolk Virginia, and by him registered as one of his hands employed in the Great Dismal Swamp, in Gates County.

LEWIS is about thirty two years of age, has a dark complexion, large nostrils, thick lips, a tolerably high fore head, and good teeth in front. He has a small scar on his left jaw, one on the thumb of his right hand, one on the fore head above the right eye, and one on his right ankle; stands without shoes five feet four inches, nearly.

(144) 152 State of North Carolina} County Court Clk's office
         Gates County.   } September 17/th/ 1849
No. 86. BEN, the property of Samuel R. HARRELL of Gates County and by him registered as one of the hands of HARRELL&Co of said county, employed in the GreatDismal Swamp.

BEN is about forty years of age, has a dark complexion, thick lips, large nostrils and a tolerably high forehead. He? has two small scars on his forehead, near his right eye, and stands without shoes five feet ten & a half inches, nearly [sic].

No. 70 Reissued No. 87. -

State of North Carolina} County Court Clk's Office
Gates County   } October 1/st/ 1849.
No. 88. NOAH, the property of Abram BRINKLEY of Nansemond County Virginia, and by him registered as one of his hands employed in the Great Dismal Swamp:

NOAH is about ten years of age of dark brown complexion, has good teeth, a high fore head and a flat nose. He has a scar about one inch long on the top of his left foot, and stands without shoes four feet half inch. Reissued June 22nd 1850 No. 61.

(145) 153 State of North Carolina} County Court Clerk's office
         Gates County.   } November 24/th/ 1849.
No. 89. POMPEY, the property of Samuel R. HARRELL of Gates County and by him registered as one of the hands of Samuel R. HARRELL &Co employed in the Great Dismal Swamp.

POMPEY is about twenty seven years of age, has a dark complexion, a decayed upper front tooth and his left leg crooked. He has a scar from a burn on the right temple and one on the wrist of his left hand - Stands without shoes five feet three inches.

State of North Carolina} Co.Court Clk's office
Gates County.   } Nov. 24/th/ 1849
No. 90   ISAAC the property of James N. HARRELL of Gates County and by him registered as one of the hands employed by SamuelR. HARRELL &Co. in the Great Dismal Swamp

ISAAC is about twenty five years of age, has a dark complexion, large eyes, thick lips, and good teeth in front. He has a scar upon his left ankle and throws his feet out in walking - stands without shoes five feet five & a half inches, nearly. Reissued March 20/th/ 1850 No. 46

(146) 154 State of No.Carolina} County Court Clerk's office
         Gates County.   } December 4/th/ 1849.

4 December 1849

(146) (Cont.) <u>No. 91</u>   WILL the property of Burwell BROTHERS of Gates County and by him registered as one of the hands of BROTHERS & SMALL employed in the Great Dismal Swamp.

WILL is about twenty one years of age, has a black complexion, a low forehead and good teeth in front. He has a scar ~~immediately~~ over his right /eye/, one upon his fore head running into the edge of his hair and a large one scar? upon his right leg from a burn – Stands without shoes five feet eight inches   [Remainder of page is blank.]

(147) 155 [Entire page is blank.]

(148) 156 State of No:Carolina} County Court Clerk's office
              Gates County   }   January 9/th/ 1850.
<u>No. 1</u>   MUNROE, the property of H. L. EPPES of Nansemond County Virginia, hired the present year by Jethro RIDDICK &Co of said County and by them registered as one of their hands employed in the Great Dismal Swamp.

MUNROE is about twenty eight years old, has a black complexion, a wide mouth, good teeth and a tolerably high forehead. He has a large scar upon the back of his left hand, and several upon his legs: Stands without shoes five feet seven inches; and when he smiles he shows a part of the inside of his upper lip.

State of North Carolina} Co. Court Clk's office
Gates County.   }   January 9/th/ 1850.
<u>No. 2.</u>   JOE, the property of H. L. EPPES of Nansemond county Virginia, hired the present year by Jethro RIDDICK &Co. of said county, and by them registered as one of their hands employed in the Great Dismal swamp.

JOE is about nineteen years old, has a dark complexion, good teeth and tolerably thick lips. He has a large scar upon the inside of the right leg, one upon theleft leg, one upon his heel string of the same leg, ~~and~~ a small scar upon the fore finger of his left hand /& one nearly over the right eye/: and stands without shoes five feet six inches.

(149) 157 State of North Carolina} County Court Clk's office
              Gates County.   }   January 9/th/ 1850.
<u>No. 3</u>   NED, the property of H L. EPPES of Nansemond County Virginia, hired the present year by Jethro RIDDICK &Co. of said county and by them registered as one of their hands employed in the Great Dismal swamp.

NED is about thirty five years old, has a dark brown conplexion, tolerably good teeth, a scar in /his/ forehead nearly in the shape of a V.; one on the left side of his face, three upon his left wrist, one upon the left arm and a large one upon his right arm: stands without shoes five feet three inches

State of No:Ca: } County Court Clerk's office
Gates County   }   January 9/th/ 1850.
<u>No. 4</u>   EDMOND, the property of Luke RABY of Nansemond County Virginia, hired the present year by Jethro RIDDICK &Co of said county and by them registered as one of their hands enployed in the great Dismal swamp.

EDMOND is about twelve years old, has a dark brown complexion, good teeth, and a wide mouth. He has several small scars upon his left leg, and one on his right knee, Stands without shoes four feet three and a quarter inches

(150) 158 State of North Carolina} County Court Clerk's office
              Gates County.   }   January 9/th/ 1850.
<u>No. 5</u>   EDOM, the property of James RIDDICK of Nansemond county Virginia, hired the present year by Jethro RIDDICK &Co. of said county and by them registered as one of

9 January 1850

(150) (Cont.) their hands employed in the GreatDismal Swamp.

EDOM is about twenty three years old, has a brown complexion, good teeth, tolerable large nose, and features. He has a scar on the right ankle, one on the left leg, two upon his left wrist and one upon each hand, stands without shoes five feet four and a half inches.

State of North Carolina} Co. Court Clk's office
Gates County.   }   January 9/th/ 1850.
No. 6   LEWIS, the property of James SAUNDERS of Nansemond county Virginia hired the present year by Jethro RIDDICK &Co. of said county and by them registered as one of their hands employed in the Great Dismal swamp.

LEWIS is about Eleven years old, has a dark complexion, good teeth, thin lips and a flat nose. He has a scar upon each Knee, a scar under the left eye, a scar on the little /finger/ of his right hand, and a scar from a burn under his left arm stands without shoes four feet two and a half inches.

(151) 159 State of North Carolina} County Court Clerk's office
        Gates County.   }   January 10/th/ 1850.
No. 7   JACK, the property of the estate of R. R. SMITH of Nansemond County Virginia, hired the present year by Willis S. RIDDICK of said county, and by him registered as one of his hands employed in the Great Dismal Swamp.

JACK is about twenty four years old, has a dark complexion, and good teeth. He has a small Scar over his the left eye, a scar on the forefinger of his right hand and a small mole upon the right side of his neck: Stands without shoes five feet nine inches.

State of North Carolina} County Court Clerk's Office,
Gates County.   }   January 10/th/ 1850.
No. 8   ABRAM, the property of the Estate of R. R. SMITH of Nansemond County Virginia, hired the present year by Willis S. RIDDICK of said County, and by him registered as one of his hands employed in the Great Dismal Swamp:

ABRAM is about twenty one years old, has a dark brown complexion, good teeth, and a full forehead. He has a small scar upon his left jaw, a scar upon his right hand, and stands without shoes five feet five and a quarter inches. In Testimony &c.

(152) 160 State of North Carolina} County Court Clerk's office
        Gates County.   }   January 10/th/ 1850.
No. 9   CHARLES, the property of the Estate of R. R. SMITH of Nansemond County Virginia, hired the present year by Willis S. RIDDICK of said County and by him registered as one of his hands employed in the Great /Dismal/ Swamp.

CHARLES is about twenty six years old, has a dark complexion, large nostrils, a full forehead and a tolerably flat head. He has a scar over his left eye, a scar above his nose, a scar upon his left jaw, and a scar upon one of his fingers of the left hand from a cut, and stands without shoes five feet four and a half inches.
        In Testimony &c.

State of North Carolina} County Court Clerk's office
Gates County.   }   January 19/th/. 1850.
No. 10.   MILLS, the property of the Estate of James COSTEN Sr of Gates County hired the present year by BROTHERS & SMALL of said County and by them registered as one of their hands employed in the Great Dismal Swamp:

MILLS is about forty five years of age, has a light complexion, thick lips, wide mouth, large nose and nostrils and a low forehead. He has two Scars upon his right leg just below the knee, and a large Scar upon his left hand and a Scar upon the thumb of the same hand: Stands without shoes five feet two and a half inches.

22 January 1850

(152) (Cont.)   In Testimony &c.

(153) 161 State of North Carolina} County Court Clerk's office
            Gates County.   } January 22nd 1850.
No. 11   GEORGE the property of Allen EDWARDS of Southampton county Virginia, hired
the present year by William B. WHITEHEAD of Suffolk Virginia and by him registered as
one of his hands employed in the Great Dismal Swamp.
     GEORGE is about twenty seven years of age, has a dark complexion, a high forehead,
flat nose and a small mouth. He has a Scar over his left eye, a scar between his
eyes, a Scar upon the under lip and a scar stands without shoes five feet seven and a
half inches. In Testimony &c.

State of North Carolina} County Court Clerk's office
Gates County.   } January 22nd. 1850.
No. 12.   TOM, the property of Francis JONES of Nansemond County Virginia, hired the
present year by William B. WHITEHEAD of Suffolk and by him registered as one of his
hands employed in the Great Dismal Swamp.
     TOM is about sixteen years of age, has a dark complexion, flat nose, a good set
of teeth, and large nostrills. He has a small scar under his right eye, a large scar
upon his left leg and a scar upon his left knee, and a scar upon his left hand:
Stands without shoes five feet three inches. In Testimony &c.

(154) 162 State of North Carolina} County Court Clk's Off___
            Gates County   } January 22nd 1850.
No. 13   ALEXANDER, the property of William B. WHITEHEAD of Suffolk Virginia and by
him registered as one of his hands employed in the Great Dismal Swamp
     ALEXANDER is about fifteen years of age, has a light complexion, a high forehead,
and a small flat nose. He has a small scar in his forehead, a scar upon his left
thumb and stands without shoes four feet nine inches. In Testimony &c.

State of North Carolina} County Court Clk's offic_
Gates County   } January 22nd 1850
No. 14   JOE, the property of Francis JONES of Nansemond County Va: hired the present
year by William B. WHITEHEAD of Suffolk Virginia and by him registered as one of his
hands employed in the Great Dismal Swamp:
     JOE is about Sixteen years of age, has a dark complexion, a low forehead, a large
flat nose. and a wide mouth. He has a small bump upon his right eye, a scar above the
right knee and a scar upon the same knee Stands without shoes four feet nine & a half
inches

(155) 163 Marked Reissued from 1?4 to 36 inclusive.
State of North Carolina} County Court Clerk's Office
Gates County.   } January 22nd 1850.
No. 37.   DAVY, the property of Daniel BRINKLEY Jr. of Nansemond County Virginia hired
the present year by Wm.B.WHITEHEAD of Suffolk and by him registered as one of his
hands employed in the Great Dismal Swamp.
     DAVY is about twenty five years of age, has a Sugar loaf head, sunken eyes, good
teeth, with a vacancy between the upper front teeth; has a spot under the corner of
his left eye and stands wide upon his feet. He has a scar upon the shin bone of his
left leg, and stands without shoes five feet six inches.

State of North Carolina} County Court Clerk's office
Gates County   } January 22nd 1850
No. 38   SAWYER, the property of James GOODMAN of Nansemond County Va. hired the
present year by Wm.B.WHITEHEAD of Suffolk and by him registered as one of his hands

(155) (Cont.) employed in the Great Dismal Swamp.

SAWYER is about thirty eight years old, has a dark brown complexion, a wild look, full eyes, small mouth, a scar in the corner of his forehead, a small scar in front ofthe right ear, a small scar on the cheek bone behind the left eye, a knot on each nuckle bone of the Great toe, and a large scar on his right /leg/ half way down from the knee to the foot. He stands five feet five and a half inches high.

(156) 164 State of North Carolina} County Court Clerk's Office,
    Gates County.   } January 22nd 1850.
No. 39 GEORGE the property of Josephus MEREDITH, of Nansemond County Virginia, hired the present year by William B. WHITEHEAD of Suffolk and by him registered as one of his hands employed in the Great Dismal Swamp.

GEORGE is about fifty two years old, has a black complexion, a heavy beard, and a peak in the forehead. He has a scar under the edge of the hair on the left side of the peak in his forehead; good teeth, a scar on each knee, a scar on the lower edge of the right breast & stands without shoes five feet seven and a half inches

No. 72 Reissued No. 40.
State of No.Carolina} County Court Clerk's Office
Gates County. } February 6th 1850.
No. 41. Mills, REED, a free boy of color, hired the present year by Willis S. RIDDICK of Nansemond County Virginia and by him registered as one of his hands employed in the Dismal Swamp:

Mills REED is about ten years of age, has a light, yellow complexion and thick lips. He has a small scar near the left corner of his mouth - has been deprived of the sight of his left eye and stands without shoes four feet four inches.

(157) 165 State of North Carolina} County Court Clerk's Office
    Gates County.   } February 6/th/ 1850.
No. 42 Daniel CHAWK, a free boy of Color, hired the present year by Willis S. RIDDICK of Nansemond County Virginia and by him registered as one of his hands employed in the Great Dismal Swamp.

Daniel CHAWK is about twelve years of == age, has a yellow complexion, good teeth, flat nose, low fore head and a full upper lip. He has no Scars about his person and stands without shoes four feet five and a half inches nearly.

State of North Carolina} County Court Clerk's Office
Gates County. } February 18/th/ 1850.
No. 43. JACK JACK the property of Admiral BRINKLEYs heirs of Nansemond County Virginia, hired the present year by Jethro RIDDICK &Co. of said County and by them registered as one of their hands employed in the Great Dismal Swamp.

JACK is about sixty three years of age, has a rusty black complexion, small features, red eyes, thin beard, thick lips, bad teeth and a large knot on the upper joint of the Great toe of the left foot and stands without shoes five feet seven and a halfinches.

(158) 166 State of North Carolina} County Court Clerk's Office
    Gates County.   } February 18/th/ 1850
No. 44 JACOB the property of Capt. Edward RIDDICK of Nansemond County Va. hired the present year by Jethro RIDDICK &Co. of Nansemond County and by them registered as one of their hands in the Dismal Swamp:

JACOB is remarkably black, has a very large nose and thick lips. He has a small scar on the right collar bone /a large scar across the left foot/ & a large scar on the right shin bone: Stands without shoes five feet six and three quarter inches.

23 February 1850

(158) (Cont.) State of North Carolina} County Court Clerk's Office
          Gates County   } February 23rd. 1850.
<u>No. 45</u>   GRANVILLE, the property of Isaac R. HUNTER of Gates County, hired the present year by James B. NORFLEET and by him registered as one of his hands employed in the Great Dismal Swamp

    GRANVILLE is about forty five years of age, has a black complexion, large nose, mouth & nostrills and a prominent fore head. He limps a little in his gait and his left leg is larger than the right: Stands without shoes five feet eight inches

No. 90 Reissued No. 46
No. 66 "   "   47

(159) 167 State of North Carolina} County Court Clerk's Office
          Gates County.   } March 25/th/ 1850.
<u>No. 48</u>   HARMON the property of Abram BRINKLEY of Nansemond County Virginia, hired the present year by Willis S. RIDDICK of said County and by him registered as one of his hands employed in the Great Dismal Swamp.

    HARMON is a small boy, about twelve years old, has a dark complexion, a large belly, flat nose and a tolerably full fore head. He has a small scar on his fore head, and throws his feet out in walking and stands without shoes three feet ten inches.

State of North Carolina} County Court Clerk's office
Gates County.   } March 25 /th/ 1850.
<u>No. 49.</u> - EDMOND the property of the Estate of John KNIGHT of Nansemond County Virginia, hired the present year by Willis S. RIDDICK of said County, and by him registered as one of his hands employed in the Great Dismal Swamp.

    EDMOND is a small boy, about ten years old, has a dark complexion, a small nose, a small scar on each eye, a large belly and stands without shoes three feet eleven and a half inches.

(160) 168 State of North Carolina} County Court Clerk's Office
          Gates County.   } March 25/th/ 1850.
<u>No. 50</u>   ISAAC the property of the Estate of Admiral BRINKLEY of Nansemond County Virginia, hired the present year by JamesB. NORFLEET, and by him registered as one of his hands employed in the Great Dismal Swamp.

    ISAAC is about thirty three years old, has a black complexion, flat face, sunken eyes, large mouth, good teeth, with a sunken place in the scull bone near the crown of the head and a scar on the shin bone. He stands without shoes five feet five inches.

State of North Carolina} County Court Clerk's Office
Gates County.   } March 25/th/ 1850.
<u>No. 51.</u>   William Henry WINSLOW son of Cate? WINSLOW of Nansemond County Virginia, hired the present year by James B. NORFLEET of Suffolk and by him registered as one of his hands employed in the Great Dismal Swamp.

    William Henry is a free boy, about ten years of age, has a black complixion, a tolerably large, flat nose, good teeth in front and thin lips. He has a small scar on his right ankle and stands without shoes four feet two and a half inches, nearly
No. 55. reissued No. 52.

(161) 169 State of North Carolina} County Court Clerk's Office
          Gates County   } May 1/st/ 1850.
<u>No. 53</u>   BOB the property of Sophia DUKES of Nansemond county Virginia, hired the present year by Jethro RIDDICK & Co of said county and by them registered as one of their hands employed in the Great Dismal Swamp.

(161) (Cont.) BOB is about sixteen years of age has a dark brown complexion, large eyes, flat nose, tolerably large nostrils, and good teeth. He has a scar below the right eye, a scar near the corner of the same eye, and a small scar on the right side of his head which runs up into his hair: and stands without shoes four feet ten inches nearly.

State of North Carolina} County Court Clerk's Office
Gates County.   }   May 7/th/ 1850.
No. 54.   ISRAEL the property of James B. NORFLEET of Suffolk Virginia, and by him registered as one of the hands employed by Jethro RIDDICK &Co in the Great Dismal Swamp, in Gates County.

ISRAEL is about Sixteen years of age, has a dark complexion, a low fore head, a sunken place over each eye, and a vacancy in /both/ his under and upper teeth in front. He has a small scar on the front part of his left leg, and stands without shoes four feet Eleven inches. In Testimony &c.

(162) 170 State of North Carolina} County Court Clerk's Office
          Gates County.   }   May 11/th/ 1850.
No. 55.   George GRIMES the property of James S. SEGUINE of Deep Creek Va. and by him registered as one of his hands employed in the Great Dismal Swamp in Gates County.

George is about fifty three years of age, has a dark brown complexion, flat wrinkled face, short teeth, full beard, full eyes and is quite gray. The forefinger of his left hand is a little stiff; has a large deep scar upon his left leg just above the knee, and two large flat scars on the out side of his right leg, and the first joint of the little /toe/ on the left foot is off: Stands without shoes five feet Eight inches.

State of North Carolina} County Court Clerk's Office
Gates County.   }   May 11/th/ 1850.
No. 56.   WILSON the property of Isaac? FLEMING? of Norfolk County Va: hired the present year by James S. SEGUINE of Deep Creek in said County and state, and by him registered as one of his hands employed in the Great Dismal Swamp:
DAVY is said to be free /WILSON is about 16 yrs. old./ has a dark brown complexion, tolerably high forehead, good teeth, small mouth, tolerably flat nose and a vacancy between his upper teeth in front. He has a small scar on his right thigh, a long scar upon the left side of his face, and a small scar upon his left leg; a large scar upon his back, & stands without shoes four feet ten & a half inches

(163) 171 State of North Carolina} County Court Clerk's Office
          Gates County.   }   May 11/th/ 1850.
No. 57   Davy SMITH, a colored boy, son of Marian SMITH of Norfolk County Virginia, hired the present year by James S. SEGUINE of Deep Creek in said county and state, and by him registered as one of his hands employed in the Great Dismal swamp.

Davy SMITH, is said to be free, is about twelve years of age, has a black complexion, wide mouth, thick lips, flat nose and full eyes. He has a small scar near the corner of his left eye, three small scars on or near the right eye, and stands without shoes four feet six and a half inches.

State of North Carolina} County Court Clerk's Office
Gates County.   }   May 13/th/ 1850.
No. 58.   LEWIS, the property of Penina EPPES of Nansemond County Virginia, hired the present year by Jethro RIDDICK &Co of said County, and by them registered as one of their hands employed in the Great Dismal Swamp:
LEWIS is about forty six years of age, of brown complexion, has one tooth missing in the upper jaw in front, with his right leg shorter than the left. He has a scar on

(163) (Cont.) the knee pan of the right leg, and stands without shoes five feet five inches.

(164) 172 State of North Carolina} County Court Clerk's Office
             Gates County   }   May 23rd 1850.
No. 59.   Henry FAULKS, a colored man, and? is? said to be free, hired the present year by RIDDICK, EPPES & NORFLEET of Nansemond County Virginia, and by them registered as one of their hands employed in the Great Dismal Swamp:
    Henry is about twenty years of age, has a dark complexion, flat nose, large nostrils, good teeth, full forehead, and a thick upper lip. He has a scar on his right leg below the knee and a small scar on his left hand from a burn: Stands without shoes five feet six inches.

State of North Carolina} County Court Clerk's Office
Gates County.   }   June 8/th/ 1850.
No. 60.   WILLIS the property of the heirs of Riddick JONES of Gates County, hired the present year by Alfred VANN of Nansemond County Va: and by him registered as one of his hands employed in the Great Dismal Swamp.
    WILLIS is crow black, with high forehead, very thin beard spare made, a small scar on the left side of the mouth, and a scar upon each shin bone: Stands without shoes five feet seven and a half inches.

No. 88 of 1849 marked "Reissued No 61."

(165) 173 State of North Carolina} County Court Clerk's Office
             Gates County.   }   July 19/th/ 1850.
No. 62   Lorenzo FAULK, said to be a free man, hired the present year by William B. WHITEHEAD of Suffolk Virginia, and by him registered as one of his hands employed in the Great Dismal Swamp:
    The said FAULK is about thirty five years of age, has a yellow complexion, flat face, good teeth, black eyes, tolerably wide mouth, and small nose. He has no scars about his person except one on the front part of his right leg, and Stands without shoes five feet seven and a quarter inches.

State of North Carolina} County Court Clerk's Office
Gates County.   }   July 24/th/ 1850.
No. 63   TONEY the property of James B. NORFLEET of Suffolk Virginia, and by him registered as one of his hands employed in the Great Dismal Swamp.
    TONEY is about forty four years of age, of black complexion, has thick lips, large mouth and bad teeth. He has a Scar on his right shoulder from a burn, and has lost the first joint of the little finger of his left hand: Stands without shoes five feet, six inches and has a scar about one and a half inches long on the back of his left hand.

(166) 174 State of North Carolina} County Court Clk's Office
             Gates County.   }   October 10/th/ 1850.
No. 64   JIM, the property of William B. WHITEHEAD of Suffolk Virginia and by him registered as one of his hands employed in the Great Dismal Swamp.
    JIM is about forty five years of age, has a brown complexion, full face; flat wide nose, and several small Scars on the outside of his left eye. He has a Scar on his left jaw-bone, three small Scars on his left arm, and a Scar upon the top of his left foot - and Stands without Shoes five feet six & three quarter inches.
              In Testimony of which &c

State of North Carolina} County Court Clerk's Office

4 January 1851

(166) (Cont.) Gates County   }   Januy. 4/th/ 1851.
[No Reg. #.]   WILLIS the property of Thomas J. BARNES, of Gates County NCarolina, and by him registered as one of his hands employed in the Great Dismal Swamp.

WILLIS is a bright mulatto about Twenty four years old with a scare on the right leg from a burn, and one on the left arm near the elbow also a scare on the left fore finger and stands five feet four 1/4 Inches without shoes.

State of N.Carolina}   County Court Clerks Offic?e?
Gates County   }   Jany 6/th/.. 1851
[No Reg. #.]   TONY belonging to Elbert? === RIDDICK and hired by John HINTON Guardian to Jethro RIDDICK of Nansemond County V/a/. and by him registered as one of his hands employed in the Great Dismal Swamp

TONY is about forty one years of age of black complexion, a little gray upon the top of his head, has a scar on

(167)   175   each eye, and one on the shin bone of the right leg, and has two fingers on his right hand drawn up, and stands five feet sevn & 3/4 inches without shoes.

State of N.Carolina}   Conty Cour?t Clerk's Office
Gates Conty   }   Jany 6/th/. 1851
[No Reg. #.]   Boy JOB belonging to Miss May R EPPS of Nansemond Conty V/a/. and registered by Messrs RIDDICK, EPPS & NORFLEET to work in the Great Dismal Swamp

JOB is a boy supposed to be about twelve years of age of black complexion, free from scars, looks well and is but four feet two and a 1/4 inches high without shoes.

State of North Carolina}   County Court Clerks office
Gates County   }   Januy 11/th/ 1851.
[No Reg. #.]   Boy RANDUL the property of Jethro RIDDICK of the County of Nansemond in the state of Virginia and Registered in the County of Gates & Statee aforesaid to work in the Great Dismel Swamp

RANDOL is about Twenty years of age, Black, with full eyes and medium mouth with thick lips, he has a scar on the right hand commenceing on the back of and extending from the senter to the first joint of the little finger, RANDOL is five feet four and a half inches high under the Stand

State of NCarolina}   Gatesville 13/th/. Jany 1851
Gates Conty   }   County Court Clks offce
[No Reg. #.]   Negro man ISAAC belonging to Allen BRIGGS and hired by him to Andrew

(168)   176   VOIGHT and by him registerd to work in the Great Dismal Swamp.

ISAAC is about twenty eight yeas of age of dark complexion, slightly disfigured on the face by a burn has a scar on the middle finger of his right hand and is five feet ten inches hight without shoes.

State of N.Carolina}   Conty Court Clerks
Gates Conty   }   Office 18/th/. Jany 1851
[No Reg. #.]   Negro Man JOE the? belonging to the estate of John MITCHELL dec/d/. and registerd by John L TROTMAN to work with Mesrs NORFLEET & EPPS in the Great Dismal Swamp.

JOE is about Twenty nine years of age black, well set has a scar on the right side of the Jaw his face, extending a little under his jaw, and is five feet eight inches high without shoes.

State of NCarolina}
Gates County   }   Gatesville 28/th/. Jany 1851

(168) (Cont.) [No Reg. #.] Negro boy JOHN the property of James B NORFLEET of Suffolk Va. and registered by him to work in the great dismal Swamp

JOHN is about twelve years of age, his complexion dark brown, has a small dark place on the right jaw, and a scar on his right foot occasioned by a burn, and is four feet five inchs high without shoes

(169) 177 State of N.Carolina} Conty Court clks Office
            Gates Conty}   Feby 1/st/. 1851
[No Reg. #.] Negro man WILLIS the property of Saml. WILKINS and hired by him to Willis RIDDICK and by the said RIDDICK registered to work in the Great Dismal Swamp.

WILLIS is about twnty three years of age, crow black, with large thick lips, with a raised place on the left cheek and is five feet four & a half inches high withoutshoes

State of NCarolina} County Court Clks
    Gates County} Office 6/th/.. Feby 1851
[No Reg. #.] Negro man LEWIS the property of Mrs Ann WILSON of Norfolk Va. and registered by James S SEQUINE of Deep Creek Va. to work in the Great Dismal Swamp

LEWIS is about is about [sic] forty four years of age of dark complexion, has a small scar on his forehead a little above the right eye, and a small scar on his face a little under the right eye and is five feet three & 3/4 inches high without shoes.

(170) 178 State NoCarolina} County Court Clerks office
            Gates County}   Februay 14/th/. 1851.
[No Reg. #.] Negro Boy HENRY belonging to the estate of C. W HAWE?S dec Nansemond County in the State of virginia and worked in the Great Dismal swamp in the County of Gates and State aforesaid by William B. WHITEHEAD and registerd by him

HENRY is about seventeen years ofld dark brown five feet 4 1/4 Inches high with a small scar == on the right leg a little below the nee [sic] joint, he has also a wen of the under side of the right Jaw pinched mouth & thick lip

State No Carolina} County Court Clerks office
    Gates County}   Februy. 14/h/. 1851.
[No Reg. #.] Negro BILLY belonging to the estate of C. W. HAWES decd of the County of Nansemon & State of Virginia and registered by W. B. WHITEHEAD to work in the Great Dismal Swamp in the County of Gates and State of No. Carolina

BILLY is about eighteen years old Black, with weedy? features pleasant countenance with a a [sic] small scar on the calf of the left leg. BILLY is five feet 5 Inches in his stocking feet high.

State No Carolina} County Court Clerks office
    Gates County} Feby. 14/th/ 1851.
[No Reg. #.] Negro SANDY, belonging to the estate of C W HAWES decd of the County of Nansemond in the State of Virginia and registered in the County Court Clerks /office/ of the County of Gates by W. B WHITEHEAD to work in the great Dismal Swamp in the County ofGates

SANDY is about Fifteen years old, Dark Brown with remarkable short fingers a scar on the front of the left arm in the bend looks as if it was caused by a burn, SANDY is fiv [sic] feet five 1/2 Inches in his Stocting

(171) 179 high givn und [sic] my hand and seal of office

State No Carolina} County Court Clerks office
    Gates County}   Februy 14/th/. 1851.

14 February 1851

(171) (Cont.) [No Reg. #.] Jim SAWYEAR represented by W B. WHITEHEAD to have been free born and registered by said WHITEHEAD as one of his hands to work in the great Dismal Swamp in the County of Gates during the year 1851.

Jim SAWYEAR is about sixteen years old Coppe Color Gray eyed and when Spoken to shows his teeth plain and plenty of them, front teath pointed large mouth and Stands in his Stocking feet four feet Ten Inches.

State No Carolina} County Court Clerks offi_e
    Gates County} Febry. 14/h/. 1851.
[No Reg. #.] MOSES the property of W B. WHITEHEAD of Suffolk Va and by him registerd as one of his hands in the Dismal Swamp

MOSES has a scar on the left eye he is of Dark brown complexion about forty five years old has a scar on the right arm cause [sic] from the bite of a negro his Great toe of the right foot has only one bone in the ceneter? and is shorter than the other toes and his left leg shorter than the right stands without shoes five feet five Inches, given [End of entry.]

(172) 180 State of North Carolina} County Court Clerks office
           Gates County} Gatesville February 20/th/ 1851
[No Reg. #.] Moses BROWN the property of the /belonging to the/ estate of Button BROWN deceased, of the State of virginia and Registered by William B. WHITEHEAD of Suffold va to work in the great Dismal Swamp in the County of Gates and State aforesaid for the Term of one year

Moses BROWN is about thirty years of age B very dark Brown has no scars smoothe Skin, averag [sic] face thick lips and wares his hae?ir Comed up and is 5 feet 41/2 Inches high in his stocking feet [Margin:] Duplicate made 6 March 1854

State of North Carolina} County Court Clerks office
           Gates County} Gatesville Febry 20/th/ 1851
[No Reg. #.] Negro Stephen RIDDICK belonging to the estate of William S. RIDDICK decd. of the State of virginia and Registered by William B. WHITEHEAD of Suffold Virginia to work in the Great Dismal Swamp in the County of Gates and State aforsaid for the term of One year

Negro Stephen is about Fifty Six years old of a Dark Copper Colour each of his thuns [sic] has an enlargenent of the joint that connects the thun with the parn of the hand has lost one of his upper Front Teeth and stands in his stocking feet five feet six 1/3 Inches.

(173) 181 State of North Carolina} County Court Clerks office
           Gates County} Gatesville Feby 20/th/ 1851
[No Reg. #.] Negro WILLIS belonging belonging to Javan FRANKLIN of Virginia an [sic] Registered by William B. WHITEHEAD of Suffolk Virginia to work in the Great Dismal Swamp in the County of Gates & Statee of No Carolina for the Term 1851 of one year

WILLIS is === of dark copper colour about Twenty seven years old with fair countenane everage face high fore head and has a scar of on the right leg near the instep on the inside, with small feet for a negro say No 7. shoes would fit, and stands five feet 1/4 Inches in his stocking feet [Margin:] #

State of No. Carolina} County Court Clerks Office
           Gates County} Gatesville Februay 20
[No Reg. #.] LAWYER the property of James GOODMAN of virginia and registered by William B WHITEHEAD of the state of Virginia to work in the Great Dismal Swamp in the County of Gates and State of North Carolina for the Term of one year from the date of this certificate

LAWYER is about forty six years of age, Black with a scar about 2 Inches long on

20 February 1851

(173) (Cont.) the front of the right ancle flat nose /and/ pointed and when spon? to has a considerable stopage in his speach and stands in his stocking feet five feet five 1/2 Inches high [Margin:] Duplicate made 6 March 1854 #

(174) 182 State of No. Carolina} County Court Clerks office
            Gates County}   Gatesville Februay 20/th/ 1851
[No Reg. #.]   Negro DAVID belonging to Daniel BRINKLEY of the state of virginia and registered by William B WHITEHEAD of the state of virginia to work in the Great Dismal Swamp in the County of Gates and State of North Carolina for the Term of one year
        DAVID is about Twenty four years old dak [sic] brown and has a Mark of birth on his left arm betwen the elbow and the hand about 4 or 5 Inches long good teeth and has a small space between the two Center upper teeth of the 16/th/ of and Inch flat face with deep eyes large flat nose & thick lips and Stands in his Stocking feet five feet Six 1/2 Inches high and well set.

State of North Carolina}   County Court Clerks office
        Gates County}   Gatesville February 20/th/ 1851
[No Reg. #.]   Negro JACKSON the property of Javan FRANKLIN of the state of Virginia and registered by William B WHITEHEAD of the state of virginia to work in the Great Dismal Swamp in the /County of Gats/ State of North Carolina for the Term of one year from the date of this Certificate
        JACKSON is about Twenty years of age ==== Black Spare built and has a scar over the left eye long lims thick lips teeth projecting outward a little and with all a likely boy & stands in his Stocking feet 5 feet 6 Inches high

(175) 183 State of No. Carolina}   County Court Clerk's office
            Gates County}   Gatesville Feby 20/th/ 1851
[No Reg. #.]   EDWARD the property of William B WHITEHEAD of Suffolk virginia and by him registered by him to work in the Great Dismal Swamp in the County of Gates and State of North Carolina
        EDWARD is very Black and appears to be about Fifty years old turning Gray slitely, & sliteely ball good front teeth slite scar on the Stomach and a scar on the right knee about 3/4 Inch long and Stands in his Stocking feet five feet Eight inches high.

State of No. Carolina}   County Court Clerks office
Gates County   }   Gatesville Febry 20/th/ 1851
[No Reg. #.]   Jack ANDERSON a free boy bound to Nathnil [sic] BOOTHE of Nansemond County virginia and hired by Wm B. WHITEHEAD the present year and by him registerd as one of his hands to work in the Great Dismall swamp in the County of Gates for the? one year. 18 [sic]
        Jack AANDERSON is about sixteen years old full over his eyes making his eyes shew very Small, his hair is grows very low down making his forehead very Small and Stands four feet Eight Inches high without Shoes.

(176) 184 State of No. Carolina}   County Court Clerk's Office
            Gats County}   Februy 24/th/ 1851
[No Reg. #.]   HARVEY the property of Jethro FRANKLIN of Nansemond County va. and hired the present year by Abram BRINKLEY of the state of Virginia to work in the Great Dismall Swamp i_ the County of Gates for the Term of one year
        HARVEY is about Twenty Seven years old has a Small scar near the corner of the left eye on the off corner, a small Scar on the right leg near the ancle, legs inclined to be hairy and a scare on his left foot about one Inch long between the large toe and the instep, Of very Dark brown Cottormplexion and Stands without Shoes five feet five Inches high

(176) (Cont.) State of No. Carolina} County Court Clerk's Office
                                Gates County}   Februry 24/th/. 1851.

[No Reg. #.] JACOB the property of Edward RIDDICK of the County of Nansemond and State of Va. and hired by Abram BRINKLEY of the state of Va. to work in the Great Dismal Swamp in the County of Gates and state aforesaid, and registerd by him for the Space of one year

JACOB is about Twenty Eight years of age Black has a scar on his breast enlarged, scars on his left foot near the instep, wares his hare Comed up tolerable smoothe Skin and Stands withoutShoes five feet six 1/2 Inches high.

(177) 185 State of No. Carolina} County Court Clerks Office
                                Gates County}   February 24/th/ 1851

[No Reg. #.] NOAH the property of Abram BRINKLEY of Nansemod County in the State of Virginia and registered by him to work in the Great Dismal Swamp in the County of Gates to the Term of One year.

NOAH is about Twelve years old very Dark Brown Complexion has a scar on the left foot projecting frm near the first toe towards the instep has a Scare on his breast near the throat, flat nose and Stands without Shoes four feet four Inches high

State of N.Carolina} County Court Clerk's Office
        Gates County}   April 6/th/.. 1851

[No Reg. #.] Boy TOM the property of Jefersn MITCHEL [sic] and hired by Elisha BLANCHARD and by him registered to work in the work? Messrs EPPS & NORFLEET /& Jethro RIDDIK/ in the great Dismal Swamp.

TOM is about Elvn? years of age Complexion dark brown, seems to be free from scars is well proportioned and four feet 6 1/4 inches high without shoes

(178) 186 State of No Carolina} Gatesville North Carolina
                                Gates County} County Court Clerks office

[No Reg. #.] Negro DICK the property of Abram BRINKLEY of the State of virginia and registered by said BRINKLEY of [sic] work in the Great Dismal Swamp in the County of Gates for the Term of one year

DICK is Black, about forty five years old small peaked face has a large scare on the right arm near the elbow has a s=care on the right leg caused by a snag and Stands without shoes five feet four 3/4 Inches high

State of No Carolina} County Court Clerks Office
Gates County   } Gatesville Gates County NC.

[No Reg. #.] Negro BEN the Property of Abram BRINKLEY of the State of virginia and registerd by him to work in the great Dismal Swamp in the County of Gates for the Term of one year

BEN is about Twenty years old, Black has a scar on the off side of the left knee caused from a burn & has a scar on the lid of the right eye rough skin and Stands without shoes five feet four Inches high

State of No Carolina} Gates ville Gates County NC.
        Gates County}   County Court Clerks office

[No Reg. #.] Negro JACK the property of Abram BRINKLEY of the State of virginia and registered by said BRINKLEY to work in the Great Dismal Swamp in the County of Gates for the Term of one year

JACK is very Black about Twenty six years old thick lip has a wen on the rist [sic] of the left hand Clear of scars and good countenance and Stands without shoes five feet seven 1/4 Inches high

(179) 187 State of No Carolina} County Court Clerks Office

(179) (Cont.)   Gates County   }   March 10/th/ 1851.
[No Reg. #.]   SAME the property of the estate of John R KNIGHT? of Nansemd County and
State of Va and hired the present year by Willis S. RIDDICK of Suffolk Va and by him
registered as one of his hands to wor_ in the Great Dismae? Swamp in the County
ofGates for the Term of one year.
     SAM is about Twenty seven years old very Dark brown Complexion full forehead and
has a scar on his fore head broad flat nose Clear smoothe skin and Stands without
Shoes five feet five /2 [sic] Inches high

State of No Carolina} County Court Clerks Office
Gates County   }   March 10/th/ 1851.
[No Reg. #.]   SAM the property of Nancy GRIFFITH of Nansemond County in the state of
Virginia and hired the present year by Abram BRINKLEY of the County of Nansemond va of
==== = & state of Va. and registered by him to work in the Great Dismal Swamp in the
County ofGates for the Term of One year
     SAM is about Twenty Eight years old very dark brown Complexion thin beard thick
lips large Mouth has a Scar on the lower mussell [sic] of the left arm caused from a
burn andStands without shoes five feet Eight 1/4 Inches.

(180) 188 State of NoCarolina} County Court Clerks Office
          Gates County   }   March 10/th/ 1851.
[No Reg. #.]   WASHINGTON belonging to the estate of John R KNIGHT of Nansemond County
state of Va and hired the present year by Willis S. RIDDICK of Suffolk' Va and
registered by him to work in the Great Dismal Swamp in Gates Cou___ for the Term of
one year
     WASHINGTON is about Fourteen years old Black everag_ face has a small Scar on the
top of the left foot and stands without shoes four feet six 1/2 Inches.

State of No Carolina} County Court Clerks Office
Gates County   }   March 10/th/ 1851.
[No Reg. #.]   TURNER the property of Daniel BRINKLEY of Nansem_d county Va. and hired
the present year by Abram BRINKLEY the present year and registered by him to work in
the Great Dismal Swamp in the County of Gates for the Term of one year
     TERNER is very Black sho==ws a good deal of the whites of his eyes, has two scars
on the off side of the knee joint of the left leg and has two scars on the off side of
the right knee joint andStand_ without shoes, five feet has a scar also X the left
brow.

(181) 189 State of No. Carolina}
          Gates County   }   County Court Clerks Office
[No Reg. #.]   PETER the property of Allen EDWARDS of Southampton County in the State
of Virginia and hired the present year by William B WHITEHEAD of Suffolk virginia and
registered by him to work in the Great dismal Swamp in the County of Gates for the
Term of one year
     PETER is about Sixty years of age Black complexion has a small scare on his right
arm near his elbow ball on the top of his head, has a pach of hair on the fromt, has
lost all his jaw teeth and some of his lower frount, and Stands without shoes five
feet five 1/2 Inches high [Margin:] #

State of N. Carolina} May 31/st/. 1851
Gates County   }   County Court Clerks Office
[No Reg. #.]   GILBERT the propety of Richard RIDDICK of V/a/. and hired by Jethro
RIDDICK of Va. and by him registered to work in the Great dismal swanp.
     GILBERT is about sixty four years of age of black conplexion, has a large and? or
something like it on the right side of his nose, just above the eye, has another on

(181) (Cont.) the right arm on the inside at the elbow joint, has scars on both legs, is gray headed and stands five feet eight inches under the standard without shoes

(182) 190 State of NCarolina}   May 31/st/. 1851
           Gates County   }   County Court Clerks office
[No Reg. #.] **REUBEN** the property of Jethro **RIDDICK** of Nansemond County Va. and by him registerd to work in the Grat dismal swamp for one year
     REUBEN is a likely looking man about thirty two years of age, rather spare of dark complexion talks well is fron fron [sic] scars and six feet high without shoes under the standard.

State of NCarolina}   May 31/st/. 1851
Gates County   }   County Court Clerks Office
[No Reg. #.] Boy **WORGHT** the property of James **BRINKLEY** and hired by Jethro **RIDDICK** of Nansemond County Va. and by him registered to work in the Great dismal Swamp for one year.
     Boy **WORGHT** is a likely boy, not of very dark complexion has a bushy head of hair, has a small scar on his fore-head on the right side, a small scar on the fore finger of the left hand and is four feet ten & a quater inches high without shoes under the standard and is about seventeen years of age from his appearance.

(183) 191 State of North Carolina, Gates County
              County Court Clerks Office July 1/st/ 1851
[No Reg. #.] **MILLS** the property of Elisha **ASHMAN** and of Nansemond County and State of Virginia and registered by Richard **HOSHIER** to Work in the Great Dismal Swamp for the Term of one year
     MILLS is very Black has a small Scar on his forehead over the left eye has also a notable Scar on the under part of the left arm near the Elbow, and the muskelar [sic] part of his ai?rms shews a good many Small scares caused from the whip, and Stands without Shoes five feet one Inch === ==== without shoes age about Twenty one

State of North Carolina Gates County
              County Court Clerks Office July 1/st/1851
[No Reg. #.] **JOE** belofonging to the estate of John **CLARK** of Nansemond County in the State of Virginia and registered by Richard **HOSHIER** to work in the Great Dismall Swamp for the Term of One year
     JOE is Black, clear of Scars on his loins with fine muskerly power everage features low well set and Stands without shoes five feet one 1/4 Inches. and wares his hare in small twist age about thirty years.

(184) 192 State of North Carolina Gates County
              County Court Clerks Office July 1/st/18__
[No Reg. #.] Richard **REED** son of Penny **REED** a free woman of Colour of Nansemond County Virginia and registered by Richard **HOSHIER** of said County to work in the Great dismall Swamp in the state of North Carolina for the spac_ of One year
     Richard is very Bright, hare very Stre?ght little curly at the ends full dark Brown eye clear of scars, has Eight small black moles on his Neck and breast and avery likely boy and Stand without Shoes five feet four 2/3 Inches high age Six teen Eighteen years.

State of North Carolina Gates County   1851
              County Court Clerks office July 1
[No Reg. #.] William **BOON** son of Patcy **BOON** dec/d/ all? ofthe County of Nansemond in the State of Virgina and registered by Richard **HOSHIER** of said County and State to work in the Great dis mal [sic] Swamp in the State of North Carolin for the Term of

(184) (Cont.) one year

William is a Brite Melato with Negro hare has a considerable scar on the right arm caused from a burn, he has a=lso ascar on the off side of the right leg extending a bove and below the knee joint he has also a small Scar on the off side of the left knee joint, age about fourteen yeas - and Stands without shoes four? feet seven Inches high.

(185) 193 State of North Carolina Gates County
            County Court Clerks office July 1/st/ 1851
[No Reg. #.] Solomon CHAPEL son of Medean CHAPEL of Nansemon County and State of North Carolina Virginia and registered by Rich/d/ HOSHIER of the County of Nansemon and State of Va., to work in the Great dis mall Swamp in the State of North Carolina for the Term of one year
      Solom [sic] is about fifteen years of age Bright yellow hair little inclined to be Streght has a notable Scare on the inside of his right foot where the Hollow ought to be, has a small scare on the top of the left hand pointing towards the first finger andStands without Shoes four feet five 1/2 Inches hight

State of N Carolina} County Court Clerks office
  Gates County   }   July 8/th/.. 1851
[No Reg. #.] Negro Boy JOE the property of Daniel BRINKLY of Nansemond Va and hired by W S RIDDICK to work in The Great Dismal Swamp for one year and by him registered for that purpose. JOE is about fourteen years of age of darke complexion has good Teeth large Nostrils Thick lips has a scar on the right cheek from a burn and severa [sic] small scars from the same cause on his knees and Legs and stands without shoes four feet eight and 1/2 inches high.

(186) 194 State of N Carolina} county court clerks office
            Gate County   } July 8/th/.. 1851
[No Reg. #.] Negro Boy EDMUND belonging to the estate of John KNIGHT Nansemond v and hired by W L RIDDICK of Suffolk va and by him registered to work in the great dismal swamp for one year. EDMUND is a boy of about elven years of age of dark complexion has a small nose and scars in each eyes and sktands without shoes four feet one and a half inches high

State of N Carolina} County Court clerks office
Gates County   } July 8/th/ 1851
[No Reg. #.] Negro Boy JIM Belongink to Daniel BRINKLY of Nansimond Va and hired by W S RIDDICK and by him registered to work in the great dismal Swamp for one year.
      JIM is a bout eleven years of age looks fearce has large white teeth and far apart and is four feet eigh inches with out sues.

State of N Carolina} County Court clks office
Gates County   } July 8/th/.. 1851
[No Reg. #.] HENRY the prroperty of Daniel BRINKLY of the State of Va. Nansimond county and hired by W S RIDDICK to work in the dismal swamp and by him registered for that purpose.
      HENRY is nineteen years of age has a sharp forehea_ and a scar just at the point of same small deep eyes and very small eye brows a small scar on the midle joint of the middle /fore/ finger and little finger an stand [sic] without shoes five feet seven and 3/4 inches high

(187) 195 State of N Carolina} County Court clks office
            Gates County   } July 8/th/. 1851
[No Reg. #.] Milles RIDDICK dese JACK the property of the estate of Milles RIDDICK

(187) (Cont.) dese of Suffolk va and hired and registered by W S RIDDICK to work in the dismal swamp for one year. JACK is forty eight years of age of dark brown colour high fore head prominent eyes=Brows - a little gray - a scar on the head near the top -a small scar on the back of the left hand and a scar on the bend of the same arm on the in side a scar on the left knees and a scar on the left Thumb and stand without shoes five six and a quarter inches high

State of N Carolina} County Court clks Office
Gates County   } July 8/th/ 1851
[No Reg. #.] HARRISON the property of the Estate of John R KNIGHT of Nansemond County Va and hired the present year by Willis S. RIDDICK of Suffolk and by him registered to work in the Great Dismal Swamp
     HARRISON is twenty /one/ years old, flat wide nose, a scar on the outside of the left wrist a scar on both knees. Stands without shoes five feet six inches high.

State of NCarolina} Conty Court Clerks Office
Gates Conty   } July 28/th/. 1851
[No Reg. #.] This is to certify that Archibald RIDDICK of Nansemond Conty V/a/. has enployed in the Great Dismal Swanp a negro by the name of Arkey MILTEAR of the following descrption: five feet nine and a half inchs high without shoes of light complexion about 24? years of age

(188) 196 has a scar on the back of the right hand.

State of North Carolina} County Court Clerks office
        Gates County } August 9/th/ 1851.
[No Reg. #.] PHILIP belonging to the estate of Joseph RIDDICK dec/d/ of Suffolk va and registered by Amos B. BADGER of the state of va. to work in the Great Dismall Swamp in the state of North Carolina for the term of one year
     PHILIP is about Sixty Nine years of age; Complexion, Black, low well set and has a considerable scar in his forehead above the right temple front teeth good lower Jaw teeth gone, has a good countenance, and stands without Shoes five feet one 1/3 Inches high

State of No Carolina} County Court Clerks office
        Gates County} August 9/th/ 1851
[No Reg. #.] John BOON represented by Amos B BADGER to be a free born boy of Collor of the state of va. and registered by him the said Amos B. BAGER to work in the great Dismal Swamp in the state of North Carolina for the term of one year
     John is of the Coper Colour about Seventeen year of age, has a scratch Scar on his forehead above the right Temple has also a small scar near the joint of the left thum and stands without shoes five feet thee Inches high

(189) 197 State of North Carolina} County Court Clerks office
        Gates County } August 31 /st/? 1851
[No Reg. #.] ISAH the property of Marmaduk [sic] JONES of the State of virginia and registered by him in this office to work in the Great Dismall Swamp in the State aforesaid for the Space of One year next presenting? ISIAH is about Twenty five years of age Black complexion has a small wort on the upper side of his right rist joint paralel with the right thum has also two small worts on the joint of the right thum has also a small wort on the left arm about three Inches below the elbow has a Scar on the joint of the right foot near the big toe, Sharp Chin and Stands without Shoes five feet four 1/4 Inches high given with my hand and seal of Office [End of entry.]

State of North Carolina} County Court clerks office

(189) (Cont.) Gates County   } Nov. 19/th/.. 1855 [sic]
[No Reg. #.]   JOSIAH, the property of Marmaduke JONES of County &State aforesaid, and registered to work in the great dismal Swamp in the State of North Carolina, for the term of one year next preceeding.

JOSIAH is about twenty six years of age, of dark Complexion, large cheek bones, good teeth,- He has a scar on his right elbow-joint, a scar on the first joint of his great right toe, a small one on the middle finger ofhis left hand, and stands without shoes five feet three & a half inches high. Given under my hand &c.

(190) 198 State of North Carolina} County Court Clerks office
                    Gates County } September 8/th/ 1851
[No Reg. #.]   LEWIS the property ofthe estate of Pinina? EPPES of the State of Virginia and registered by Jethro RIDDICK &C of the State of va to work in the Great Dismal Swamp in the State of North Carolina for the Term of one year

LEWIS is about forty seven years of age of brown Complexion has one upper frount tooth Missing with his right leg shorter than the left He has a Scar on the knee pan of the right leg and Stands with out shoes five feet five Inches.   [Margin:] duplicate of this present? Master 6/th/ day Jany 1855

State of North Carolina} County Court Clerks office
                    Gates County } September 9/th/ 1851.
[No Reg. #.]   EDOM the property of James RIDDICK of Nansemn? County in the State of virginar [sic] and registered by Jethro RIDDICK &co to work in the Great Dismal Swamp in the State of North Caroliner for the space of one year

EDOM is about Twenty five years old has a dark brown Complexion has lost one of his upper Corner teeth on the right side of his Mouth, large Nose at the lower extremity, He has a scar on the right wrist and one upon each hand and Stands with outshoes five feet four Inches

(191) 199 State of North Carolina} County Court Clerks office
                    Gates County } September 9/th/ 1851
[No Reg. #.]   SIMOND belonging to the estate of Arch BRINKLEY dec/d/. and hired the present year by Jetho RIDDICK & co to work in the Great Dismal Swamp in the State of North Carolina for the Space of One year next preceeding

SIMON is about Twenty Seven years of age brown Complexionhas a Scar on the off side of the right leg with that exception Clear of Scars large face, has a small scar on his forehead and Stands without Shoes Boots? five feet two 1/4 Inches

State of North Carolina} County Court Clerks Office
                    Gates County } September 9/th/ 1851
[No Reg. #.]   JACK the property of Jethro RIDDICK and registered by Jethro RIDDICK &co of the State of Virginia to work in the Great Dismal Swamp in the State of North Carolina for one year

JACK is about Sixty four years old Black Complexion small features, thicklip, red eyes, tolerable good teeth of his age has a knot on the upper joint of the great toe of the left foot and Stands without shoes five feet seven and a half Inches.

(192) 200 State of North Carolina} County Court Clk office
                    Gates County } September 9/th/ 1851
[No Reg. #.]   JOE belonging to the estate of Miles GRIFFITH dec/d/ and hired the present year by H L. EPPES of the State of Va, and registered by Jethro RIDDICK and co to work in the Great dismal Swamp in the State of North Carolina for the term of year [sic]

JOE is about Sixteen years old very dark Brown Complexion has a Considerable burn on the back of his Neck & behind each ear and Stands without shoes five feet

15 November 1851

(192) (Cont.) State of North Carolina} County Court Clerks office
Gates County } Nov. 15/th/ 1851.
[No Reg. #.] ELBERT the property of Benjami JOHNS? and Hired the presnt year by W B.? JUDKINS to work in the great Dismaill Swamp in the State of North Carolina for the Term of one year

ELBERT is about twenty years of age Black clear of Scars well proportioned thick lips and Stands without shoes five feet three 1/2 Inches high

(193) 201 State of North Carolina}
Gates County } County Court Clerks office
November 12/th/ 1851.
[No Reg. #.] BEN the property of William BEEMAN of said County and State hired the present year by Isaac S HARRELL and is now in the employment of Andrew VOIGHT Who has hired BEN from the present time till the first day of Jany Next from the said Isaac S HARRELL and said BEN is registered by the said Andrew VOIGHT for the purpose of Working in the Dismal Swamp

BEN is about Twenty five years of age Stands five feet three and a half inches in height when in his shoes weighs about One hundred and forty pounds has a scar on the Shin bone of the left leg occasioned by a burn and another Scar on the inside of the left knee In Testeamony whereof I do hereunto set my hand and affix the seal of my office the day and year above written [End of entry. Remainder of page is blank.]

(194) 202 State of North Carolina} County Court Clerks
Gates County } office Janury 1/st/ 185_
[No Reg. #.] GEORGE the property of Dempsey KNIGHT asf? the County and state aforesaid and hired the present year by Jordan PARKER and registered by him to Work in the great Dismal swamp in the state of NCarolina for the present year

GEORGE is about Twenty Eight years of age dark brown Complexion clear of scars fine muscular powener? and Stands without shoes five feet nine Inches in witness whereof I have hereunto set my hand and affixed my the seal of Office == the day and date above written   WGDAUGHTY CC
                                    FM DAUGHTY DC

State of North Carolina} County Court Clerks office
Gates County } January 3/rd/. 1852.
[No Reg. #.] WASHINGTON the property of John C GORDAN, and hired the present year by Jacob BENTON, and registered by said BENTON to work in the Dismill swamp for the term of one year

WASHINGTON is about fifty five years of age Brown Complexion Has lost one of his upper front teeth and two under, clear of scars and stands without shoes five feet Ten Inches hight given under my hand and seal of office the date above written [End of entry.]

State of No. Carolina}   {1852
Gates, County} Gatesville 8/th/.. Jan
[No Reg. #.] LUKE belongs to the estate of Joseph RIDDICK /and hired the presant year by Jethro RIDDICK/ of Nansemond County Va. and by him registered to work in the Great Dismal Swamp

LUKE is about twenty six years

(195) 203 of age, of dark complexion a little scared on the front of each leg, by burns, is well marked or pitted with the effect of the Small-Pox and is four feet ==
Nine nine [sic] inches high, without shoes
                          WGDAUGHTEY CCC

(195) (Cont.) State of N Carolina} County Court Clerks office
                    Gates County} Gatesvile 8/th/.. January 1852
[No Reg. #.]   MILES belongs to Reuben RIDDICK and hired the presant year Jethro
RIDDICK of Nanesemond County, Va. and by him registered to Work in the Great Dismal
Swamp for this year
     MILES is about twenty years of age of dark complexion well set; free from scars,
is broad across the face at the cheek bone. The white of his eyes a little red and is
five feet three inches high without Shoes
                    WGDAUGHTEY CCC

                              {offic
State of N Carolina} County Court Clerk_
        Gates County} January 8/th/.. 1852
[No Reg. #.]   TONY belongs to Elbert RIDDICK and hired the peseant [sic] year by
Jethro RIDDICK of Va. and by him registered to work in the Great Dismal Swamp for the
year 1852
     TONY is about forty two years of age black complexion a little greay upon the top
of his head, has a scar over each eye and one on the shin bone of his right leg and
has two finges on his right hand, drawn up and is

(196) 204 five feet seven and a half inches high withou_ shoes WGDAUGHTEY CC.C

State of NCarolina} County Court Clerk's office
     Gates County } January 8/th/.. 1852
[No Reg. #.]   JOSIAH belong [sic] to the estate of Joseph RIDDICK and hired by Jethro
RIDDICK and by him registered to work in the Great Dismal Swamp for the year 1852
     JOSIAH is about forty one years of age of dark complexion, has a small or sl?ight
scar on his fore-head, is otherwise free from scars and is five feet two and quarter
inches in height without shoes
                    WGDAUGHTEY C.C.C.

State of North Carolina} County Court Clks off___
Gates County   } January 9/th/ 1852
[No Reg. #.]   Man WILLIS, the property of Jason BRINKLY and hired the present year by
Archibald RIDDICK of Suffolk, Virginia and by him registered by him to work in the
Great Dismal Swamp the present year.
     WILLIS is about 25 years old of Brown complexion, well set, big flat nose, large
mouth, and broad across the face at the cheek bones, free from scars and is five feet
= three and a Quarter inches high without shoes   WGDAUGHTRY CCC

State of North Carolina} County Court Clerks of___
          Gates County } January 9/th/. 1852
[No Reg. #.]   Man ===== SOLOMON property of Jason BAINS? and hired by Archibald
RIDDICK of Suffolk V.a. and by him registered

(197) 205 to work in the Great dismal Swamp the present year
     SOLOMON is about 24 years of age of dark complexion, Two scars on the right wrist
- has lost one uper & thwo lower /of his/ front teeth and stands five feet 8ix? five &
three quarter inches high without shoes
                    WG DAUGHTRY CCC

State of North Carolina} County Court Clerk Offi__
          Gates County } January 9/th/ 1852
[No Reg. #.]   Boy SAM the property of Henry ROGERS and hired by Jethro RIDDICK of
Nansemon_ Co Va and by him Registered to work in the great Dismal Swamp the present

9 January 1852

(197) (Cont.) year.

Boy SAM is of a brown complexion looks to be about ten or leven [sic] years of age. A Scar on the right side of his neck well set & is four feet two inches without shoes   W G DAUGHTRY CCC

State of North Carolina} County Court Clk office
        Gates County   } January 9/th/ 1852
[No Reg. #.] Boy CHARLES the property of Jason BRINKLY and hired by Archibald RIDDICK of Suffolk Va. and by him registered to work in the Great Dismal Swamp the present year.

CHARLES is about thirteen years of age brown complexion A scar on the left hand of slend [sic] form and is four feet four inches high without shoes   W G DAUGTRY CCC

(198) 206 State of North Carolina} County Court Clks offic_
        Gates County   } January 9/th/. 1852?
[No Reg. #.] Man HARRY belongs to the Estate of Archibald BRINKLY and hired by Archibald RIDDICK of Suffolk Va. and by him registered to work in the Great Dismal swamp for the present year

HARRY is about nineteen years old - brown complexion - A scar on the litle finger which is contracted - large neck weel set and five feet four inches higth without shoes   W G DAUGHTRY CCC

State of North Carolina} County Court Clks. office
        Gates County   } Januaary 9/th/. 1852
[No Reg. #.] Dempay JONES a free man of colour and hired by Archibald RIDDICK of Suffolk va and by him registered to work in the Great Dismal swamp for the present year

Dempcy is of light complexion - a small scar on the right hand above the fourth finger also a small one about the midle of the fore head - hair nearly straight and is five feet ten and a half inches without shoes   W G DAUGHTRY CCC

State of North Carolina} County Court Clks offic_
Gates County   } January 9/th/. 1852
[No Reg. #.] Boy Milles son of Patcy BOON a free woman of color and hired by Archibald RIDDICK and of Suffolk va and by him registered to work in the Greate Dismal Swamp for the present year Milles is of light complexion long head from the chin to the top of his head and narrow from ear to ear a defect in the left eye - a scar on the left arm thick upper lip

(199) 207 and is four feet Six and a quarter inches high without shoes WG DAUGHTRY CCC

State of North Carolina} County Court Clerks office
Gates County   } January 9/th/. 1851 [sic]
[No Reg. #.] Man WHIT the property of Archibald NELMS and hired by Archibald RIDDICK and by him registered to work in the Great Dismal Swamp for the present Year. Man WHIT is about fifty seven years of Age - light Brown complexion. The nails of two fingers have been split - has lost one of his uper front teeth and is fiouve feet six inches high without shoes   W G DAUGHTRY CCC

State of North Carolina} County Court Cleks Office
Gates County   } January 9/th/ 1852
[No Reg. #.] Man DAVY belongs to the estate of Will/m/ GARVY and hired by Archibald RIDDICK /of Suffolk/ and by him registered to work in the Great Dismal Swamp for the present year

9 January 1852

(199) (Cont.) DAVY is about twenty five years of age light complexion - bushy hair.
A scar to the left of the nose - well set and is five feet four inches high without
Shoes   W G DAUGHTRY CC_

State of North Carolina} County Court Clk office
Gates County   } January 9/th/. 1851 [sic]
[No Reg. #.]   Man GATES belonging to Charles BALDEL and by him registered to work in
the Great Dismal Swamp through the present year
     Man GATES is about Sixty four years old - of Brown complexion - prominent fore
head hair not? g? - small eyes and is free from scars - five feet four and three
quarter inches high without shoes   W G DAUGHTRY CCC

(200) 208 State of N.Carolina} County Court Clerks /{office/
               Gates County } January 9/th/. 1852
[No Reg. #.]   Man ISAAC the property of Huldae? KNIGHT and hired by Archibald RIDDICK
of Suffolk Va, and by him registered to work in the Great Dismal Swamp the presant
year   ISAAC is about thirty year of age, of a dark complexion a scar on the right
corner of the mouth prominent fore-head, and has a wide nose, mostrils well expanded,
He is five feet, four and a quarter inche in height, with out Shoes
                    W.G.DAUGHTRY. C.C.C.

State of North Carolina} County Court Clk Offic_
     Gates County } January [sic]   . •·
[No Reg. #.]   Dick JONES a free man of colour and hired by Archibald RIDDICK and by
him registered to work in the Great Dismal Swamp for the present year
     Dick JONES is of light complexion about twenty five years of age - thick head of
hair A scar on his forhead over the right eye rather slender built and is five feet
eight inches high without Shoes   W G DAUGHTRY CCC

(201) 209 State of North Carolina} County Court Clerks office
               Gates County   } January 10/th/. 1851 [sic]
[No Reg. #.]   Man ISAC belonging to the Estate of Miles GRIFIN and hired by Archibald
RIDDICK of Suffolk Va and by him hiredt? registered to work in the Great Dismal Swamp
for the present Year ISAC has a dark complexion two scars = one on the left hand the
other on the left cheek - upper front teeth very mutch decayed - rather a small head -
he is about twenty three years of age and is five feet five inches high without shoes
                    W G DAUGHTRY C C C

State of North Carolina} County Court Clks offi__
     Gates County } January 10/th/ 1851
[No Reg. #.]   LAWYER the property of James GOODMAN and hired by Archibald RIDDICK and
by him registered to work in the Great Dismal Swamp for the present Year.
     LAWYER is about forty seven years of Age - black A scar about two inches long on
the front of the right ankle has a flat nose and when spoken to has a considerable
stopage in his speech - with expresion out of the eyes and is five feet five and a
half inches high with out shoes   WGDAUGHTRY C C C

State of North Carolina} County Court Clerks Off [sic]
     Gates County } February 2/nd/ 1852
[No Reg. #.]   JACK? belonging to the Estate of Edward RIDDICK deceased and hired by
Archibald RIDDICK of Suffolk Va and by him register

(202) 210 State of North Carolina} County Court Clks off___
               Gates County } January 10/th/.. 1851?
[No Reg. #.] NOAH the property of Abram BRINK__ of Nansimond Va and registered by him

75

(202) (Cont.) to work in the Great Dismal Swamp in the county of Gates to the term of One Year

NOAH is about thirteen years old of a dark brown complexion has a scar on the left foot progescting from the first toe towards the instep - has a scar near the throat flat nose and stands without shoes four feet six inches W GDAUGHTRY C C C

State of North Carolina} County Court Clerk Off___
        Gates County } February 2/th/? 1852
[No Reg. #.] JACK belonging to the Estate of Edward RIDDICK deceased and hired by Archibald RIDDICK of Suffolk Va and by /him/ registerd by him to work in the Great Dismal Swamp for one year.

JACK is about forty years of age c?row blac_ complexion - sunken jaws, sharp mouth, thin visage - free from scars and stands five feet seven inches. WGDAUGHTRY CCC

State of North Carolina} County Court Cherk Off___
        Gates County } February 2/th/ [sic] 1852
[No Reg. #.] BRISTO the property of Josiah MILLER and hired the pressent year by Archibald RIDDICK of Suffolk Va and by him registered to

(203) 211 work in the Great Dismal Swamp one year

BRISTO is about fifty five years of age has two Scars on the left leg just belowe? the knee and a smal one on the fore hed? and one on the right hand across the fingers occasioned by cut, a bald streak on his head running from the front of the forehead - his hair on each side of his head is nearly black below that it is gray. He is five feet five and half inches in height. WGDAUGHTRY CCC

State of North Carolina} County Court Clerk Office
        Gates County } February 2/th/ 1852
[No Reg. #.] JOSIAH the property of Jessie IVES and hired by Archibald RIDDICK of Suffolk V and by him registered to work in the Great Dismal swamp one year.

JOSIAH is about forty five years of age crow black complexion - long narrow head ==== small eyes - a scar on the forehead just above the nose - and one on the fourth finger of the right hand, has lost one under jaw toothe on the left side Height is five feet eight inches WGDAUGHTRY CCC

State of North Carolina} County Court Clerks Office
        Gates County } February 2/nd/ 1852
[No Reg. #.] Boy BRISTO the property of Mitchel PHILIPS and and [sic] hired by Archibald RIDDICK of Suffolk Va and by him registered to work in the

(204) 212 Great Dismal Swamp one year.

BRISTO has a dark complexion - large head short neck - prominent chest - thick upe [sic] lip has a scar on the left leg otherwise well set and is four feet three and half inches high without shoes W G DAUGHTRY CCC

State of North Carolina} County Court Clerks of____
        Gates County } February 10/th/ 1852
[No Reg. #.] Man ISAAC belonging to HamlinL EPS [sic] and hired by Edward RIDDICK of Nansemo__ Va and by him registered to work in the Great Dismal Swanp for one year

ISAC is five feet eight high is of black skin - has a scar on his right thigh occasioned by a burn - also a scar on his right leg - also a scar on his left hand just above his thunb - thick under lip with projesting mouth is about thirty years of age W G DAUGHTRY CCC

State of North Carolina} County Court Clks o____

10 February 1852

(204) (Cont.)   Gates County }   February 10/th/ 1852
[No Reg. #.]   Man MOSES belonging to Grt [sic] RIDDICK of Nansemond County Va and by
him riestered to work in the Great Dismal Swamp for one year.
    MOSES is about twenty three years of age has a scar on the left leg Caused by a
cut - black complexion - projecting mouth long narrow face and is five feet three and

(205) 213 a half inches high without shoes. W G DAUGHTRY CCC

State of North Carolina} County Courty Clerk Office
        Gates County }   February 10/th/ 1853?
[No Reg. #.]   Man JACOB belonging to Edward RIDDICK and by him registered to work in
the Great Dismal Swamp.
    JACOB is about twenty nine years of age has a scar on his back a large scar on his
left ~~leg~~ foot near the Instep smoothe skin and stands without shoes five feet seven
and a half inches high W G DAUGHTRY CCC

State of North Carolina} County Court Cherks Offic_
        Gates County }   February 16/th/ 18532
[No Reg. #.]   Man BUREL belonging to Edward RIDDICK of nancemond County Va and by him
registered to work in the Great Dismal Swamp for one year.
    BURELL is a bout twenty one years of age - has a dark complection has rought? skin
A scare on the right foot just above his big toe joint a scare on the left hand just
abov_ the forth finger, a scare between the ear & right eye, and has a large neck, and
stands without shoes five feet seven & three quater inchis WGDAUGHTRY C C C.

(206) 214 State of North Carolina} County Court Cherks Offi__
            Gates County }   February 16/th/ 1852
[No Reg. #.]   PAUL belonging to Edward RIDDICK of Nansemond County Va and by him
registered to work in the Great Dismal Swamp for one year
    PAUL is about forty eight years of age of brown complexion has enlargement on the
left ankle and badly scared on both of his legs from his knesss [sic] to his ankles
the middle finger of his left hand has been masked [sic] off just above the nails has
a sm?al scar on the lid of the left eye and stands five feet six and o a half inches
without shoes W G DAUGHTRY CCC

State of North Carolina} County Court Clerks Off__
        Gates County }   February 16/th/ 1852
[No Reg. #.]   Boy JOE belonging to Eddwar [sic] RIDDICK of Nansemond County Va and by
him registered to work in the Great Dismal Swamp for one year.
    JOE is about thirteen years of age - of brown complexion - has a Wort on his right
leg just below the kness - has a scar about the middle of the fore head inclined to
the right - hair inclined to be thin and speaks readily when spoken to and stands
without shoes four feet seven and half inches. W G DAUGHTRY

(207) 215 State of North Carolina} County Court Cherks Office
            Gates County }   February 16/th/.. 1852
[No Reg. #.]   Man LOUIS belonging to Edward RIDDICK of Nansemond Co Va and by him
registered to work in the Great Dismal Swamp one Year.
    LOUIS is about fifty sxix years of age has a dark complexion - has lost several of
his front teeth has a large scar on his left arm caused by a burn - also a small scar
on the wrist of the right arm, round head well set and proportional in form - and is
five feet eight inches without shoes W G DAUGHTRY CCC

State of North Carolina} County Court Clerk's Office
        Gates County }   February 16/th/.. 1852

16 February 1852

(207) (Cont.) [No Reg. #.] Man RANDAL belonging to Edward HARRELL and registered by James B NORFLEET of Suffolk Va to work in the Great Dismal Swamp for one year.

RANDAL is about twenty one Years of age - of Black complexion - a scar under his right arm caused by a rising - a large scar on the back of the right hand - thick pouting lips and is five feet five inches high without shoes.

W GDAUGHTRY CCC

State of North Carolina} County Court Clerks Office
     Gates County } February 16/th/ 1852
[No Reg. #.] Boy BOB belonging to Mrs DUKES and hired by Archibald RIDDICK of Suffolk Va and by him registered to work in the Great Dismal Swamp for one year - BOB has a Brown complexion, long narrow head, dull expression out the eye, has a scars on the right temple and is five feet two inches high, & about

(208) 216 Seventyeen years of age

W G DAUGHTRY Clerk

State of North Carolina} County Court Clerk office
  Gates County } February 16/th/ 1852
[No Reg. #.] Boy JIM belonging to Mrs GARY and hired by Archibald RIDDICK of Suffolk Va and by him registered to work in the great Dismal Swamp for one year

JIM has a dark complixion, free from scars flat nose - full prominent eyes, the white Slightly yellowend? - he is about fourteen years of age and Stands without Shoes four feet and six inches.

W G DAUGHTRY ClErk

State of North Carolina} County Court Clerk Office
  Gates County } Februay 16/th/ 1852
[No Reg. #.] Hardy REED a free man of color and hired by Archibald RIDDICK of Suffolk Va and by him registered to work in the Great Dismal Swamp for one year - Hardy is about thirty years of age, a bright mulatto of prominent nose inclined to turn up, free from scars and stands five feet eight inches without shoes

W G DAUGHTRY Clerk

State of North Carolina} County Court Clerk Office
Gates County } Februay 16/th/ 1852
[No Reg. #.] Boy Emanuel WHITE belonging to the Widow WHITE and hired by James SEAGUINE of Deep Creek Va and by him registered to work in the great dismal Swamp for one year - Boy Emanuel is nine years of age, of black complexion, prominent forehead wide nose, has a impediment in his Speech, free from Scars and is four feet hig=h

(209) 217 without Shoes.

W G DAUGHTRY C C C

State of North Carolina} County Court Clerk office
  Gates County } February 16/th/ 1852
[No Reg. #.] ALFRED belonging to Estate of John MILLER and hired by Archibald RIDDICK of Suffolk Va and by him registered to work in the great dismal Swamp for one year - ALFRED is about fourteen yeas of age - black complexion, full eyes, and the white yellowo?ed - has a wart on his right knee - has an impediment in his speech - smal mouth, & prominent nose and is four feet eight inches high without shoes.

W G DAUGHTRY C C Cl

State of North Carolina} County Court Clerk Office
  Gates County } February 16/th/ 1852

(209) (Cont.) [No Reg. #.]   Daniel a free boy of color son of Jack **CHORK** hired by Archibald **RIDDICK** of Suffolk Va and by him registered to work in the great dismal Swamp for one year

Daniel is a bright Mullatto, has a scar on the ball of his right thumb, about sixteen years of age, his hair grows somewhat to a point on the fore head and is well proportioned. Stands without Shoes four feet, ten & half inches high

W G **DAUGHTRY** C C C

State of North Carolina} County Court Clerk Office
   Gates County   }   February 16/th/ 1852
[No Reg. #.] Man **JACK** the property of Hamilin L **EPS** and hired by Isaac **HARRELL** and registered by ~~him to~~ HARRELL & PARKER to work in the great dismal

(210)   218 Swamp for one year. **JACK** is about forty years of age, black complexion, crossed in one eye, has a scar over the right eye - small teeth & stands without shoes five feet nine & half inches in h̲ight.

W G DAUGHT̲Y̲ CCC

State of North Carolina} County Court Clerk Office
         Gates County }   February 16/th/ 1852
[No Reg. #.]   **PHILIP** belonging to Isaac **HARRELL** and registered by **HARRELL & PARKER** to work in the great dismal Swamp for one year.

PHILIP is about fifty five years of age, brown conplexion, large mouth, thi̲ck lips, has a scar on the nail of the fouth finger of the left hand and Stands without Shoes five feet eight inches & half

W G **DAUGHTRY** CCC

State of North Carolina} County Court Clerk Office
         Gates County }   February 16/th/ 1852
[No Reg. #.] Man **NED** belonging to the Estate of Henry **COSTEN** & hired by **PARKER** & **HARRELL** & by them registered to work in the gr̲at dismal Swamp for one year

NED is about forty five years of age black complexion, eyes rather small, large nose, thik? under lip, has lost several of the front upper teeth & a few of the gaw teeth, has a scar on both feet caused by a cut, Also a smal̲ scar onthe left arm & Stands without shoes five feet nine & half inches high

W G **DAUGHTRY** C C C

(211) 219 State of North Carolina} County Court Clerk Office
           Gates County }   February 16/th/ 1852
[No Reg. #.]   **JIM** belonging to Wm **BEEMAN** and hired by Harry **HOFLER** and by him registered to work in the Great Dismal Swamp for one Year

JIM is about thirt̲ey-four years of age - has a burn on his left foot and a scar on his left fore arm - well set and stands without shoes five feet five inches in height.

WGDAUGHTRY C C C

State of North Carolina} County Court Clerk's Office
         Gates County }   February 16/th/ 1852
[No Reg. #.]   Man **TONY** belonging to Joseph **HURDLE** and hired by Harry **HOFLER** and by him registered to work in the Great Dismal Swamp for one Year

TONY is about sixty years of age black complexion - has a long narrow head - has a scar on his uper lip under the right nostril-has been frost bitten on his two toes of the right foot - he stands without shoes five feet five inches high.

WGDAUGHTRY C C C

State of North Carolina} County Court Clerk's Office

16 February 1852

(211) (Cont.) Gates County } February 16/th/ 1852
[No Reg. #.]   Man MINGO belonging to Elizabeth RIDDICK and hired by HARRELL & PARKER
and by them registered to work in the Great Dismal Swamp for one Year
     MINGO is about twenty five years of age dar̲ek complexion-few small scars on the

(212) 220 fou̲th finger of the left hand - large fu̲l face - has lost one front uper
toothe - well set and stands without shoes five feet four inches
                    W G DAUGHTRY C C C

State of North Carolina} County Court Clerk's Office
         Gates County }   February 24/th/.. 1852
[No Reg. #.]   JACKSON belonging to Javan R FRANKLIN & hired by Wm. B WHITEHEAD of
Suffolk Va and by him registered to work in the Great Dismal Swamp one Year.   JACKSON
is about twenty years of age - of dark complexion - large mouth thick lips - small
narrow forehead - a small scar on the left of the f̶a̶c̶e̶ left eye - spare built and
stands without shoes five feet eight inches in height
                    WGDAUGHTRY CCC

State of North Carolina} County Court Clerk Office
         Gates County }   Februy 24/th/.. 1852
[No Reg. #.]   MOSES belonging to Mrs. Sarah SMITH of Somerton Va and hired by Wm.. B
WHITEHEAD of Suffolk Va and by him registered to work in the Great Dismal Swamp one
year
     Boy MOSES is about sixteen years old - dark complexion - wide flat nose projecting
mouth with thick lips - a long head from his chin to the crown of his head small eyes
- free from Scars and is five feet high without shoes
                    WGDAUGHTRY CCC

(213) 221 State of North Carolina} County Court Clerk's Office
                 Gates County }   February 24/th/.. 1852
[No Reg. #.]   Edmund BOOTHE a free man and hired by Wm.. B WHITEHEAD of Suffolk Va
and by him registered to work in the Great Dismal Swamp one year.
     Edmund is about forty seven years old - black complexion - four feet nine inches
high without shoes - has a scar on the right hand one on his breast one on the left
side of the face below the eye and stoutly built
                    WGDAUGHTRY CCC

State of North Carolina} County Court Clerk's Office
         Gates County }   Febury 24/th/. 1852
[No Reg. #.]   Man RICHARD the property of William WILSON and hired by James S SEGUINE
of Deep Creek Va and by him registered to work in the Great Dismal Swamp one year
     RICHARD is about fifty years old - jaws sunken rather dark complexion; - flat nose
with wide nostrils - gray headed - spare built and stands without shoes five feet
nine inches in height
                    WGDAUGHTRY CCC

State of North Carolina} County Court Clerk's Office
         Gates County }   March 16/th/.. 1852
[No Reg. #.]   William PERKINS a free boy of color hired by Archibald RIDDICK of Suffolk Va and by him registered to work in the Great Dismal Swamp one year.
     William is about thirteen years of age - black complexion - thick under lip - the
white? of his eyes very much reddened and stands without shoes four feet eight inches
                    WGDAUGHTRY CCC

(214) 222 Gates County March 18/th/1852

(214) (Cont.) [No Reg. #.] persuant to the actof our Legislature & anorder from Chs. E. BALLARD, I measured boy STEPEN [sic] & described him in a certificate given him as follows, five feet 8 1/2 to 9 inches in height, of a dark copper colour, a fine high forehead, a scar & one /the/ left of the same, one other scar /on/ cheek - right - and goes to workin the great Dismal swam [sic] as one of the hands of Iaac R.HARRELL & E/d/PARKER

not pd.   Signed by H. M. DAUGHTERY Dpy Clk.

[No Reg. #.] Persuant to the same act, and an order from E/d/.R.HARRELL I gave his boy JOHN a certificate as followes, Boy JOHN is five feet 10 inches in height dark complected, = has a pleasan_ & earnest countenance when spoken to, a fine forehead, between forty & 43 years of age - and is turning gray - has good teeth, and a scar on his left foot across the instep - & goes in the great Dismal swam to work as the hand of JnoC. JGORDON, signed the 18/th/ Mch 1852. paid WmG. DAUGHTRY Clk

H.M. DAUGHTERY Dpy Clk
Mr.? GWBUSH - agt-

[No Reg. #.] HARMAN the property of James E. BARNES &by him [sic] for this year to JnoC. GORDON of Gates Co & employed by him as one of his hands to work in the Dismal Swamp - HARMAN is about 35 years old, Black, has a scar on his left forehead, which is round, full a pleasant coutenance, has a small scar on his lef knee & is 5feet 6/8 /inches/ in height - Gates Co. Co. C. C.lkes [sic] office Mch 22/52- not paid

(215) 223 Gates Co. Clks office.
[No Reg. #.] Negro NELSON - the property of Fredrick JONES & hired by him to Jno.C. GORDON to work as one of his hands for this year, in the Dismall swamp
  NELSON is 5 feet 4 & 3/4 inches in height, dark complected, Good teeth, fine forehead & has a scar on the left side of the same, one also on the left hand - &is about 26 years of age
  Gates Co. Co. Co. Clks office
    Mch 22/d/?1852   not pd

Gates County N.C.
[No Reg. #.] Negro. ISAAC the property of Chas. E. BALLARD & by him hired this year to Jno.C. GORDON to work in the Dismal Swamp.
  ISAAC is 5 feet 7 & 1/2 inches in height, quite Black, good forehead, has a pleasant countenance when adoressed, only - has lost his upper teeth, has ascar on the left cheek & is about 40 years of age
  Gates Co. Co. Clks office}
    Mch 26/th/.. 1852 } not pd

(216) 224 State of North Carolina} County Court Clerks office
      Gates Carolina [sic]} 21/st/ Feby 1854 [sic]
[No Reg. #.] Negro Man ISAAC the property of Allen BRIGGS of the County and State aforesaid and Hired the present year by James S SEGUIN of Norfolk County in the State of virginia to work in the Great Dismale Swamp in the State of North Carolina
  ISAAC is about thirty two years of age of dark brown colour his face a little disfigured by a burn has a small scar on the middle finger of his wright hand & stanes without shoes five feet Nine 1/2 Inches high

[Remainder of page is blank.]

(217) 225 [Entire page is blank.]

(218) 226 State of NoCarolina} County Court Clerk's office

9 June 1852

(218) (Cont.) Gates County } June 9/th/ 1852.
No. 1. C. Sam ALPHIN, who is said to be a free man of color, is hired the present year by RIDDICK & HOSIUR of Suffolk Va and by them registered as one of their hands employed in the Great Dismal swamp in the County of Gates aforesaid.

The said Sam ALPHIN is about thirty years of age, of light, yellow complexion, tolerably high forehead, has good teeth, black eyes, a scar upon his ==== right hand, and stands without shoes five feet four 1/2 inches high.

In Testimony &c.

State of North Carolina} County Court Clerk's office
Gates County } June 12/th/ 1852.
C. No. 2. Jack ANDERSON, of color, who is said to be a free man, is hired the present year by William B. WHITEHEAD of Suffolk Va. and by him registered as one of his hands employed in the Great Dismal Swamp in the County of Gates aforesaid.

The said Jack is about twenty one years of age, of dark complexion, very low forehead, small eyes, wide mouth, bad teeth and tolerably thick lips. His hair Comes down very near his eyes and he stands without shoes four feet nine & half inches high.

In Testimony &c.

(219) 227 State of North Carolina} County Court Clerk's office
Gates County } June 12/th/ 1852
C. No. 3 MOSES, the property of the estate of Britton BROWN of Nansemond County, is hired the present year by William B. WHITEHEAD of Suffolk Virginia and by him registered as one of his hands employed in the Great Dismal Swamp, in the County of Gates aforesaid.

The said MOSES is about thirty years of age, of dark complexion, small eyes, tolerably large nostrils, small mouth, thick lips and bad teeth. He has no scars upon his person and stands without shoes five feet four & half inches high.

In Testimony &c.

State of North Carolina} County Court Clerks Office
Gates County } June 12/th/ 1852.
C. No. 4 TURNER, the property of the estate of Luke RABY of Nansemond County Virginia, is hired the present year by William B. WHITEHEAD of Suffolk, and by him registered as one of his hands employed in the Great Dismal Swamp, in the County of Gates aforesaid.

TURNER is about twenty four years of age, of dark complexion, has large cheek bones, wide mouth, tolerably flat nose, black eyes, good teeth in front - is a low thick set man, wide across the shoulders. He has == two large scars upon his left arm, a large scar upon the Calf of his left leg, a scar upon his back, and stands without shoes five feet two and a half inches.

In Testimony &c.

(220) 228 State of North Carolina} County Court Clerk's office
Gates County } June 12/th/ 1852.
No. 5 C. SANDY, the property of the Estate of C. W. HAWES of Nansemond County Virginia, is hired the present year by William B. WHITEHEAD of Suffolk, and by him registered as one of his hands employed in the Great Dismal Swamp in the County of Gates aforesaid.

The said SANDY is about fifteen years of age, of dark complexion, low forehead, small nose and mouth, good teeth, black eyes, - has no scars about his person and stands without shoes four feet eight inches high.

In Testimony &c.

State of North Carolina} County Court Clerk's office

(220) (Cont.) Gates County } June 12/th/ 1852.
No. 6. C. ABRAM, the property of Dr. Samuel C. HOLLAND of Nansemond County Virginia, is hired the present year by Wm. B. WHITEHEAD of Suffolk and by him registered as one of his hands employed in the Great Dismal Swamp in the County of Gates aforesaid.

The said ABRAM is about nineteen years of age, of tolerably dark complexion, high forehead, flat nose, and black eyes. He has a scar at the corner of his mouth upon the right side of his face, several small scars upon his left leg, and stands without shoes five feet three inches high.

(221) 229 State of North Carolina} County Court Clerk's office
      Gates County } June 12 1852
No 7 C. DAVY, the property of Danl. BRINKLEY of Nansemond County Virginia, is hired the present year by William B. WHITEHEAD of Suffolk, and by him registered as one of his hands employed in the Great Dismal Swamp in the County of Gates aforesaid.

DAVY is about twenty five years of age, of dark brown complexion, high forehead, small eyes, high Cheek bones, flat nose, and good teeth. He has a scar upon his left elbow, and stands without shoes five feet seven inches high.
         In Testimony &c.

State of North Carolina} County Court Clerk's office
  Gates County   } June 12/th/ 1852
No 8 C. STEPHEN, the property of the estate of William S. RIDDICK of Nansemond County Virginia, is hired the present year by William B. WHITEHEAD of Suffolk and ' by him registered as one of his hands employed in the Great Dismal Swamp in the County of Gates aforesaid.

STEPHEN is about fifty eight years of age, of a dark copper color, high forehead, high cheek bones, large nostrils, wide mouth and thick lips. He has a scar upon his left arm, has lost one of his upper front teeth and stands without shoes five feet Six inches.   In Testimony &c.

(222) 230 State of North Carolina} County Court Clerk's office
     Gates County   } June 12/th/ 1852.
No. 9 C. PETER, the property of Allen EDWARDS of Southampton County Virginia, is hired the present year by William B. WHITEHEAD of Suffolk, and by him registered as one of his hands employed in the Great Dismal Swamp in the County of Gates aforesaid.

The said PETER is about Sixty two years of age, of black complexion, grey & ball head, wide mouth, flat nose, – has a small scar on his right arm near his elbow – has but lost his jaw teeth, and some of his front teeth and stands without shoes five feet five inches high.
        In Testimony &c.

State of North Carolina} County Court Clerk's office
  Gates County   } June 12 1852.
No 10. C. ALLEN, the property of Edward BROTHERS of Nansemond County Virginia, is hired the present year by William B. WHITEHEAD of Suffolk, and by him registered as one of his hands employed in the Great Dismal Swamp in the County of Gates aforesaid.

The said ALLEN is about twenty years of age, of black complexion, has good teeth, a scar on his forehead, running up into his hair, a scar near the left corner of his mouth, thick lips, several scars on each leg, and stands without shoes five feet four inches high.
        In Testimony &c.

(223) 231 State of North Carolina} County Court Clerk's office
     Gates County   } June 12th 1852
No. 11 C. HENDERSON is the property of the estate of Matthew JOYNER of Southampton

(223) (Cont.) County Virginia, and hired the present year by William B. WHITEHEAD of suffolk, and by him registered as one of his hands employed in the Great Dismal swamp in the County of Gates aforesaid.

The said HENDERSON is about thirty years of age, of dark brown complexion, stout beard, has good teeth in front, black eyes, long nose, large nostrils, a small scar on the left cheek a small scar on the back of the left hand, a scar across the right thigh about one and a half inches long, a scar on the inside of this [sic] calf of his left leg and stands without shoes five feet nine and a half inches high.

State of North Carolina} County Court Clerk's office
  Gates County   }   June 14 1852.
No. 12 C. SAM, the property of Albert BRINKLEY of Nansemond County, is hired the present year by ~~Daniel~~ /Abram/ BRINKLEY of said County and by him registered as one of his hands employed in the Great Dismal swamp in the county of Gates aforesaid.

SAM is about thirty years of age, of dark brown complexion, thin beard, thick lips, large mouth and long face. He has a scar upon his left arm, and stands without shoes five feet eight inches high.

In Testimony &c.

(224) 232 State of North Carolina} County Court Clerk's office
        Gates County   }   June 14 1852.
No. 13 C. TURNER, the property of Daniel BRINKLEY of Nansemond County Virginia, is hired the present year by Abram BRINKLEY of said County, and by him registered as one of his hands employed in the Great Dismal swamp, in the County of Gates aforesaid.

The said TURNER is about eighteen years of age, of black complexion, has a wide mouth, thick lips, large nostrils, and tolerably low forehead. He has two scars on the off side of the knee joint of his left leg, several scars on his right leg, a scar on the back of his right hand, and stands without shoes five feet three and a half inches high.

In Testimony &c.

State of North Carolina} County Court Clerk's office
  Gates County   }   June 12/th/ [sic] 1852.
No. 14 C. WILLIS, the property of Samuel WILKINS of Nansemond County Virginia, is hired the present year by Abram BRINKLEY of said County, and by him registered asone ofhis hands employed in the Dismal Swamp in the County of Gates aforesaid.

WILLIS is about twenty four years of age, of black complexion, has large thick lips, very thin beard, and a small round nose. He has a small scar on the left side of his face and shows his teeth and gums when laughing – Stands without shoes five feet five inches and a quarter high

In Testimony &c

(225) 233 State of North Carolina} County Court Clerk's Office
        Gates County   }   June 16/th/ 1852.
No. 15 C. SAM, the property of the estate of John R. KNIGHT of Nansemond County Virginia, is hired the present year by Willis S. RIDDICK of Said County, and by him registered as one of his hands employed in the Great Dismal swamp in the County of Gates aforesaid.

The said SAM is about twenty eight years of age, of dark brown complexion, has a full forehead, flat nose, smoothe clear skin, good teeth, and a scar on his forehead over the left eye, and stands without shoes five feet 5 1/2 inches high.

In Testimony &c.

State of North Carolina} County Court Clerk's office
  Gates County   }   June 16/th/ 1852.

(225) (Cont.) <u>No. 16 C.</u> WASHINGTON, the property of the estate of Jno. R. KNIGHT of Nansemond County Virginia, is hired the present year by Willis S. RIDDICK of said County, and by him registered as one of his hands employed in the Great Dismal Swamp in the County of Gates aforesaid.

The said WASHINGTON is about fifteen years of age, of black complexion, has a small flat nose, small mouth, good teeth, a scar on the left wrist, a scar on the left foot and a small wart on the left leg and stands without shoes four feet nine inches high.

In Testimony &c.

(226) 234 State of North Carolina} County Court Clerk's office
Gates County   }   June 16/th/ 1852.

<u>No. 17 C</u> WILLIS, the property of Jason BRINKLEY of Nansemond County Virginia, is hired the present year by RIDDICK & HOSIUR of said County, and by them registered as one of their hands employed in the Great Dismal Swamp in the County of Gates aforesaid.

The said WILLIS is about twenty six years of age, of light brown complexion, has a high forehead, large cheek bones, wide mouth, and a flat nose. He has a scar upon the calf of his left leg, and stands without shoes five feet three inches high.

In Testimony &c.

State of North Carolina} County Court Clerk's office
Gates County   }   June 16/th/ 1852.

<u>No. 18 C.</u> CHARLES, the property of Jason BRINKLEY of Nansemond County Virginia, is hired the present year by RIDDICK & HOSIUR of said County, and by them registered /as/ one of their hands employed in the Great Dismal Swamp in the County of Gates aforesaid.

The said CHARLES is a small boy, about fourteen years of age, has dark brown complexion, small face, thin visage, small mouth and thick lips. He has two scars upon the knee joint of his right leg from a burn, several small scars upon his left leg, and stands without shoes four feet six and a half inches high.

In Testimony &c.

(227) 235 State of North Carolina} County Court Clerk's office
Gates County   }   June 16/th/ 1852

<u>No. 19 C.</u> WASHINGTON, the property of A. RIDDICK of Suffolk Virginia, is hired the present year by RIDDICK & HOSIUR of Nansemond County, and by them registered as one of their hands employed in the Great Dismal Swamp in the County of Gates aforesaid.

The said WASHINGTON is about thirty years of age, of dark complexion, has large nostrils small nose, full forehead and thick lips. He has a scar upon his /left/ wrist about four inches long, /a scar upon the top of his head about three inches long/ a scar upon the knee joint of his left leg, and stands without shoes five feet three and a half inches high.

In Testimony &c.

State of North Carolina} County Court Clerk's office
Gates County   }   June 16/th/ 1852.

<u>No. 20 C</u> CHARLES, the property of the estate of R. R. SMITH of Nansemond County Virginia, is hired the present year by RIDDICK & HOSIUR of said County, and by them employed registered as one of their hands employed in the Great Dismal Swamp in the County of Gates aforesaid.

The said CHARLES is about thirty years of age, of dark complexion, has a high full forehead, large cheek bones, large nostrils small mouth and thick lips. - He has a scar upon his forehead, running up into his hair, a scar upon his left jaw, a scar upon his right leg, and stands without shoes five feet five inches high.

(227) (Cont.)   In Testimony &c.

(228) 236 State of North Carolina} County Court Clerk's Office
            Gates County   }   June 17/th/ 1852.
No. 21. C Arkey MILTEER, who is said to be a free man of color, is hired the present
year by RIDDICK & HOSIUR, of Nansemond County Virginia, and by them registered as one
of their hands employed in the Great Dismal Swamp in the County of Gates aforesaid.
    The said MILTEER is about twenty five years of age, has light yellow complexion,
small features and good teeth in front. He has a scar on the back of his right hand,
and stands without shoes five feet nine and a quarter inches
                            In Testimony &c.

State of North Carolina} County Court Clerk's Office
    Gates County   }   June 18/th/ 1852
No. 22. C. GILBERT, the property of Edward Richard RIDDICK of Nansemond County Va:,
is hired the present year by Jethro RIDDICK of said County, and by him registered as
one of his hands employed in the Great Dismal Swamp
    The said GILBERT is about sixty five years of age, of dark complexion, grey hair,
and thin features. He has a large wind, or something like it, on the right side of
his nose, just above his eye, has another wind on the right arm, at the elbow joint, -
several scars on both of his legs and stands without shoes five feet eight inches
high.

                    In Testimony &c

(229) 237 State of North Carolina} County Court Clerk's Office
            Gates County   }   June 19th 1852.
No. 23 C. JACK the property of the estate of Robert R. SMITH of Nansemond County
Virginia, is hired the present year by RIDDICK & HOSIER of said County, and by them
registered as one of their hands employed in the Great Dismal Swamp in the County of
Gates aforesaid.
    The said JACK is about twenty six years of age, has a black complexion, and good
teeth in front. He has a small scar over his left eye, a scar on the fore finger of
his right hand, a scar on his left wrist, a small mole upon the right side of his
neck, and stands without shoes five feet nine inches, nearly.
                    In Testimony &c.

State of North Carolina} County Court Clerk's Office
    Gates County.   }   June 19/th/ 1852.
No. 24 C. GEORGE, the property of the estate of Robert R. SMITH of Nansemond County
Virginia, is hired the present year by RIDDICK & HOSIER of said County, and by them
registered as one of their hands employed in the Great Dismal Swamp in the County of
Gates aforesaid.
    The said GEORGE is a small boy, about fourteen years years [sic] of age, has dark
brown complexion, two small white spots upon the left side of his face, a scar on his
left foot, a scar on his right thumb, small mouth and thick lips. He stands without
shoes four feet seven inches.
                    In Testimony &c.

(230) 238 State of North Carolina} County Court Clerk's Office
            Gates County   }   July 7 th 1852.
No. 25 C. REUBEN, the property of Jethro RIDDICK of Nansemond County Virginia, and
by him registered as one of his hands employed in the Great Dismal Swamp in the County
aforesaid.
    The said REUBEN is about thirty three years of age, of dark complexion, has a
tolerably low forehead, long nose, wide mouth and thick lips. He is a tall spare made

(230) (Cont.) man and has a scar upon the back of his left hand and stands without shoes six feet half inch high.

In Testimony &c.

State of North Carolina} County Court Clerk's Office
Gates County.   }   July 7 th 1852.
No. 26 C. LEWIS, the property of Travis FLANAGAN of Weldon North Carolina, is hired the present year by Jethro RIDDICK of Nansemond County Virginia, and by him registered as one of his hands employed in the Great Dismal swamp in the County of Gates aforesaid.

The said LEWIS is about forty eight years of age, of brown complexion, has large cheek bones, high forehead, has lost one of his upper front teeth, and has a space between two of his under teeth in front.

He has a large scar upon the knee pan of his right leg and stands without shoes five feet six inches high

In Testimony &c

(231) 239 State of North Carolina} County Court Clerk's Office
Gates County.   }   August 4 1852.
No. 27 C. DRED, the property of Charles BARNES of said County is hired the present year by James S. SEGUINE of Deep Creek Virginia and by him registered as one of his hands employed in the Great Dismal swamp in the County of Gates aforesaid.

The said DRED is about fifty eight years of age, of light complexion, has straight hair, thin visage, a scar on his left under Jaw, a scar on his left thumb, a scar on the inside of his right arm about two and a half inches long from his hand, and several bad scars on his right leg and stands without shoes five feet nine inches high.

In Testimony &c.

State of North Carolina} County Court Clerk's Office
Gates County.   }   August 7 th 1852
No. 28 C JACK, the property of Albert BRINKLEY of Nansemond County Virginia, is hired the present year by Frederick JONES of Gates County, and by him registered as one of his hands employed in the Great Dismal swamp in the County of Gates aforesaid.

JACK is about twenty three years of age, of black complexion, has thick lips, large nostrils, large cheek bones, and a tolerably small /narrow/ forehead. He has a small scar on his right wrist, a scar on his left leg, a scar on his right leg, and stands without shoes five feet Eight inches.

In Testimony &c.

(232) 240 State of North Carolina} County Court Clerk's Office
Gates County. }   August /September/ 20 th 1852.
No. 29 C. RODEN, the property of Elizabeth COSTEN of Gates County, is hired the present year by BROTHERS & SMALL of said County, and by them registered as one of their hands employed in the Great Dismal Swamp in the County of Gates aforesaid.

RODEN is about thirty Eight years of age, of yellow complexion, is a little grey - has a large nose, with large nostrils, thick lips and good teeth in front. He has a mole near the left corner of his mouth, a small scar under the left nostril, and stands without shoes five feet Eight and a half inches, nearly.

In Testimony &c.

State of North Carolina} County Court Clerk's office
Gates County.   }   September 23rd 1852.
No. 30. C. John MATTHEWS, a free man of color, is hired the present year by RIDDICK

(232) (Cont.) and HOSIER of Nansemond County Virginia, and by them registered as one of their hands employed in the Great Dismal Swamp in the County of Gates aforesaid.

The said John MATTHEWS is about twenty one years of age, of very light complexion, has straight hair, small pointed nose, a small scar upon the left side of his face, a small scar under his right jaw, a scar upon the top of his left foot from a burn, a scar upon his right foot, and stands without shoes five feet six inches high.

In Testimony &c.

(233) 241 State of North Carolina} County Court Clerk's Office
Gates County. }   September 23rd 1852.
No. 31 C. Hardy BOYT, who is said to be a free man of color, is hired the present year by RIDDICK and HOSIER of Nansemond County Virginia, and by them registered as one of their hands employed in the Great Dismal Swamp in the County of Gates aforesaid.

The said Hardy BOYT is about twenty four years of age, of very light complexion - nearly white - straight hair, and has a long sharp nose. He has a scar upon the right side of his fore head about an inch long, running up to the hair, and stands without shoes five feet three inches high

In Testimony &c.

State of North Carolina} County Court Clerk's Office
Gates County.   }   September 23rd 1852.
No. 32 C. Frank SKEETER, who is said to be a free man of color and a resident of Nansemond County Virginia, is hired the present year by RIDDICK and HOSIER of said County, and by them registered as one of their hands employed in the Great Dismal Swamp in the County of Gates aforesaid.

The said Frank is about twenty one years of age, of a copper Color, or yellow Complexion - has a tolerably high forehead, high cheek bones, tolerably large nose and thick lips. He has a scar upon his right breast, and stands without shoes five feet six and a half inches high.

(234) 242 State of North Carolina} County Court Clerk's Office
Gates County.   }   October 16/th/ 1852
No. 33. C ISAIAH, the property of Marmaduke JONES of Gates County, is hired the present year by Andrew VOIGHT of said County, and registered as one of his hands employed in the Great Dismal Swamp.

ISAIAH is about twenty four years of age, of dark Complexion, large Cheek bones. thick lips and good teeth. He has a scar on his right elbow joint, a scar on the first joint of his great, right toe, a small scar on his left wrist, a small scar on the middle finger of his left hand, and stands without shoes five feet three and a half inches high.

In Testimony &c.

[Margin:] Duplicate Made 28/th/ May 1854.

State of North Carolina} County Court Clerk's office
Gates County. }   October 23rd 1852
No. 34 C. BOB, the property of Willis W. HARRELL of Gates County, is hired by Andrew VOIGHT &Co. of said County and by them registered as one of their hands employed in the Great Dismal swamp.

BOB is about thirty two years of age, of dark complexion, has lost two of his teeth - nearly in front - has a scar three inches long on the outside of his right leg, a scar near his left eye, and stands without shoes five feet six inches high.

In Testimony &c

(235) 243 State of North Carolina} County Court Clerk's Office
Gates County. }   November 29 1852.

(235) (Cont.) <u>No. 35.</u> HENRY, the property of the Estate of Jesse WIGGINS of Gates County, is hired the present year by Thomas PARKER and employed by Andrew VOIGHT and by him registered as one of his hands in the Great Dismal swamp.

The said HENRY is about twenty nine years of age, of black complexion, with projecting lips and flat nose. He has a scar upon his left shin bone, a scar upon his right leg - a small scar on /the middle toe of/ his right foot and stands without shoes five feet seven inches high.

In Testimony &c.

State of North Carolina} County Court Clerk's Office
     Gates County.   }   January 3rd 1853.
     ABRAM the property of the Estate of James COSTEN deceased, is hired the present year by James R. DOUGHTY /of said County/ and by him registered as one of his hands

Mr H L EURE
You will please give ISIAH a certificate for the Swamp by him paying you for it he will inform you who he works for   For Jos.. JONES
          May 27/54   pr James TAYLOR

(236) 244 [Entire page is blank.]

(237) 245 State of North Carolina} County Court Clerk's Office
          Gates County.   }   January 3rd 1853.
<u>No. 1.</u> ABRAM the property of the Estate of James COSTEN deceased, of Gates County is hired the present year by James R. DOUGHTY of said County, and by him registered as one of his hands employed in the Great Dismal swamp.

The said ABRAM is about twenty one years of age, of dark complexion, has a long face, large head, small flat nose, and tolerably thick lips. - He has a small scar on his right wrist, a small scar on his right cheek, and several small /scars/ on each knee and stands without shoes five feet seven inches high, nearly.

In Testimony &c.

State of North Carolina} County Court Clerks Office
     Gates County.   }   January 8 th 1853.
<u>No. 2.</u> PHILIP the property of Isaac S. HARRILL of Gates County, is registered the present year by HARRILL and PARKER of said County, as one of their hands employed in the Great Dismal swamp in the County of Gates aforesaid.

The said PHILIP is about fifty six years of age, of brown complexion, has a very large mouth, thick lips, a scar on the nail of the fore finger of his left hand, a small scar on his fore head and stands without shoes five feet eight inches.

In Testimony &c.

(238) 246 State of North Carolina} County Court Clerk's Office
          Gates County.   }   January 8/th/ 1853.
<u>No. 3</u> NED the property of the estate of Jesse WIGGINS of Gates County, is hired the present year by HARRELL and PARKER of said County, and by them registered as one of their hands employed in the Great Dismal swamp in the County of Gates aforesaid.

The said NED is about thirty eight years of age, of yellow complexion, has high cheek bones, sunken eyes, wide mouth and tolerably high forehead. He has a scar on or near his right thumb, a scar under his left eye, a small mole on the right side of his chin, a scar on his right shoulder and stands without shoes, five feet seven and a half inches. In Testimony &c.

State of North Carolina} County Court Clerk's Office
     Gates County. }   January 8 /th/ 1853

(238) (Cont.) No. 4. JACK, the property of Hamlin L. EPPES of Nansemond County Virginia, is hired the present year by HARRELL and PARKER of Gates County and by them registered as one of their hands employed in the Great Dismal Swamp in the County of Gates aforesaid.

The said JACK is about forty one years of age, of black complexion, is crossed in one eye, has a scar over his right eye, small teeth, a scar on the Middle finger of his left hand and right hand with skinned places on each leg and stands without shoes five feet nine inches high.

In Testimony &c.

(239) 247 State of North Carolina} County Court Clerks Office
Gates County. } January 8/th/ 1853.
No. 5. DANIEL the property of the estate of Willis R. BOND deceased of Gates County, is hired the present year by HARRELL and PARKER of said County, and by them registered as one of their hands employed in the Great Dismal Swamp in the County of Gates aforesaid.

The said DANIEL is about thirty years of age, of black complexion, has a flat nose, large nostrils and bad teeth in front. He has a scar on his nose, a scar near the corner of his right eye, several small scars upon his forehead, a scar near the corner of his left eye, and several large scars on each leg, and stands without shoes, five feet one and a half inches, nearly. In Testimony &c.

State of North Carolina} County Court Clerk's Office
Gates County. } January 18/th/ 1853.
No. 6. MILES, the property of Reuben RIDDICK of Gates County, is hired the present year by Jethro RIDDICK of Nansemond County Virginia, and by him registered as one of his hands employed in the Great Dismal swamp in the County of Gates aforesaid.

The said MILES is about twenty One years of age, of dark complexion, - is well set, free from scars, is broad across the face at the cheek bone - the white of his eyes a little red - and stands without shoes five feet three inches high.

In Testimony &c.

(240) 248 State of North Carolina} County Court Clerk's Office
Gates County } January 18th 1853
No. 7. JOSIAH, the property of Elbert RIDDICK of Gates County, is hired the present year by Jethro RIDDICK of Nansemond County Virginia, and by him registered as one of his hands employed in the Great Dismal Swamp in the County of Gates aforesaid.

JOSIAH is about forty two years of age, of dark complexion, has a small scar on his forehead, three small scars near his right eye, a large scar on his left wrist - has lost One of his teeth in front, and stands without shoes five feet two inches high.

In Testimony &c.

State of North Carolina} County Court Clerk's Office
Gates County. } January 18/th/ 1853.
No. 8 LUKE, the property of Francis RIDDICK of Gates County, is hired the present year by Jethro RIDDICK of Nansemond County Virginia, and by him registered as one of his hands employed in the Great Dismal Swamp in the County of Gates aforesaid.

LUKE is about twenty Seven years of age, of dark complexion, is a little scared on the front of each leg, by burns and is well marked with the effects of the small pox, and stands without shoes five feet nine inches high

In Testimony &c.

(241) 249 State of North Carolina} County Court Clerk's Office
Gates County. } January 18 th 1853.

(241) (Cont.) No. 9 TONEY, the property of Elbert RIDDICK of Gates County, is hired the present year by Jethro RIDDICK of Nansemond County Virginia, and by him registered as one of his hands employed in the Great Dismal swamp in the County of Gates aforesaid.

TONEY is about forty three years of age, of black complexion, is a little grey, has a scar over each eye, a scar on the shin bone of his right leg, a scar on each wrist - has two fingers on his right hand drawn up - and stands without shoes five feet seven and a half inches high.

In Testimony &c.

State of North Carolina} County Court Clerk's office
    Gates County.   }   January 18 1853.
No. 10. GRANBURY, the property of Joseph RIDDICK of Gates County, is hired the present year by Jethro RIDDICK of Nansemond County Virginia, and registered as one of his hands employed in the Great Dismal Swamp, in the County of Gates aforesaid.

GRANBURY is about thirty three years of age, of yellow complexion /has nearly straight/ [sic] has a wide mouth and thick lips. He has a scar on his left cheek, a scar on his left foot and several scars on his right leg and a scar on the left leg and stands without shoes five feet nine inches high

In Testimony &c.

(242) 250 State of North Carolina} County Court Clerk's office
        Gates County.   }   January 18 th 1853.
No. 11. SAM, the property of Elbert RIDDICK of Gates County, is hired the present year by Jethro RIDDICK of Nansemond County Virginia, and by him registered as one of his hands employed in the Great Dismal Swamp in the County of Gates aforesaid.

SAM is about twenty six years of age, of dark Complexion, has a small narrow face, a small scar under his mouth, a small scar near his right eye, a scar on his right arm, a small scar on the forefinger of his right hand and stands without shoes five feet four and a half inches high.

In Testimony &c.

State of North Carolina} County Court Clerk's office
    Gates County.   }   January 18 1853.
No. 12 CHARLES, the property of Francis HARRELL of Gates County, is hired the present year by Jethro RIDDICK of Nansemond County Virginia, and by him registered as one of his hands employed in the Great Dismal Swamp in the County of Gates aforesaid.

CHARLES is about seventeen years of age, of black complexion, has a low, full forehead, small mouth and thick lips. - He has a small scar on the little finger of his left hand, a small scar on the little toe of his left foot and stands without shoes four feet ten inches high.

In Testimony &c.

(243) 251 State of North Carolina} County Court Clerk's office
        Gates County.   }   January 18 1853.
No. 13 DANZY, the property of Francis HARRELL of Gates County, is hired the present year by Jethro RIDDICK of Nansemond County Virginia, and by him registered as one of his hands employed in the Great Dismal Swamp in the County of Gates aforesaid.

DANZY is about fourteen years of age, of dark complexion, has a small forehead and thick lips. - He has a scar on his head from a burn (and the hair is off) a scar on his right hand, a large scar on his left hip from a burn, and stands without shoes four feet seven & a === half inches. In Testimony &c

State of North Carolina} County Court Clerk's office
    Gates County.   }   January 18 1853.

(243) (Cont.) No. 14 SAM, the property of Francis HARRELL of Gates County, is hired the present year by Jethro RIDDICK of Nansemond County Virginia, and by him registered as one of his hands employed in the Great Dismal Swamp in the County of Gates aforesaid.

SAM is a small boy about fourteen years of age, of dark complexion, has a small scar on his forehead, wide mouth, low full forehead and a large head - stands without shoes four feet Eight (blank) inches high.

In Testimony &c.

(244) 252 State of North Carolina} County Court Clerk's office
Gates County.   }   January 18 1853.
No. 15. JOHN, the property of the Estate of Henry COSTEN of Gates County, is hired the present year by Jethro RIDDICK of Nansemond County Virginia and by him registered as one of his hands employed in the Great Dismal Swamp in the County of Gates aforesaid.

JOHN is about fifteen years of age, of brown or yellow Complexion, brown hair, low forehead, has a small scar over his left eye, two small scars near his left knee, and stands without shoes four feet ten and a half inches high

In Testimony &c.

State of North Carolina} County Court Clerk's office
Gates County   }   January 26 1853.
No. 16. HARMAN, the property of Christian BARNES of Gates County, is hired the present year by Jethro RIDDICK of Nansemond County Virginia, and by him registered as one of his hands employed in the Great Dismal swamp in the County of Gates aforesaid.

HARMAN is about forty two years of age, of black complexion, has a high forehead, wide face, large cheek bones, a scar on his right hand, a small scar on his forehead, a small scar on his right foot, and stands without shoes five feet six inches high.

In Testimony &c.

(245) 253 State of North Carolina} County Court Clerk's office
Gates County. }   January 26 1853.
No. 17. George GRIMES, the property of James S. SEGUINE of Deep Creek Virginia, is registered the present year by said SEGUINE as one of his hands employed in the Great Dismal swamp in the County of Gates aforesaid

The said George is about fifty six years of age, of dark complexion, rinkled face, short teeth, full beard, and is quite gray. - The fore finger of his left hand is a little stiff - has a large deep scar upon the left leg just above his knee; two long flat scars on his right leg - has lost the first joint of the little toe of his left foot and stands without shoes five feet Eight and a half inches.

In Testimony &c.

State of North Carolina} County Court Clerk's office
Gates County.   }   February 4/th/ 1853.
No. 18. GEORGE the property of the estate of Dempsey KNIGHT of Gates County, is hired the present year by John A. KNIGHT of said County and by him registered as one of the hands of Andrew VOIGHT employed in the Great Dismal Swamp in the County of Gates aforesaid.

GEORGE is about thirty years of age, of dark brown complexion, has very thick lips and a wide mouth. - He has a scar on his right wrist and stands without shoes five feet nine inches high.

In Testimony &c.

(246) 254 State of North Carolina} County Court Clerk's Office
Gates County.   }   February 4 1853

(246) (Cont.) <u>No. 19</u> STEPHEN, the property of the estate of Dempsey **KNIGHT** of said County, is hired the present year by Jno. A. **KNIGHT** of said County, and by him registered as one of the hands of Andrew **VOIGHT** employed in the Great Dismal Swamp in the County of Gates aforesaid.

STEPHEN is about twenty one years of age, of dark complexion, thin beard, has a scar in his left thumb nail, a small scar on his left wrist, a long scar on his right foot, a scar on the third toe of the same foot, and stands without shoes five feet seven and a half inches high.

In Testimony &c.

State of North Carolina} County Court Clerk's Office
    Gates County.   }   February 4/th/ 1853.
<u>No. 20</u> WILLIS, the property of Christian **BARNES** of said County, is hired the present year by James E. **BARNES** and by him registered as one of the hands of Andrew **VOIGHT** employed in the Great Dismal swamp in the County of Gates aforesaid.

WILLIS is about twenty seven years of age, is a very bright mulatto, has thin lips, full face, tolerably wide mouth, a small scar on his left arm, just above the elbow, a scar on his breast, and stands without shoes five feet five inches, nearly.

In Testimony &c.

(247) 255 State of North Carolina} County Court Clerk's Office
            Gates County. }   Februay 21st 1853.
<u>No. 21</u> Allen **REID**, who is said to be a free man of Color, is hired the present year by Andrew **VOIGHT** of Gates County and by him registered as one of his hands employed in the Great Dismal swamp in the County of Gates aforesaid.

Allen **REID** is about twenty five years of age, of dark Complexion, has a scar on on the right side of his chin, a scar from a burn on the left wrist, and several scars in his face and one on his neck, from the small pox, and stands without shoes five feet Eight and a quarter inches high

State of North Carolina} County Court Clerk's Office
    Gates County.   }   Februay 26 1853.
<u>No. 22.</u> ABRAM, the property of Humphrey **PARKER** of Gates County, is hired the present year by Seth **BENTON** of said County and by him registered as one of the hands of James S. **SEGUINE** employed in the Great Dismal Swamp.

The said **ABRAM** is about fifty four years /of age/ Complexion dark, yet slightly yellow, has grey hair, a scar directly over his right eye occasioned by the kick of an ox and stands without shoes five feet seven and a quarter inches high.

In Testimony &c

(248) 256 State of North Carolina} County Court Clerk's Office
            Gates County.   }   April 11th 1853.
<u>No. 23.</u> JOHN is the property of James S. **SEGUINE** of Deep Creek Virginia and by him registered as one of his hands employed in the Great Dismal Swamp in the County of Gates aforesaid.

JOHN is about sixty two years of age, has dark complexion, large cheek bones very bad teeth flat nose and wide nostrils He has a scar on his left leg from a burn, a scar on his right leg, and stands without shoes five feet seven and a half inches high.

In Testimony &c.

State of North Carolina} County Court Clerk's Office
    Gates County.   }   April 11/th/ 1853.
<u>No. 24</u> Dick **BARTIE** is the property of James S. **SEGUINE** of Deep Creek Virginia, and by him registered as one of his hands employed in the Great Dismal Swamp in the County

(248) (Cont.) of Gates aforesaid.

Said Dick is about fifty five years of age, of dark complexion, is quite bald, has a wide mouth, large nose and wide nostrils. He has a scar on his left breast a scar on his left knee and one just above it, and stands without shoes five feet nine and a half inches high.

In Testimony &c.

(249) 257 State of North Carolina} County Court Clerk's Office
Gates County } April 11/th/ 1853.

No. 25 ROBERT, the property of James MOORE of Norfolk Virginia, is hired the present year by James S. SEGUINE of Deep Creek, Virginia, and by him registered as one of his hands employed in the Great Dismal Swamp in the County of Gates aforesaid.

ROBERT is about fourteen years of age – not well grown – of dark Complexion, has a small mouth, but thick lips and very small ears. He has a small scar over his right eye, a small scar on his upper lip, a small scar under his right eye, several small scars on both knees, has lost a part of his little toe of his left foot and stands without shoes four feet four and a half inches. In Testimony &c.

State of North Carolina} County Court Clerk's Office
Gates County. } April 29 1853.

No. 26. TONEY, the property of Joseph HURDLE of Gates County, is hired the present year by Jethro RIDDICK of Nansemond County Virginia, and registered as one of his hands employed in the Great Dismal Swamp in the County of Gates aforesaid.

TONEY is about sixty years old, of dark complexion, is getting bald, has a scar on his upper lip, the great toe of his right foot and the one next to it is a little frost-bitten. He has a full forehead and a long head – a little flat on top and stands without shoes five feet five inches high.

In Testimony &c.

(250) 258 State of North Carolina} County Court Clerk's office
Gates County. } May 14 1853

No. 27. Edmond BOOTHE, said to be a free man, is hired the present year by Wm. B. WHITEHEAD of Suffolk Virginia and by him registered as one of his hands employed in the Great Dismal Swamp in the County of Gates aforesaid.

Said Edmond is about forty eight years of age, of black Complexion, is stoutly built, has a scar on his right hand, one on his breast, one on the left side of his face below the eye and stands without shoes five feet eight inches high.

In Testimony &c

State of North Carolina} County Court Clerk's Office
Gates County. } May 14 th 1853.

No. 28 JACKSON, the property of Javan R. FRANKLIN of Nansemond County Virginia, is hired the present year by Wm. B. WHITEHEAD of Suffolk, and by him registered as one of his hands employed in the Great Dismal swamp in the County of Gates aforesaid.

JACKSON is about twenty two years of age, of dark complexion, large mouth, thick lips, small narrow forehead, a small scar near his left eye, spare built, and stands without shoes five feet eight inches high.

In Testimony &C.

(251) 259 State of North Carolina} County Court Clerk's Office
Gates County } May 14/th/ 1853.

No. 29 Jack ANDERSON, of color, said to be a free man, is hired the present year by W.B. WHITEHEAD of Suffolk Virginia and by him registered as one of his hands employed in the Great Dismal swamp in the County of Gates aforesaid.

The said Jack is about twenty two years of age, of dark Complexion, very low

(251) (Cont.) forehead, small eyes, wide mouth, bad teeth and tolerably thick lips. His hair comes down very near his eyes - is free from scars and stands without shoes four feet eleven and a half inches high.

In Testimony &c.

State of North Carolina} County Court Clerk's Office
Gates County.   }   May 14/th/ 1853.
No. 30   MOSES, the property of the estate of Robert R. SMITH of Nansemond County Virginia, is hired the present year by W. B. WHITEHEAD of Suffolk, and by him registered as one of his hands employed in the Great Dismal Swamp in the County of Gates aforesaid.

MOSES is about seventeen years of age, of dark complexion, has a wide flat nose, projecting mouth, with thick lips, a long head from his chin to the Crown of his head, a scar on his left cheek, a small scar near his left eye and stands without shoes five feet three & half inches high, nearly.

In Testimony &c

(252) 260 State of North Carolina} County Court Clerk's Office
Gates County. }   May 14 th 1853.
No. 31   TURNER, the property of the estate of Luke RABY of Nansemond County Virginia, is hired the present year by Wm.B.WHITEHEAD of Suffolk and by him registered as one of his hands employed in the Great Dismal Swamp in the County of Gates aforesaid

TURNER is about twenty five years of age, of dark complexion, has large cheek bones, wide mouth, tolerably flat nose, black eyes, good teeth in front - is a low thick set man, wide across the shoulders. He has two large scars upon his left arm, a large scar upon the calf of his left leg, a scar upon his back, and stands without shoes five feet three inches, nearly.

In Testimony &C.

State of North Carolina} County Court Clerk's Office
Gates County   }   May 14/th/ 1853.
No. 32   TURNER the property of Daniel BRINKLEY of Nansemond County Virginia, is hired the present year by Wm. B. WHITEHEAD of Suffolk and by him registered as one of his hands employed in the Great Dismal Swamp in the County of Gates aforesaid.

The said TURNER is about Nineteen years of age, of black Complexion, has a wide mouth, thick lips, large nostrils and a tolerably low forehead. He has two scars on the off side of the knee joint of his left leg - several scars on his right leg, a scar on the back of his right hand, and stands without shoes five feet five inches high

In Testimony &c

(253) 261 State of North Carolina} County Court Clerk's Office
Gates County. }   May 14/th/ 1853.
No. 33   DENNIS the property of Ann BROWN of Nansemond County Virginia, is hired the present year by Wm. B. WHITEHEAD of Suffolk, and by him registered as one of his hands employed in the Great Dismal swamp in the County of Gates aforesaid.

DENNIS is about twenty One years of age, of dark Complexion, has a full face, large eyes and mouth and thick lips. He has a small scar on his chin, and stands without shoes five feet five & a quarter inches high.

In Testimony &c.

State of North Carolina} County Court Clerk's Office
Gates County }   May 14 1853.
No. 34   HARVEY, the property of Ann BROWN of Nansemond County Virginia, is hired the present year by Wm.BWHITEHEAD of Suffolk, and by him registered as one of his hands

14 May 1853

(253) (Cont.) employed in the Great Dismal Swamp in the County of Gates aforesaid.

HARVEY is about twenty two years of age, of dark complexion, has a small nose, small mouth, a scar at the corner of his right eye, a large scar on his left arm, a small scar on his right hand and stands without shoes five feet six and a half inches high.

In Testimony &C

(254) 262 State of North Carolina} County Court Clerk's Office
Gates County.   }   May 14 th 1853.

No. 35. STEPHEN, the property of the estate of William J. RIDDICK of Nansemond County Virginia, is hired the present year by Wm. B. WHITEHEAD of Suffolk, and by him registered as one of his hands employed in the Great Dismal swamp in the County of Gates aforesaid.

STEPHEN is about fifty nine years of age, of a dark copper Color, high forehead, high cheek bones, large nostrils, wide mouth and thick lips. He has a scar upon his left arm - has lost one of his upper front teeth, and stands without shoes five feet six inches.

In Testimony &C.

State of North Carolina} County Court Clerk's Office
Gates County. }   August 15 1853.

No. 36   Watson , SMITH, said to be a free boy of Color, is hired the present year by James S. SEGUINE of Norfolk Va County Virginia, and by him registered as one of his hands employed in the Great Dismal Swamp.

The said Watson is about twelve years of age, of black Complexion, has a full fore head, a small scar near the right eye, and stands without shoes four feet Eight inches high.

In Testimony &c.

(255) 263 State of N.Ca} County Court Clerks office
Gates County }   Der 10/th/ 1853

[No Reg. #.]   Peter JONES the propert [sic] of W/m/.. AJONES of Nansemond County Va. and by him registered as one of his hands employed in the great Dismel Swamp

Peter is about thirty seven years of age of dark complexion with a Small head of hair and face whiskers and Stands in his boots five feet and seven inches high

State of N.Carolina} County Court Clks.
Gates County } office Jany 6/th/ 1854.

[No Reg. #.]   ISAAC the property of Joseph HURDLE of Gates County, is hired the present year by Wm.. T. PARKER of this County and by him registered as one of his hands imployed in the Great Dismal swamp in the County & State aforesaid

ISAAC is about Twenty six years of age of Black complexion with a high fore head a good countenance and has all of his frount Teeth effected [sic] and Stands in his boots four feet and seven inches high

In Testimony of which I hereunto subscribe my name and affix the seal of my office at Gates Ville the day and year above written.
Henry L EURE C C C

(256) 264 State of N.Ca} County Court Clks office
Gates County }   January 6/th/ 1854

[No Reg. #.]   STEPHEN the property of Henry HURDLE of Perquimons N.Ca. is hired the present year by Wm.. T. PARKER of this County and by him registered as one of his hands employed in the Great Dismal swamp in the County & State aforesaid.

STEPHEN is about forty one years of age of Black complixion is a little gray has a

(256) (Cont.) large scar on the left side of his fore head, has a small scar near the left corner of his mouth and Stands in his boots five feet, and nine inches high

> In Testimony of which I here unto subscribe my
> name and affix the seal of my office at Gates
> Ville the day and year above written
>   Henry L EURE C C C

State of N.Ca} County Court Clk's office
 Gates County}   Jany 6/th/ A D 1854
[No Reg. #.]   JOSIAH the property of Elbert RIDDICK of Gates County, is hired this present year by W/m/. T PARKER of this County and by him registered as one of his hands imployed in the Great Dismal Swamp in the County & State aforesaid

   JOSIAH is about forty three years of age, of Dark complexion has a small scar on his forehead three small scars near his right erye [sic]
>   forward

(257) 265 a large scar on his left wrist has lost one of his teeth in front and is? without shoes five feet two inches high

> In Testimony of which I here unto subscribe my
> name and affix the seal of my office at Gates
> Ville the day and year above written.
>   Henry L EURE C C C

State of NCa} County Court Clks
Gates County} office Janry 6/th/ 1854
[No Reg. #.]   SAM the propert of Elbert RIDDICK of Gates County is hired the present year by Wm.. T. PARKER of this County, and by him registered as one of his hands employed in the Great Dismal Swamp in the County of Gates aforesaid

   SAM is about Twenty seven years of age of dark complexion has a small narrow face, a small scar under his mouth a small scar near his right eye a scar on his right arme, a small scar on the forefinger of his right hand and stands without shoes five feet four and a half inches hight

> In Testimony of which I here unto subscribe my
> name and affix the seal of my office at Gates
> Ville the day and year above written.
>   Henry L EURE C C C

(258) 266 State of NCa} County Court Clks. office
         Gates County }   Januy 6/th/ 1854
[No Reg. #.]   LUKE the property of Francis RIDDICK of Gates County is hired the present year by W/m/.. T PARKER of this County and by him registered as one of his hands imployed in the Great Dismal swamp in the County & State aforesaid

   LUKE is about Twenty eight years of age, of dark complixion is a little scared on the fround of each leg by burns, and is well marked with the effects of the small pox, and stands == without Shoes five feet nine inches high

   In Testimony of of [sic] which I here unto subscribe my name and affix the seal of my office at Gates Ville the day and year above written.
>   Henry L EURE C C C

(259) 267 State of N.Ca} County Court Clks office
         Gates County }   Janu?y 6/th/ 1854.
[No Reg. #.]   TONEY the property of Elbert RIDDICK of Gates County -is hired the present year by W/m/.. T PARKER of this County, and by him registered as one of his hands imployed in the Great Dismal swamp in the County & State aforesaid

6 January 1854

(259) (Cont.) TONEY is about forty four years of age of black complexion is a little gray, has a scar over each eye, a scar on the shin bone of his right leg, a scar on each wrist has two fingers on his right hand drawn up - and stands without shoes five feet seven and a half inches high

In Testimony of which I here unto subscribe my namd and affix the seal of my office at Gates Ville the day and year above written.

Henry L. EURE C C C

(260) 268 (State of North Caroline} County Court Clerks office
Gates County} March 6/th/ 1854

[No Reg. #.] GRANVILE the property of Abram BRINKLY andhired the present year /by Mills ROGERS/ and registered by him to work in the great Dismal Swamp in the State of North Carolina the present year

GRANVIL is about Twelve years of age Dark brown Complexion has a scar over the left eye and has a large burn on his back andstands without shoes four feet four inches high Given under my hand and seal of Office

HL E?URE CCC

State of North Caroline} County Court Clerks
Gates County} Office March 6/th/ 1854

[No Reg. #.] James Edward DICKERSON son of Zelpha COPELAND and represented by Mills ROGERS as free born and registered by him to work in the Great Dismal Swamp in the State of North Carolina

Jim is about fifteen years old Dark brown Complexion clear of Scars good countenance rather Small mouth for a negro and Stands without Shoes four feet Teen and a half incheshigh Given under my hand and seal of Office date above written

H. L. EURE CCC

(261) 269 State of North Carolina} County Court Clerks
Gates County} Office March 6/th/ 1854

[No Reg. #.] JOE the property of Nancy Ann BROWN andhired the present year by Mills ROGERS of the State of Virginia and registered by him to work in the Great Dismal Swamp in the state of North Carolina for one year.

JOE is about fifteen years old Black very likely clear of Scars andstands without Shoes five feet high

Given under myhand andseal of Office this date abve [sic] written

H L EURE C C C

State of North Caroline} County Court Clerks
Gates County} Office March6/th/ 1854

[No Reg. #.] Boy Dick SAWYER son of Perny SAWYER and represented by Mills ROGERS as being free born and registered by him to work in the Great Dismal Swamp in the State of North Caroline

Dick is about Twelve years Old brown complexion has a scar on the ellbow of the right arm caused from a burn and heis back well scared with the whip andstand [sic] without shoes four feet three and a half inches high given under my hand andseal of Office date abov written

H. L. EURECCC

(262) 270 (State of North Carolina} County Court Clerks office
Gates County} March 6/th/ 1854.

[No Reg. #.] HARRY the property of James GOODMAN of the State of virginia and registered by Mills ROGERS to work in the Great Dismal Swamp in the State of North Carolina the present year.

(262) (Cont.) **HARRY** is about Twelve years of age Black, clear of scars very likely
good face pleasant countenance his under lip a little too thick and heavy andstands
without shoes four feet four inches high given under my hand and seal of Office
H L. EURE C CC

State of North Caroline} County Court Clerk
Gates County} office March [sic]
[No Reg. #.] **WILLIAM** the property of Nancy A. **BROWN** of Suffolk virginia and registered by Mills **ROGERSS** of virginia to work in the Great Dismal Swamp in the State of
North Caroline?
  WILLIAM is about Thirteen years old Black but not very black good pleasant
countenance clear of scars the 8 whites of his eyes has a brown cast over them
andstands without shoes four feet six inches high
  given under my hand andSeal of office H L. EURECC

(263) 271 State of N.Ca} County Court Clerks office
Gates County } March 13/th/ 1854.
[No Reg. #.]   **JACK** of **RIDDICK** the property of Mrs Nancy **RIDDICK** of Nansemond Co Va.
is hired the present year by Mills **ROGERS** of Nansemond Co Va and by him registered as
one of his hands employed in the Great Dismal swamp in the County of Gates aforesaid
  JACK is about Fourty eight years of age of a dark complexion, high forehead with
dark eyes, and stands without shoes Five feet &Seven inches high

> In Testimony of which I Henry L. **EURE** Clerk of
> the Court of Pleas & Quarter sessions of the
> County aforesaid have hereunto set my hand &
> affix the seal of my office at Gates Ville the ay
> [sic] & year first before written.
> Henry L **EURE** C C C

(264) 272 State of NCa} County Court Clks office
Gates County} March 13/th/ 1854
[No Reg. #.]   Sam **ALPHIN**, who is said to be a free man of color is hired the present
year by Mills **ROGERS** of Nansemond Co Va and by him registere_ as one of his hands
employed in the Great Dismal Swamp in the County of Gates aforesaid
  The said Sam **ALPHIN** is about thirty one years of age of light yellow complexion
tolerably high four head has good teth black eyes a scar upon his right hand and
Stands without shoes five feet four and a half inches high

> In Testimony where of I Henry L **EURE** clk of the
> Court of Pleas & Quarter sessions of the County
> aforesaid hereunto set my hand & affix the seal
> of said Court at office in Gates Ville the day
> and year above written.
> Henry L **EURE** {clk

(265) 273 State of North Carolna} County Court Clerk's office
Gates County.} June 2/nd/. 1854.
[No Reg. #.] **GID** the property of Richard **BAUGH** of Norfolk County Virginia is hired
the present year by James S. **SEQUINE** of Norfolk County Va. and by him registered as
one of his hands employed in the Great Dismal Swamp in the County of Gates & State of
North Carolina.
  GID is about Forty seven years of age, of a dark Complexion, has a high fore head
with bright eyes - And Stands (in his shoes) five feet seven & ahalf inches high, has
on his breast a scar about an inch long, a scar on his left hand near his fore finger.
  In Testimony of which I have here unto set my hand & affixed my seal ofoffice, the
day & date first before written. [End of entry.]

(265) (Cont.) State of North Carolina} County Court Clerks office
Gates County. } June 2nd, 1854.

[No Reg. #.] DANIEL of COWPER the proper [sic] of John COWPER of Norfolk County Va. is hired the present year by James S. SEQUINE of Deep Creek, Norfolk County Va. and by him registered as one of his hands employed in the Great Dismal Swamp in the County of Gates &State aforesaid N. Ca. -

DANIEL is about thirty seven years of age, of light complexion with dark eyes, has two scars on his right hand near his thumb, & stands in his shoes five feet five inches high

In Testimony &c.

(266) 274 State of North Carolina} County Court Clerks office
Gates County. } June 2/nd/ 1854

[No Reg. #.] HENRY of COWPER the property of John COWPER of Norfolk County Va. is hire [sic] the present year by James /S/. SEGUINE of Deep Creek Norfolk County Va, And by him registered as one of his hands employed in the great Dismal Swamp in the County of Gates &State of N. C.

HENRY is about Ten years old of a bright complexion, has a scar on his right leg. And stands without shoes about four feet high.

In Testimony &c.

State of North Carolina} County Court Clerk's office
Gates County. }   June 2/nd/. 1854.

[No Reg. #.] FRANK of SIKES, the property of Jesse /D/ SIKES of Norfolk Va County Va., is hired the present year by James S. SEGUNE, of Deep Creek Norfolk County Va. and by him /registered/ employed as one of his hands employed in the Great Dismal Swamp in the County of Gates & State of N. Ca. - FRANK is about thirty years ofage, of light complexion has dark eyes, has a small scar on the right side of his forehead, a scar on his left hand near his little fingers, & stands /in/ his shoes five feet five & a half in high [sic].

In Testimony &c.

(267) 275 State of North Carolina} County Court Clerk's office
Gates County }   June 2?/nd/. 18534

[No Reg. #.] CHARLES of MILLER of Norfolk County Va. who is supposed to be a free boy of color is hired the present year by James S SEGUINE of Deep Creek Norfolk County Va. and by him registered as one of his hands employed in the great Dismal swamp in the CountyofGates&state of N. Ca.

CHARLES is about sixteen years ofage of a dark complixion with dark eyes, has a scar on his right leg, & a small scar on his right hand near his thumb, & stands in his shoes five feet & ==== one inch high.

In Testimony &c.

State of NCa}
Gates County} County Court Clerks office
June 12/th/ 1854

[No Reg. #.] ARMSTED the property of Mills ROGERS of Nansemond Co. Va is hired the present year by Wm..B.WHITEHEAD of Suffolk Va. and by him registered as one of his hands employed in the Great Dismal Swamp in the County of Gates aforesaid

ARMSTEAD is about sixteen years of age of a very dark copper color has a slight scar on the right side of his face & fore head which was caused by a burn when small, has a scar under his right eye & a small scar on each one of his knees and stands without shoes Four feet & Eleven inches high In Testimony &c.

(268) 276 State of NCa} County Court Clerks Office

12 June 1854

(268) (Cont.)
          Gates County}   June 12/th/ 1854
[No Reg. #.]   STEPHEN the property of Doctr W/m/.. S RIDDICK's Estate of Portsmouth
Norfolk County Va. is hired the present year by Wm..B.WHITEHEAD of Suffolk Nansemond
Co Va. and by him registered as one of his hands employed in the Great Dismal swamp in
the County of Gates aforesaid
     STEPHEN is about sixty years of age of a dark copper color, high fore head, high
cheek bones, large nostrils, wide mouth, and thick lips. He has a scar upon his left
arm, has lost one of his upper front teeth and stands without shoes Five feet six
inches high
                         In Testimony &C.

(269) 277 State of NCa} County Court Clerks office
          Gates County}   July 6/th/ AD 1854
[No Reg. #.]   HIRAM the property of James B NORFLEET of Suffolk Nansemond Co Va. and
by him registered as one of his hands employed in the Great Dismal swamp in the County
of Gates.
     HIRAM is about Twenty nine years of age of rather a brown complexion has a high
forehead a good countenance with a good sett of teeth with a deformed little finger on
his lef hand and stands without shoes five feet five & a half inches high
In Testimony &C.

State of N.Caro} County Court Clerks office   , .
  Gates County}   July 6/th/ A D 1854
[No Reg. #.]   BEN the property ofElisha ASHBURN of Nansemond Co. va is hired the
present year by James B NORFLEET of Suffolk Nansemond Co Va and by him registered as
one ofhands [sic] employed in the Great Dismal swamp in the County of Gates aforesaid
     BEN is about Twenty four years ofage of a dark complixion, has a high forehead
with a good countenance &a good sett of teeth &? has a large scar on his right heel
and a scar on the forefinger of his right hand & stands without shoes five feet six
and a half inches
In Testimony &C.

(270) 278 State of NC} County Court Clerks office
          Gates County}   July 6th 1854
[No Reg. #.]   HARRY the property of Archibald BRINKLYs Estate of Nansemond Co. Va is
hired the present year by James B. NORFLEET of Suffolk - Nansemond Co. Va and by him
registered as one of his hands employed in the Great Dismal Swamp in the County of
Gates aforesaid
     HARRY is about Twenty one years of age, of rather a brown complexion has a full
mouth with a good sett of teeth, has a scar on his right, little finger and stands
with shoes five feet five inches high In Testimony &C.
                         H L EUR Clek

(271) 279 State of NCa} County Court Clerks office
          Gates County}   July 7/th/ AD 1854
[No Reg. #.]   WILLIS the property of Frederick R JONE [sic] of Gates County NCa is
hired the present year by James B NORFLEET of Suffolk Nansemond Co Va and by him
registered as one of his hands employed in the Great Dismal swamp in the County of
Gates aforesaid
     WILLIS is about thirty years of age, of a dark complexion has a high fore head,
with a scar uppon his fore head, has a scar uppon his right rist has several scars
uppon his left hand and Stands without shoes five feet seven & a half inches high In
Testimony &C.

7 July 1854

(271) (Cont.)   State of NCa} County Court Clerks office
                Gates County}   July 7/th/ 1854
[No Reg. #.] PETER the property of James GOODMAN of Nansemond Co. Va is hired the
present year by James B NORFLEET of Suffolk Nansemond Co. Va and by him registered as
one of his hands employed in the Great Dismal swamp in the County of Gates aforesaid.

    PETER is about forty five years of age of a copper color has a flat nose a scar on
his right hand which was caused by a burn when small, his left rist is a little
deformed has two small scars uppon his breast and Stands without shoes five feet four
& a half inches high In Testimony &C.

                    H L EURE CCC

(272) 280 State of NCa} County Court Clerks officee
                Gates County}   July 10/th/ 1854
[No Reg. #.]   ISAAC of SKINNER the property of Abram SKINNERs Children of Nansemond
Co. Va is hired the present year by James B. NORFLEET of Suffolk Nansemond Co. Va and
by him registered as one ofhis hands employed in the Great Dismal /swamp/ in the
County of Gates afore said

    ISAAC is about Twenty five years of age of a dark complexi__ with all of his front
upper teeth affected has a scar near the left corner of his mouth has several Small
scars on each of his hands & Stands without shoes five feet five inches high In
Testimony &C.

              Henry L EURE CC Clk

State of NCa} County Court Clerks office
Gates County}   July 19/th/ A D.. 1854.
[No Reg. #.]   EDMOND of BOOTH a free Boy of Color is hired the present year by Mills
ROGERS of Nansemond Co. Va and by him employed and registered as one of his hands
employed in the Great dismal swamp in the County of Gates afore said

    Said EDMOND is about forty eight years of age, of black complexion, is stoutly
built, has a scar on his right hand one on his breast one on the left side of his face
below the eye, and stands without shoes five feet eight inches high In Testemony of
which &C.

             Henry L EURE C CC

(273) 281 State of NCa} County Court Clerks office
                Gates County}   July 19/th/ 1854.
[No Reg. #.]   Jack ANDERSON of Color, said to be a free boy is hired the present year
by Mills ROGERS of Nansemond Co. Va and by him reg==istered as one of his hands
employed in the Great dismal swamp in the County of Gates aforesaid

    The said Jack is about Twenty three years of age, of a dark complexion, very low
fore head, small eyes, wide mouth bad teeth and thick lips, his hair comes down very
near his eyes, is free from scars and stands without shoes five feet two inches high.
              In Testimony &C.
             Henry L EURE C C C

State of N.Ca}
Gates County} County Court Clerks office
                July 1st [sic] A D 1854
[No Reg. #.]   EDWARD of James S. SEGUINE, the property of sd James S SEGUINE is
registered by him of Norfolk Co Va and by him registered as one of his hands employed
in the Great dismal swamp in the County of Gates afore said

    EDWARD is about forty eight years of age, of a dark complixion has a good counten-
ance has a full sett of teeth, has a scar Just below his lip? ==== lips, a scar on his
left hand near the rist joint has a scar on his left foot and stands without shoes
five feet Seven inches high In Testimony &C.   Henry L EURE C C C

(274) 282 State of NCa} County Court Clerks office
Gates County}   July 21 st 1854
[No Reg. #.] CHARLES of James S SEGUINE the property of sd James S SEGUINE ~~and by~~
~~him registered as one of his~~ of Norfolk Co Va and by him registered as one of his
hands employed in the Great Dismal swamp in the County of Gates afore said
CHS. is about Ten years of age very likely, ha=s a Large Scar on his left hip a
scar under neath his left rist a scar on the back of his head which was caused by a
burn and stands without shoes four feet four & a half inches In Testimony &C.
Henry L EURE

(275) 283 State of NCa} County Court Clerks office
Gates County}   April 5/th/ 1855 [sic]
[No Reg. #.] PETER of Jas S. SEGUINE the property of sd Jas S. SEGUINE of Deep creek
Norfolk County Va. and by him registered as one of his hands employed in the Great
Dismal Swamp in the County of Gates afore said
PETER is about Thirty Thee [sic] years of age of dark Complixion has a full sett
of teeth has a scar on the inside of his left & [sic] stands with out shoes five feet
Ten inches high In Testamony of which I hereunto set my name & affix my seal the day &
date first before written   HenryLEURE clk?

(276) 284 [Entire page is blank.]

(277) 285 State of NCa} County Court Clerks office
Gates County}   July 24/th/ A D 1854
[No Reg. #.] JACK the property of Abram BRINKLY of Nansemond Co. Va is hired the
present year by James B NORFLEET of Suffolk Nansemond Co. Va and by him registered as
one of his hands employed in the Great Dismal Swamp in the County of Gates afore said
JACK is about Thirty five years of age of dark complexion, has a good sett of
frount teeth, has four small scars on the lower part of his breast all of which are in
a row. And Stands without shoes five feet &seven inch high In Testimony &C.
Henry L. EURE

State of N.Ca} County Court Clerkers [sic] office
Gates County}   July 24/th/ 1854
[No Reg. #.] CALVEN of LAWRENCE, supposed to be a free boy of color is hired the
present year by James B NORFLEET of Suffolk Nansmond Co Va and by him registered as
one of his hands employed in the Great Dismal swamp in the County of Gates aforesaid
CALVIN is about fiften years of age of a bright Bacon color has two small scars on
his right foot two small scars on his right knee has two small scars on the inside of
the fleft [sic] leg near the ancle, has two small scars near the knee pan over? the
kne joint of his left knee & Stands with shoes four feet seven inches high In
Testimony &C.
H. L. EURE

(278) 286 State of NCa} County Court Clerks office
Gates County}   July 24/th/ A D 1854
[No Reg. #.] Basset MACKEY a free man of color is hired the present year by James B
NORFLEET of Suffolk Nansem___ Co. Va and by him registered as one of his hands
employed in the Great Dismal swamp in the County of Gates afore said
Basset is about thirty five years of age is of a dark copper Color, has a high
fore head with a thin head of hair has a scar over the right eye has three other scars
upon his fore head has two scars on his left hand, has a scar on the right side of his
right leg - has lost one of his frount upper teeth and stands without shoes five feet
four & a half inches high In Testimony &C. Henry L EURE C.C.C.

(279) 287 State of N.Carolina} County Court Clks office
          Gates County   }   January 6/th/ 1855
[No Reg. #.] MILLS, beloning [sic] to the Estate of Arc RIDDICK Decd.. and hired the present year by Jethro RIDDICK of the Sate of ==Va? to work in the great dismal Swamp in the State of North Carolinia for the Term of one year

    MILLS is about Thirty Eight years of age of a dark brown complixion high forehead, has one of his front teeth missing his Seckond finger on his left hand stiff in the first Joint and Stands without Shoes five feet six Inches high given under my hand and Seal of office date above written

State of NCa} County Court clk office
Gates County}   Jany 27/th/ 1855
[No Reg. #.] WILLIS the property of Allin BRIGGS of the County & State aforesaid is hired the present year by James S SEGUINE of Norfolk Co Va & by him registered as one of his hands employed in the Great Dismal Swamp in the County & state aforesaid for the Term? of one year only

    WILLIS is about Twenty one years of age is of a dark brown complexion a good countena__ has a good sett of teeth & stands with out shoes full five feet seven inches high Given under my hand & seal of office the dy [sic] & date first before written Test Henry L EURE

(280) 288 State of North Carolina} County Court Clerks office
          Gates County }   February 11/th/.. 1855.
[No Reg. #.] TONY the property of Elbert RIDDICK of Gates County is hire [sic] the present year by Jesse EASON of this County, and by him registered as one of his hands, employed in the great Dismal Swamp, in the County &State aforesaid. TONY is about Forty five years of age, black complexion, is a little [sic], has a scar of over each eye, a scar on the shin bone of his right leg, a scar on each wrist, has two fingers on his right hand drawn up, and stands without shoes Five feet seven & a half inches high.

                    In Testamony of which I have here unto subscribed
                    my name, and affixed the seal of my office at
                    Gatesville, the day & year above written.
This certificate is good for one year only
                    Henry L EURE Clk C C.

State of North Carolina [End of entry.]

(281) 289 State of North Carolina} County Court Clerk's
          Gates County } office, Feb. 11/th/. 1855.
[No Reg. #.] PETER, the property of Jesse EASON, of this County, and by him registered, as one of his hands employed in the great Dismal Swamp in the County &State aforesaid. PETER is about sixty five years of age, /black complexion is a little gray/ has a scar over each eye, has two scars on his throat, his right leg swollen, and stands without shoes Five feet & full seven inches high.

                    In Testamony whereof I have hereunto set my hand
                    and affixed the seal of my office, at Gatesville,
                    the day & year as above written.
This certificate is good for one year only
                    Henry L EURE clk C C

(282) 290 State of No.Ca.} County Court Clerks office
          Gates County. }   May 6/th/. 1855.
[No Reg. #.] Jacob SKETER is a free man of Color, is hired the present year by James B. NORFLEET of Suffolk va. and by him registered as one of his hands in the great

(282) (Cont.) Dismal Swamp in Gates County aforesaid

Jacob SKETER is about ===== ==== Twenty two years old bright complexion, thick head of hair, and stands without shoes five feet five inches high.

In witness &c.

H. L. EURE C.C.C. By W. L.? BOOTHE DC.

State of No.Ca.} County Court Clerks office
Gates County } May 6/th/. 1855.
[No Reg. #.] Kinsey SKETER is a free boy of Color, is hired the present year by James B NORFLEET of Suffolk va. and by him registered as one of his hands imployed in the Great Dismal swamp in Gates County aforesaid.

Kinsy SKETER is about fifteen years old, bright compliexion, & stands without shoes four feet eight inches high.

In witness &c.

H. L. EURE C. C. C. By W. L. BOOTHE DC.

(283) 291 State of NCa} County Courts clks office
Gates County} May 11/th/ 1855
[No Reg. #.] ELISHA the property of Reubin RIDDICK of Gates County is hired the present year by Messs [sic] T. = C HINES &Co, and by them registered as one of their hands employed in the Great Dismal swamp in the County and State afore said

ELISHA is about Twenty three years of age of dark complexion has a scar on his fore head Just in the edge of his hare has a scar over the left corner of his left eye & stands without shoes five feet & nine inches high In Testamony &c.

Henry L EURE

(284) 292 State of NorthCarolina} County Court Clerks offic_
Gates County } May 11/th/. 1855
[No Reg. #.] LUKE the property of Francis RIDDICK of Gates County is hired the present year by Messrs T. C. HINES &Co and by them registered as one of their hands employed in the Great Dismal Swamp in the County &State aforesaid

LUKE is about twenty nine years of Age, of Dark complexion, has little? scar on the front of each leg by burns, and is well marked with the Effects of the Small Pox, and stands without shoes five feet nine Inches high.

In Testimony &c.

Henry L. EURE C C C

State of NorthCarolina} County Court Clerks office
Gates County. } May 11/th/ 1855
[No Reg. #.] JOSIAH the property of Elbert RIDDICK of Gates County is hired the present year by Messrs T. C. HINES &Co. and by them registered as one of their hands employed in the Great Dismal Swamp in the County & State aforesaid

JOSIAH is about forty four years of age of Dark complexion has a small scar on his forehead, three small scars near his right Eye, a large scar on his left rist has lost one of his teeth in front and stands without shoes five feet two inches high. In Testimony &c.

H. L EURE C. C C

(285) 293 State of North Carolina} County Court Clerk's office
Gates County } May 11/th/. 1855
[No Reg. #.] MILES the property of Reuben RIDDICK of the County of Gates, is hired the present year by Messers T. C. HINES &Co. and by them registered as one of their hands employed in the Great Dismal Swamp in the County & State aforesaid

MILES is about twenty five years of age, of Dark complexion, is well set and free of scars, is Broad across the face, at the Cheek bone the white of his Eyes a little red and stands without shoes five feet three inches high.

11 May 1855

(285) (Cont.)   In Testimony of which I hereunto affix my name
                                 and the seal of my Office at Gates ville, the day
                                 and date above written
                                          HenryL. EURE, C C C.

(286) 294 State of North Carolina} County CourtClerks Office
                 Gates County   }   May 11/th/ 1855
[No Reg. #.]   EDMOND ofBOOTHE a free man of color is hired the present year by W. B.
WHITEHEAD of Nansemond County Virginia, and by him Registered as one of his hands
employed in the Great Dismal Swamp in Gates County aforesaid.
       Said EDMOND is about forty nine years of Age. Black Complexion is stoutly built
has a scar on his right hand one on his breast, one on the left side of his face below
the Eye, and stands without shoes five feet Eight inches high
                              In Testimony &C. H. L EURE C C C

State of NorthCarolina} County Court Clerks Office
        Gates County }   May 11/th/ 1855
[No Reg. #.]   ISAAC the property of Abram SKINNER of Nansemond Co. Va is hired the
present year by W. B. WHITEHEAD of Suffolk Va and by him registered as one of his
hands, employed in the Great Dismal Swamp in the County of Gates aforesaid
       ISAAC is about thirty years of Age, Black Complexion has a scar near the left
Corner of his Mouth also several small scars on each hand bad upper teeth & stands
without shoes five feet four & a half inches high In Testimony &c.
                                          Henry L. EURE C C C

(287) 295 State of NorthCarolina} County Court Clerks Office
                 Gates County   }   May 11/th/ 1855
[No Reg. #.]   VESTARD the property of Javan R. FRANKLIN of Nansemond Co. Va. is hired
the present year by W. B. WHITEHEAD of Suffolk Nansemond Co. Va. and by him Registered
as one of his hands employed in the Great Dismal Swamp in the County of Gates aforesaid
       VESTARD is about thirty four years of Age, of Dark Complexion, fair Countenence,
thick under lip and stands without shoes five feet six inches high
                              In Testimony &C.
                              Henry L. EURE C C C.

State of NorthCarolina} County Court Clerk's Office
        Gates County }   May 11/th/ 1855
[No Reg. #.]   STEPHEN the property of Doctor Wm. S. RIDDICK's Estate of Portsmouth
Norf. Co. Va. is hired the present year by W.B. WHITEHEAD Nansemond Co. Va. and by him
registered as one of his hands Employed in the Great Dismal Swamp in the Countyof
Gates aforesaid
       STEPHEN is about Sixty one Years of Age, ofa Dark Copper Color, high forehead,
high Cheek Bone, large Nostrils wide Mouth & thick lips, he has a scar upon his left
arm has lost one of his upper front teeth, and stands without shoes five feet six
inches high   In Testimony &c.
                              Henry L EURE. C C C

(288) 296 State of NorthCarolina} CountyCourtClerks Office
                 Gates County }   May 11/th/ 1855
[No Reg. #.]   STEPHEN the property of Javan R FRANKLIN of Nansemond Co. Va is hired
the present year by W. B. WHITEHEAD of Suffolk, Nansemond Co. Va. and by him
registered as one of his hands Employed in the Great Dismal Swamp in the County
ofGates aforesaid
       STEPHEN is about twenty five years of Age, has a large scare? on the inside of his

11 May 1855

(288) (Cont.) right leg, high forehead, thick lips, and stands without shoes five feet five inches high In Testimony &C. HenryL. EURE C C C.

State of NorthCarolina} County Court Clerks Office
     Gates County }   May 11/th/.. 1855
[No Reg. #.]   JACKSON the property of Javan R. FRANKLIN of Nansemond Co. Va. is hired the present year by W.B. WHITEHEAD of Suffolk Nansemond Co. Va. and by him registerd as one of his hands employed in the Great Dismal Swamp in the County of Gates aforesaid
    JACKSON is about twenty yeas of age, Black Complixion, has a scar near the left Corner ofthe left Eye, good Countenance, thick lips and stands without shoes five feet eight inches high

In Testimony &c.
Henry L EURE C. C C

(289) 297 State of NorthCarolina} CountyCourtClerks Office
     Gates County }   May 11/th/ 1855.
[No Reg. #.]   JEFFREY the property of Javan R. FRANKLIN of Nansemond County Va. is hiredthe present year by W.B. WHITEHEAD of Suffolk, Nansemond Co. Va. and by him registerd as one of his hands employed in the Great Dismal Swamp in the County ofGates aforesaid
    JEFFREY is about nineteen years of age Copper Color has agood set ofteeth and a fierce Eye: and Stands with out shoes five feet six inches high.

In Testimony &C.
HenryL. EURE C C C

State ofNorthCarolina} CountyCourtClerks Office
     Gates County }   May 11/th/ 1855
[No Reg. #.]   JOE the property of Nancy Ann BROWN of and hired the present year by W. B. WHITEHEAD of the State of Virginia and registerd by him to work in the Great dismal Swamp of in the State of North Carolina for One Year Only.
    JOE is about sixteen years of Age, Black, very likely Clear ofScars, and stands without shoes five feet two inches high given? under my hand and seal this day above written   HenryL. EURE. C C C

(290) 298 State ofNorthCarolina} CountyCourtClerks Office
     Gates County }   May 11/th/. 1055
[No Reg. #.]   Jack ANDERSON a free boy of Color, is hired the present year by W.B. WHITEHEAD of Suffolk, Nansemond Co. Va. and by him registered as one of his hands Employed in the Great Dismal Swamp in the County of Gates aforesaid
    Jack is about twenty three yeas ofage, of a dark Complexion, very low forehead, small Eyes wide mouth, bad teeth & thick lips his hair comes down very near his eyes, free from scars and stands without [sic] five feet two inches high In Testimony &c.

HenryL. EURE C. C C

State of NorthCarolina} CountyCourt Clerks Office
     Gates County }   May 11/th/ 1855
[No Reg. #.]   ALBERT the property of Owen R. FLYNN of Suffolk Nansemond Co. Va. is hired the present year by W.B. WHITEHEAD of Suffolk, Nansemond Co. Va. andby him registered as one of his hands employed in the Great Dismal Swamp in the County ofGates aforesaid
    ALBERT is about Eighteen years of age, of dark Complexion, is free of scars, and stands without shoes five feet three inches high In Testimony &C.

HenryL. EURE C C C

11 May 1855

(291) 299 State of NorthCarolina} CountyCourtClerks Office
              Gates County   }   May 11/th/ 1855
[No Reg. #.]   JERRY the property of Thomas JONES of the County & State aforesaid is hired the present year by WB WHITEHEAD and by him registered as one of his hands employed in the Great Dismal Swamp in the County aforesaid.
     JERRY is about eleven years of age of Black Complexion, has three small scars on his forehead and a set of good teeth, and stands with out shoes four feet six inches high   In Testimony &c.
                                        HenryL EURE EC C C

Stat [sic] of NorthCarolina} County Court Clerks Office
              Gates County }   May 11/th/ 1855
[No Reg. #.]   ARMSTEAD the property of Mills ROGERS of Nansemond Co. Va. is hired the present year by W.B WHITEHEAD of Suffolk Nansemond Co. Va. and by him registered as one of his hands employed in the Great Dismal Swamp in the County ofGates aforesaid
     ARMSTEAD is about Nineteen Years of age is of a dark Copper Color ful forehead has a scar on the left cheek one on the left side of the forehead both ofwhich were? caused by a burn when small, also has a scar under his right Eye, a small scar on each one of his knees and stands without shoes five feet and a half inch high
                                   In Testimony &c.
                                   H. L. EURE C C. C.

(292) 300 State of NorthCarolina} CountyCourtClerks Office
              Gates County }   May 11/th/. 1855
[No Reg. #.]   WILLIS the property of Javan R. FRANKLIN of Nansemond Co. Va. is hired the present year by WB. WHITEHEAD of Suffolk Nansemond Co. Va. and by him registered as one of his hands employed in the Great Dismal Swamp in the County ofGates aforesaid
     WILLIS is about thirty four years of Age of Dark Complexion slightly bow leged high forehead, has quite an intilegent [sic] look, agreable Counternanc? a good set of teeth, he has a scar on the top of his middle finger of the left hand And stands without shoes five feet high
                                   In Testimony &c.
                                   HenryL EURE C C C

State of NorthCarolina} CountyCourtClerks Office
              Gates County }   May 11/th/ 1855
[No Reg. #.]   DEMPSEY the belonging to the Estate of Abram RABEY of Nansemond Co. Va. is hired the present year by Wm B. WHITEHEAD of Suffolk Nansemond Co. Va andby him registered as one of his hands Employ [sic] in the Great Dismal Swamp in the County of Gates aforesaid
     DEMPSEY is about twenty eight yeas ofage, is of a copper color has a scar on the top of his left hand, one on his left arm caused from vaxinating and stands without shoes five feet five and a half inches high
                                   In Testimony &c
                                   HL EURE C C. C

(293) 301 State of NorthCarolina} CountyCourtClerks Office
              Gates County }   May 11/th/. 1855
[No Reg. #.]   Siah PEARCE of Matilda PEARCE a free boy of Color is hired the present year by Wm.B WHITEHEAD of Suffolk Nansemond Co. Va and by him registered as one of his hands Employed in the Great Dismal Swamp in the County ofGates aforesaid
     Siah is about sixteen years of age of a copper Color has large features, a scar over his left Eye, one on his left arm caused from vaxinating and stands without shoes five feet one and a half inches high
                                   In Testimony &C.   HenryL EURE C C C

(293) (Cont.) State of NorthCarolina} County CourtClerks office
                    Gates County }   May 11/th/ 1855
[No Reg. #.]   Calvin BUKE a free boy of Color is hired the present year by Wm.B.
WHITEHEAD of Suffolk Nansemond Co. Va. and by him registered as one of his hands
employed in the Great Dismal Swamp in the County ofGates aforesaid
      Calvin is about seventeen years of age of light copper color has a small scar on
his nose between his eyes one on his forehead, also two small scars on the top of his
foot and stands without shoes four feet eight inches high
                         In Testimony &c.
                         HenryL. EURE C C C

(294) 302 State of NorthCarolina} CountyCourtClerks Office
                    Gates County }   May 11/th/ 1855
[No Reg. #.]   CALVIN the property of John RIDDICK of Nansemond Co. Va is hired the
present year by Wm.B. WHITEHEAD of Suffolk Nansemond Co. Va. and by him registered as
one of his hands employed in the Great Dismal Swamp in the County ofGates aforesaid
      CALVIN is about twelve years of age of Black Complexion stout built, has four
small scars on the top of his left hand and stands without shoes four feet two inches
high.   In Testimony &C.
                         HenryL. EURE C C C

State of NorthCarolina} CountyCourtClerks Office
      Gates County }   May 11/th/ 1855
[No Reg. #.]   John PEARCE of Martha PEARCE a free boy of Color is hired the present
year by Wm.B. WHITEHEAD of Suffolk Nansemond Co. Va. and by him registerd as one of
his hands employed in the Great Dismal Swamp in the County of Gates aforesaid
      John is about thirteen years of age ofa dark copper color, has a scar on his
forehead, one on his left cheek several small scars on each hand and stands without
shoes four feet six & three quarters inches high In Testimony &C.
                              Hery L EURE C C C

(295) 303 State of NorthCarolina} CountyCourtClerks Office
                    Gates County. }   May 11/th/. 1855.
[No Reg. #.]   Davey PEARCE a free boy of Color is hired the present year by W.B.
WHITEHEAD of Suffolk Nansemond County Virginia and by him registered as one of his
hands employed in the Great Dismal Swamp in theCounty ofGates aforesaid
      Davy is about fourteen years of age, of a dark Copper Color has a good Countenance
is free of scars and stands without shoes four feet seven inches high
                         In Testimony &c.
                         HenryL. EURE C C C

State of No.Carolina} County /Court/ Clerks office
      Gates County}   May 21st. 1855.
[No Reg. #.]   Will BROTHERS the property of Martha BROTHERS of Gates County, is hired
the present year by NORFLEET & HOSIER of Nansemond County Va. & by them registered as
one of their hand [sic] employed to work in the great Dismal Swamp in Gates County &
State of N. C. aforesaid. Will BROTHERS is of dark Complexion, & says that he is
about 26 yrs. old, has a scar over his right eye, & another scar over on his right
leg, nearly from his k=ne to his ancle, and stands without shoes Five feet nine inches
high.   In witness &c
                         H. L. EURE clk pr. W. L. BOOTHE D.C

(296) 304 State of NCa} County Court clk office
                    Gates County}   July 24th 1855
[No Reg. #.] John BRINKLY the property of Daniel BRINKLY OF Nansemond County virginia

(296) (Cont.) is hired the present year by Willis S. RIDDICK of the County and State last mentioned and by him registered as one of his hands employed to work in the great Dismal swamp in Gates County & State of NCa aforesaid

John is of dark complexion, says that he is about twenty eight years old, has a high fore head & is free or clear of scars and stands with out shoes five feet nine inches high

In Testimony of which I have hereunto set my hand &Seal of office at Gates Ville the day & date as above written

Test Henry L EURE

(297) 305 State of NCa} County Court clks office
          Gates County}   July 24th 1855
[No Reg. #.] Isaac BRINKLY the property of Daniel BRINKLY of Nansemond County va is hired the present year by Willis S. RIDDICK of the County & State last mentioned and by him registered as one of his hands employed to work in the great Dismal Swamp in Gates County and State of N..Ca aforesaid

Isaac is of dark complexion is about fourteen years old has a scar at the left corner of his left eye, his great toe & the toe next to it, are deformed and Stands without shoes four feet six inches high

In testimony of which I have hereunto set my hand & affix the seal of my office at Gates Ville the day & date as above written

Test Henry L EURE

(298) 306 State of NCa} County Court clks
          Gates County}   office Aug. 18/th/55
[No Reg. #.] Jack RIDDICK the property of of [sic] James RIDDICK of Nansemd Co. va. hired the present year by Willis S RIDDICK of the County of Nansemond and State of Va aforesaid and by him registered as one of his hands imployed in the great ‐ Dismal Swamp in the County of Gates and State of NCa aforesaid

Jack is of a dark copper color has a good set of frount teeth has a good countenance has a scar near the cormer of his left right eye and is about Twenty seven year year [sic] of age, and stands without shoes five feet five and a half inch high

In Testamony &Co

Henry LEURE clk

(299) 307 State of North Carolina} County Court Clerks office
          Gates County }   Oct. 29/th/. 1855
[No Reg. #.] BASSET a free man of Color is hired the present yea by Jas. B. NORFLEET of Suffolk Nansemond County va., and by him registered as one of his hands employed to work in the great dismal Swamp == in the County of Gates aforesaid.

BASSET is about thirty six years ofage, is of a dark Copper color, has a high forehead, with a thin head of hair, has a scar over the right eye, has three other scars upon his fore head, has two scars on his left hand, has a scar on the right side of his left /right/ leg, has lost one of his upper teeth, and stands without shoes five feet four & a half inches high. In Testimony &c.

H. L. EURE Clerk

State of North Carolina} County Court clerks
       Gates County   } office, Oct. 29/th/. 1855.
[No Reg. #.] HYRAM, the property of Jas. B. NORFLEET, of Suffo. Nansemond Co. va. and by him registered as one of his hands, employed in the great dismal Swamp in the County ofGates aforesaid. HYRAM is about thirty years of age, of rather a brown

(299) (Cont.) complexion, has a high fore head, a good Countenance, a good set of teeth, with a deformed little finger on his left hand, & stands without shoes five feet, five & a half inches high. In Testimony &C.

H. L. EURE Clerk

(300) 308 State of North Carolina} County Court Clerks office
Gates County } Oct. 29/th/. 1855
[No Reg. #.] BEN the property of Elisha ASHBORN of Nansemond County va. is hired the present year by Jas. B. NORFLEET OF Suffolk Nansemond County va. & /by him/ registered as one of his hands employed to work in the great dismal swamp in the County of Gates aforesaid. BEN is bout [sic] twenty five years of age, of a dark complexion has a high forehead, with a good Countenance, & a good set of teeth, has a large scar on his right heel, a scar on the fore finger of his right [sic], & stands without shoes five feet six & a half inches high.

In Testimony &c.
H. L. EURE Clerk

State of North Carolina} County Court clerks office
Gates County } Oct. 29/th/. 1855.
[No Reg. #.] Charles SEGUINE the property of Jas. S. SEGUINE of Deep Creek Norfolk County va. & by him registered as one of his hands employed in the great dismal swamp in the County of Gates aforesaid. Charles is about twelve years of age, very likely, has a large scar on his left hip, a scar underneath his left wrist, a scar on the back part of his head which was Caused by a burn, & stands without shoes four feet five & a half inches high.

In Testimony &c.
H. L. EURE Clk

(301) 309 State of North Carolina} County Court Clerks office,
Gates County } Oct. 29/th/. 1855.
[No Reg. #.] Negro Man ISAAC, the property of Allen BRIGGS of the County &state aforesaid, is hire [sic] the present year by Jas. S. SEGUINE of Norfolk County va. to work in the great dismal swamp in the County of Gates aforesaid,
ISAAC is about thirty three years of age, of dark Complexion, his face a little disfigured by a burn, has a small scar on the middle finger of his right hand, & stands without shoes five feet nine & a half inches high. Given under my hand &seal &c. In Testimony &c.
H. L. EURE clerk.

State of North Carolina} County County [sic] Court office,
Gates County } Oct. 29/th/. 1855.
[No Reg. #.] Negro Man LEWIS, the property of Sarah REID of Norfolk County va. & registered by Jas. S. SEGUINE of deep Creek va. to work in the great dismal swamp in the County of Gates aforesaid.
LEWIS is about forty three years of age, of dark Complexion, has a small scar on his forehead, a little above the right eye, & a small scar his [sic] face a little under the right eye, & is five feet three & three quarter inches high, without shoes.

In Testimony &c.
H. L. EURE Clk

(302) 310 State of North Carolina} County Court Clerks offic_
Gates County. } Oct. 29/th/. 1855.
[No Reg. #.] DREAD, the property of Charles BARNES of said County, is hired the present year by Jas. S. SEGUINE of deep creek va. & by him registere_ as one of his hands employed in the great dismal Swamp in the County of Gates aforesaid The said

(302) (Cont.) **DREAD** is about sixty one years ofage, of a light complexion has streight hair, thin visage, a scar on his left under jaw, a scar on his left thumb, a scar on the inside of his right arm, about two & a half inches from his hand, several bad scars on his right leg, & stands without shoes five feet nine inches high.

In Testimony &c.
H. L. **EURE** Clk.

State of North Carolina} County Court Clerks office
      Gates County }   Oct. 29/th/. 1855.

[No Reg. #.] **GEORGE**, the property of Jas. S. **SEGUINE** of deep Creek va. is registered the present year by said **SEGUINE** as one of his hands employed in the great dismal swamp, in the County of Gates aforesaid, GEORGE is about fifty eight years ofage, of dark Complexion, wrinkled face, short teeth, full beared & is quite grey, the fore finger of his left hand is a little stiff, has a large deep scar upon the left leg just above his knee, two long flat scars on his right leg, has lost first joint of the little toe of his left foot, &stands without shoes five feet eight & a half inches high.

In Testimony &C.
H. L. **EURE** Clerk.

(303) 311 State of North Carolina} County Court Clerks office
      Gates County }   Oct. 29/th/. 1855.

[No Reg. #.] **MILLS**, the property of Elisha **ASHBORN** of Nansemond County va., is hired the present year by Messrs. **NORFLEET & HOSIER** of Nansemond County va., &by them registered asone oftheir hands employed to work in the great dismal swamp in the County ofGates aforesaid.

    MILLS is about twenty six years of age, of a very dark complexion, has a scar on the left side of his chin, has a scar on the left big toe, has a scar on his left hand, & stands without shoes full five feet one inch high.

In Testimony &C.
H. L. **EURE** Clerk

State of North Carolina} County Court Clerks office
      Gates County }   Oct. 29/th/. 1855.

[No Reg. #.] **DENNIS**, the property of Mrs. Nancy **BROWN** of Nansemond County va., is hired the present year by Messrs. **NORFLEET & HOSIER**, of Nansemond Co. va. & by them registered as one of their hands employed to work in the great dismal swamp in the County ofGates aforesaid. DENNIS is about twenty five years ofage, of a dark brown complexion, has a good Countenance, a scar between his mouth & chin, & stands without shoes five feet five inches high.

In Testimony &C.
H. L. **EURE** Clk

(304) 312 State of North Carolina} County Court Clerk's office
      Gates County }   Oct. 29/th/. 1855,

[No Reg. #.] **VERGIL** the property ofthe estate of Margaret **BRINKLY** dec/d/., of Nansemond Co. va., is hired the present year by Messrs **NORFLEET & HOSIER** of Nansemond Co. va. & by them registered asone of their hands employed as one of their hands to work in the great dismal swamp in the County of Gates aforesaid.

    VERGIL is about fifty years ofage, of a dark Complexion, has a scar on the left side of the left leg, has a high forehead & stands with out shoes full five feet six inches high.

In Testimony &c.
H. L. **EURE** Clerk

(304) (Cont.) State of North Carolina.} County Court Clerk's office
     Gates County. } Oct. 29/th/. 1855.
[No Reg. #.] PHILIP belonging to the estate of Burwell BROTHERS dec/d/. of the County of Gates, is hired the present year by Messrs. & [sic] HOSIER of Nansemond County va. & by them registered as one of their hands employed to work in the great dismal swamp in the County of Gates aforesaid. PHILIP is about Thirty seven years of age, of dark Complexion, has a scar on his upper lip, has several small scars on his hands, & stands without shoes five feet eight inches high 5ft. 8 in.
       In Testimony
       H. L. EURE clk.

(305) 313 State of North Carolina} County Court Clerks office
     Gates County. } Oct. 29/th/.. 1855.
[No Reg. #.] DICK, the property [sic] Elisha ASHBORN, of Nansemond Co. va, is hired the present year by Messrs. NORFLEET & HOSIER of Nansemond Co. va. & by them registered as one of their hands to work in the great dismal swamp in the County of Gates aforesaid,
 DICK is about twenty five years of age, of dark complexion, has a scar just between his eyes, & stands without shoes full five feet three inches high.
       In Testimony &c.
       H. L. EURE clerk.

State of North Carolina} County Court Clerks
   Gates County } office, Oct. 29/th/. 1855.
[No Reg. #.] Arkey MELTEER, a free Man of Color, of Nansemond Co. va. is hired the present year by Messrs. NORFLEET & HOSIER of Nansemond County va. & by them registered as one of their hands employed to work in the great dismal swamp in the County of Gates aforesaid.
 Arkey is about Twenty five years of age, a bright Mulatto, has a scar on the back of his right hand, & stands without shoes five feet nine inches high.
       In Testimony &c.
       H. L. EURE Clerk.

(306) 314 State of North Carolina} County Court Clerks office
     Gates County. } Oct. 29/th/.. 1855.
[No Reg. #.] Juston REID, a free man of Color of Nansemond Co. va. is hired the present year by NORFLEET & HOSIER of Nansemond Co. va, and by them registered as one of their hands /employed/ to work in the great dismal swamp in the County of Gates aforesaid.
 Juston is about Nineteen years of age, a bright Mulatto, with his face much disfigured from itch or some other cause, has a scar on the top of his right foot near his toes, & stands without shoes five feet two & a half inches high.
       In Testimony &c.
       H. L. EURE clk.

State of North Carolina} County Court Clerks office
   Gates County } Oct. 29/th/. 1855.
[No Reg. #.] SOLOMON a free Man of Color, Nansemond County va. is hired the present year by Messrs. NORFLEET & HOSIER of Nansemond County va., & by them registered as one of their hands, employed in the great dismal swamp in the County of Gates aforesaid
 SOLOMAN is a bright Mulatto, has a scar just under his left eye, a scar between his under lip & chin, has a scar on the inside of his right leg just below the knee, has a scar on his left hand & stands without shoes five feet & one fouth inch high.
       In Testimony &c.
       H. L EURE clk.

29 October 1855

(307) 315 State of North Carolina} County Court Clerks office
Gates County. }   Oct. 29/th/. 1855.
[No Reg. #.] LEWIS the property of Mrs. Martha BROTHERS of Gates County, is hired
the present year by Jas. S. SEGUINE of deep creek Nofolk County va. & by him registered as one of his hands employed to work in the great dismal swamp in the County
ofGates aforesaid.   LEWIS is about sixty eight years of age, quite Gray, has bad
teeth, has a number of small marks upon both of his hands, has a scar on the left
instep, & stands without shoes five feet six inches high.
In testimony &c.
H. L. EURE clk.

State of North Carolina} County Court Clerks office
Gates County }   Oct. 30/th/. 1855.
[No Reg. #.] Mallory DIXON, a free boy of Color, is hired the present year by Messrs.
RIDDICK & NORFLEET of Nansmond County va. & /by/ them registered as one of their hands
employed to work in the great dismal swamp in the County of Gates aforesaid.
   Mallory is about seventeen years of age, a bright Mulatto, has a scar below the
left shoulder, and stands without shoes five feet three &ahalf inches high.
In testimony &c.
H. L. EURE clk.

(308) 316 State of N.Carolina} County Court Clerks office
Gates County. }   Oct. 30/th/. 1855.
[No Reg. #.] ISAAC, the property ofJas. B. NORFLEET of Nansemond County va. and by
him registered to work in the great dismal spamp in the County ofGates aforesaid.
   ISAAC is about thirty eight years ofage, has a black complexion, flat face, large
mouth, good teeth with a sunken place on the scull bone near the corner of the head, &
a scar on the shin bone, & stands without shoes five feet five inches high.
In testimony &C.
H. L. EURE clk.

State of N.Carolina} County Court Clerk office
Gates County }   Oct. 30/th/. 1855.
[No Reg. #.] Joe WEBB, the property ofJas. S. SEGUINE of deep Creek Norfolk Co. Va.
& by him registered as one of his hands employed in the great dismal swamp in the
County of Gates aforesaid.
   Joe WEBB is about forty five years of age, bright brown complexion sharp feature;
with high forehead, wide nostrils, bad teeth, a small scar on the breast, a scar on
the left hand below the thumb & forefinger a scar on the outside ofthe right knee, & a
bad scar a cross the top ofthe right foot, & one on the instep of the leftfoot, &
stands without shoes five feet seven & a half inches & weighs 165 lb.
In testimony &c.
H. L. EURE clk.

(309) 317 State of N.Carolina} County Court Clerks office
Gates County }   Oct. 30/th/. 1855.
[No Reg. #.] TONY, the property of Jas B. NORFLEET of Suffo. Nansemond County Va.,
is hired the present year by Messrs. RIDDICK & NORFLEET of Nansemond County Va. &by
them registered asone of their hands employed to work in the great dismal swamp in the
County of Gates aforesaid,
   TONY is about forty six years of age, of a dark brown Color, has a scar on his
left hand, also the end of his little finger on the same hand is off and stands
without shoes five feet & five & three quarter inches high.
In testimony
H. L. EURE clk.

(309) (Cont.) State of N.Carolina} County Court Clerks office
Gates County. }   Oct. 30/th/. 1855.
[No Reg. #.]   MOSES, the property of Jethro RIDDICK of Nansemond County va. is hired the present year by Messrs. RIDDICK & NORFLEET of Nansemond County va. & by them registered as one of their hands to work in the great dismal swamp in the County of Gates aforesaid. MOSES is about 26/th/. [sic] years ofage, is of a dark complexion, has a full mouth & thick lips, has a scar on the left side of his left leg near the shin bone, & stands without shoes five feet three & a half inches high.
In testimony &c.
H. L. EURE clerk.

(310) 318 State of N.Carolina} County Court Clerks
Gates County. }   office. Oct. 30/th/. 1855.
[No Reg. #.]   TOM the property of Edward RIDDICK of Nansemond County va. is hired the present year by Messrs. RIDDICK & NORFLEET of Nansemond County Va. & by them registered asone of their hands employed to work in the great dismal swamp in the County of Gates aforesaid.
TOM is about sixty years of age of a dark brown Color, some what gray free of scars, & stands without shoes five feet three & a half inches high.
In Testimony &c.
H. L. EURE clk.

State of N.Carolina} County Court Clerks office
Gates County }   Oct. 30/th/. 1855.
[No Reg. #.]   JOHN, the property of Jas. B. NORFLEET of Suffo. nansemond County va. is hired the present year by Messrs. RIDDICK & NORFLEET of Nansemond County va. & by them registered as one of their hands employed in the great dismal swamp in the Co. of Gates aforesaid. JOHN is about Fifty years of age, of a dark brown color, has a wide mouth, & thick lips, & a large forehead, grey whiskers (when worn) has several small moulds [sic] on his face below his eyes, has several scars on his left hand & wrist, has a scar on his right hand, & stands without shoes five feet, four & a quarter inches high.
In Testimony &c.
H L EURE clk.

(311) 319 State of N.Carolina} County Court Clerk's office
Gates County }   Oct. 30/th/. 1855.
[No Reg. #.]   ISRAEL the property of Jas. B. NORFLEET of Nansemond County va. is hired the present year by Messrs. RIDDICK & NORFLEET of Nansemond County va. & by them registered as one of their hands employed to work in the great dismal swamp in the County of Gates aforesaid.
ISREAL is about Twenty one years of age, of a dark brown Color, has a good Countenance, has a scar on the left knee pan & stands without shoes five feet three &a half inches high.
In testimony &c.
H. L. EURE clerk

State of N.Carolina} County Court Clerks office
Gates County }   Oct. 30/th/. 1855.
[No Reg. #.]   TONEY the property of Jethro RIDDICK of Nansemond County va. is hired the present year by Messrs. RIDDICK & NORFLEET of Nansemond County va. & by them registered as one of their hands employed to work in the great dismal swamp in the Co. of Gates aforesaid.
TONEY is about thirty five years of age, of dark Complexion, has a scar just over his right eye, has two of his fingers deformed on his left hand, has a scar underneath

(311) (Cont.) his left Arm, And stands without shoes Five feet six & a fourth inches
high.   In Testimony &C.
                                 H. L. EURE clk.

(312) 320 State of N. Carolina} County Court Clerks office
                Gates County. }   Oct. 30/th/ 1855.
[No Reg. #.]   GILBERT the property belonging to the estate of Josipah RIDDICK
dec/d/., of Nansemond County va.. is hired the present year by Messrs. RIDDICK &
NORFLEET of Nansemond County va., & by them registered as oneof their hands to [sic]
employed to work in the great dismal swamp in the County ofGates aforesaid.

    GILBERT is about sixty eight years of Age, of dark Complexion, his right eye some
what inflamed, very gray - free from scars, has a wind on the top of his right arm
just below the arm joint, & stands without shoes Five feet seven & a fourth inches
high.
                              In testimony &c.
                                 H. L. EURE Clk.

State of N. Carolina} County Court clerks office
     Gates County }   Nov. 1st. 1855.
[No Reg. #.] Daniel COWPER the property of John COWPER of Norfolk Co. va. is hired
the present year by Jas. S. SEGUINE of deep Creek Norfo. Co. va. & by him registered
as one of his hands employed to work in the great dismal swamp in the County of Gates
aforesaid.

    Daniel is about thirty seven /eight/ years of age, light complexion with dark
eyes, has two scars on his right hand near his thumb, & stands in his shoes five feet
& five inches high.
                              In Testimony
                                 H. L. EURE clk.

(313) 321 State of N. Carolina} County Court Clerks office
                Gates County. }   Nov. 1st. 1855.
[No Reg. #.]   Edward SEGUINE, the property ofJas. S. SEGUINE of Norfolk County va. &
by him registered as one of his hands employed to work in the great dismal swamp in
the County of Gates aforesaid.

    Edward is about Forty nine years of age of dark complexion has a good Countenance,
has a full sett of teeth, has a scar just below his mouth, has a scar on his left hand
near the wrist joint, a scar on his left foot & stands without shoes five feet Seven
inches high.
                              In testimony &c.
                                 H. L. EURE clk.

State of N. Carolina} County CourtClerk's office
     Gates County }   Nov. 1st. 1855.
[No Reg. #.]   HENRY ofCOWPER the property of John COWPER of Norfolk County va. is
hired the present year by Jas. S. SEGUINE of Deep Creek Norfolk County va. & by him
registered as one of his hands employed to work in the great dismal swamp in the
County of Gates aforesaid.

    HENRY is about eleven years of age of bright Complexion has a scar on his right
leg, & stands without shoes four feet high.
                              In testimony &c.
                                 H. L. EURE clk.

(314) 322 State of North Carolina} County ===== ==== Court Clk's offic_
                Gates County. }   Jany. 23rd. 1856.
[No Reg. #.]   MILLS belonging to the estate of Joseph RIDDICK Dec/d/., is hired the

(314) (Cont.) present year by Jethro RIDDICK of Va. to work in the great dismal Swamp in the State of N. Carolina for the term of one year.

MILLS is about Thirty Nine years of age of a dark complexion, high forehead, has lost one of his lower or under front teeth, his second finger on === the left hand is stiff (by a cut) And stands without shoes five feet six inches high, Given under my hand &seal of office

Test H. L. EURE Clk.
By W. L. BOOTHE D.C.

State of N.Carolina} County Court Clerks office
Gates County } Jany. 23/rd./ 1856.
[No Reg. #.] LEWIS the property of Travis FLANAGAN of Va. is hired the present year by Jethro RIDDICK of Va. &by him registered as one of his hands to work in the great dismal swamp in the state of N. C. for one year.

LEWIS is about fifty years of age of brown Complexion, has one upper front tooth missing, his right leg shorter than the left, he has a scar on the knee pan of the right leg, & stands without shoes, five feet five inches high
Given under my hand &c.
H. L. EURE clk.
By W. L. BOOTHE D.C.

(315) 323 State of No.Carolina} County CourtClerks office
Gates County } February 18/th/. 1856.
[No Reg. #.] BRATT, the property of belonging to the estate of Burwell BROTHERS, /Dec/d/./ & hired the present year by James TAYLOR [blank] registered to work in the great dismal swamp in the state of N. C. for the /term of/ year.

GRATT, is about Twelve years of age, of rather a light dark Complexion has three scars on his face, one over the corner of his left /right/ eye, one under the Corner of the left eye & one Across the left eye brow, & stands without shoes four feet & one inch high. Given under my hand &seal of office
H. L. EURE Clk.
By W. L. BOOTHE D.C.

(316) 324 State of NCa} County Court clerks offic_
Gates County} March 3 rd 1856
[No Reg. #.] TONY the property of Elbert RIDDICK of Gates County is hired the present year by Charles J. BARNES of the State and County aforesaid & by him registered as one of his hands imployed to work in the Great Dismal Swamp in the County of Gates &C.

TONY is about forty six years of age, of a dark complexion has a scar on his forehead just over each eye has a scar on the back of his right hand and one on the back of his left hand and stands without shoes Five feet seven & a half inches in Testamony &C
Henry L.. EURE

State of NCa}
Gates County} County Court clerks office
March 17/th/ 1856
[No Reg. #.] GRANVILLE the property of Isaac HUNTER of Gates County is hired the present year by Mills ROGERS of Nansemond Co va & by him registered as one of his hands imployed to work in the Great Dismal Swamp in the County of Gates & state aforesaid

GRANVILLE is about Fifty three years of age, of very dark complexion is free of scars & stands without shoes? boots Five feet Eight & 1/4 inches high In Testamny &C.
HL EURE cll

117

(317) 325 State of NCa} County Court clerks office
    Gates County} March 17/th/ 1856
[No Reg. #.] LEWIS the property [sic] Isaac HUNTER and registered by him to work in the Great Dismal swamp in the State of N Ca with Mills ROGERS the present year

 LEWIS is about forty six years of age remarkable high forehead har?e pointed on the forehead, has two scars on his breast a scar on the right arm just above the elbow, a scar on the left arm on the outside at the elbow, a scar on the out side of the rights leg & stands with out shoes five feet seven inches high
     In Testamony &C
     Henry L.. EURE clk

State of North Carolina} County Court Clerks office
    Gates County. } March 27/th/. 1856.
[No Reg. #.] DAVID the property of James S. SEGUINE of Deep Creek Va. & by him registered as one of his hands employed in the great dismal swamp in the County of Gates aforesaid. - DAVID is about Twenty five years of age, of a dark complexion, has a scar on his left leg just below? above his ankle, & stands without shoes five feet four & ahalf inches high.
     In testimony &c.
     H. L. EURE Clk. By W. L. BOOTHE D.C.

(318) 326 State of NCa} County Court clerks office
    Gates County} March 27/th/ 1856
[No Reg. #.] JOHN the property of James S. SEGUINE of Deep Creek Virginia & by him registered as one of his hands employed in the Great Dismal swamp in the County of Gates aforesaid

 JOHN is about sixty five years of age has dark complixion large cheek bones very bad teeth - flat nose and wide nostrils He has a scar on his left leg from a burn a scar on his right leg and stands without shoes five feet seven & a half inches high
    In Testamoy &C. H. L: EURE clk C.C.

State of NCa } County Court clerks office
Gates County.} March 27/th/ A D 1856
[No Reg. #.] ROBERT the property of James S. SEGUINE of Deep creek Creek [sic] Virginia & by him registered as one of his hands employed in the Great Dismal Swamp in the County of Gates afore said

 ROBERT is about Twenty five years of age of yellow complexion with bushy Hair he has a purple mark on the right shoulder and a tumor over the right collar-bone & stands without shoes Five feet high
     In Testamony &C.
     Henry LEURE clk

(319) 327 State of N Carolina} County Court Clerks office
    Gates County } March 29/th/. 1856.
[No Reg. #.] HENRY the property of C. E. BALLARD, ofthe County &state aforesaid, is hired the present year by Jos. MATHIAS of Gates County, &by him registered as one of his hands employed to work in the great dismal swamp, in the County of Gates aforesaid.

 HENRY is of dark complexion, has a grey beard, has lost the first joint of his forefinger on his right hand, is about sixty five years ofage, & stands without shoes five feet & full six inches high.
     In testimony &c.
     H.L. EURE clk.

State of N Carolina} County Court Clerks office

(319) (Cont.)   Gates County }   March 29/th/. 1856.
[No Reg. #.]   WILLIS, the property of Frederick R. JONES of the County &state aforesaid, &by him registered as one of his hands employed in the great dismal swamp in the County ofGates - WILLIS is very black, has a scar on his forehead, has several scarn? on each hand, & stands without shoes five feet seven inches high & is 33 yearofage In testimony &c.

H L. EURE clk.

(320) 328 State of N Carolina} County Court Clerks
          Gates County }   office March 29/th/. 1856
[No Reg. #.]   NELSON, the property of Frederick R JONES ofthe County &State afore-said, & by him registered as oneof his hands employed in the great dismal swamp swamp [sic] in the County ofGates - NELSON is of dark complixion, with a high & broad fore head, has a scar on the left side of his forehead, has a scar on the back of his lefthand, has large eyes, and stands without shoes five feet three & a half inches high, & is about thirty years of age.

In testimony &C.
H. L. EURE clk.

State of N. Ca.}
Gates County } County Court Clerks office
              May 3/d/ 1856
[No Reg. #.]   PETER, the property of Edward HARRELL of Nansemond Co. Va is hired the present year by Mills ROGERS of Nansemond Co. Va. & by him registered as one of his hands employed in the Great Dismal Swarmp in the County of Gates aforesaid. PETER is about nine years of age, of dark complexion, very likely, and is free of scars & stands without shoes four feet, two & 3/4 inches high. In testimony of which I, Henry L EURE Clerk of the Court of Pleas & Quarter Sessions at office in Gatesville &c?

Henry L. EURE Clerk

(321) 329 State of NCa} County Court Clerks office
          Gates County}   May 3rd 1856
[No Reg. #.]   RANDOL the property of Edward HARRELL of Nansemond Co V.a. is hired the present year by Mills ROGERS of Nansemond Co V.a and by him registered as one of his hands imployed in the Great Dismal Swanp in the County of Gates aforesaid

RANDOL is about Twenty six years of age of dark complexion has a large scar on the back of his right hand. has a scar on his little finger on the left hand where it joins the hand and stands without shoes Five feet five & 3/4 inches high

In Testamony &C.
H. L. EURE Clerk

State of NCa}
Gates County} County Court Clerks office
              May 3rd 1856
[No Reg. #.]   JOHN WESLY the property of Miss Sarah A. COSTIN of Gates County is hired the present year by Mills ROGERS of Nansemond Co va & by him registered as one of his hands imployed in the Great Dismal in the County of Gates aforesaid

JOHN WESLY is about sixteen years of age of a dark complixion Color? very likely has full eyes has lost one of his frount under teeth and stands with out shoes Five feet & a half inch high   In Testamony &C.

H. L EURE Clerk

(322) 330 State of NCa} County Court Clerks office
          Gates County}   May 3rd 1856
[No Reg. #.]   JERRY the property of Thos. JONES of Gates County is hired the present

3 May 1856

(322) (Cont.) year by Wm.. B **WHITEHEAD** of Nansemond County Va & by him registered as one of his hands imployed to work in the Great Dismal Swamp in the County of Gates aforesaid

JERRY is about Twelve years of age of a very dark Color & has several small scars on his fore head &face & stands without shoes Four feet seven inches high

In Testamony &C.

H L EURE Clerk

State of NCa} County Court Clerks office
Gates County}   May 3rd 1856
[No Reg. #.]   **TURNER** the property of Mills **RGERS** [sic] of Nansemond Co V.a. & by him registered as one of his hands imployed in the Great Dismal swamp in the County of Gates aforesaid

TURNER is about thirteen years of age of a very dark Color, has a small scar in his left eye brow & stands without shoes Five feet full 3/4 of an inch high

In Testamony &C.

HL. EURE Clerk

(323) 331 State of NCa} County Court Clerks office
        Gates County}   Mar?y 3rd 1856
[No Reg. #.]   **EDGAR** the property of Javan **FRANKLIN** of Nansemond Co Va is hired the present year by Mills **RGERS** of Nansemond Co Va & by him registered as one of his hands imployed in the Great Dismal Swamp in the County of Gates aforesaid

EDGAR is about Twelve years of age of a dark Copper Color & is free of scars, likeley & stands without shoes Four feet Ten & a half inches high

In Testamony &C.

H. L. EURE Clerk

State of No.Carolina} County Court Clerks office
    Gates County. }   May 12/th/. 1856
[No Reg. #.]   **ROBERT**, the property of Jethro **RIDDICK** of Nansemond County va, & by his overseer W. G. **WILKINS** registered /the present year/ as one ofhis hands employed to work in the great dismal swamp in said County.

ROBERT is about seventeen years old, of dark complexion, full & bright eyes, large Mouth, & stands without shoes five feet three & a half inches high. (nearly)

In testimony whereof&C.

Henry H L. EURE clk

By W. L. BOOTHE D.C.

(324) 332 State of N. Carolina} County Court Clerk offic_
        Gates County}   May 12/th/. 1856.
[No Reg. #.]   **BASSET** a free man of color, is hired the present year, by J. B. **NORFLEET** of Suffolk, va. & by him registered as one of his hands employed to work in the great dismal swamp in the County of Gates aforesaid.

BASSET is about thirty six or thirty seven years of age - is of a dark Copper Color, has a high fore head, with a thin head of hair - has a scar over the right eye, has three other small scars upon his forehead - has two scars on his left hand, a scar on the right side of the right leg - has lost one of his upper teeth, and stands without shoes five feet 4 1/2 inches high.

In testimony &C.

H. L. EURE Clk

By W. L. BOOTHE D.C.

State of NCa} County Court Clerks office
Gates County}   July 30/th/ 1856

(324) (Cont.) [No Reg. #.] **GEORGE** the property of James S. **SEGUINE** of Deep Creek Norfolk County va, for the present year & by him registered as one of his hands imployed to work in the Great Dismal swamp in the County of Gates aforesaid **GEORGE** is about thirteen years of age is of a dark copper Color has a scar under neath his right arm just below the elbow is free of scars in all other respects and Stands without shoes four feet seven & a half inches high In testamony &C. Henry L **EURE** Clk

(325) 333 State of NC} County Court clerks office
        Gates County}   July 30/th/ 1856
[No Reg. #.] **ROBERT** the property of James S. **SEGUINE** of Deep creek Norfolk County va. for the present year, and by him registered as one of his hands employed to work in the Great Dismal swamp in the County of Gates aforesaid
    ROBERT is about sixteen years of age is very black has a small scar on his upper lip, has a scar on the left knee just above the knee pan has lost his little toe on the left foot and = Stands with out shoes four feet ten and a half inches high
                In Testamony &C.
                Henry L **EURE**

State of NCa} County Court Clerks office
Gates County}   July 30/th/ 1856
[No Reg. #.] **OWIN** the property of James S **SEGUIME** of Deep Cree [sic] Norfolk County va and by him registered as one of his hands employed to work in the Great Dismal swamp in the County of Gates aforesaid
    OWIN is about Fifty two years of age is of a dark copper color his middle Finger on his right hand is drawn crooked has a scar on the top of his right foot has a scar on the top of his right arm & stands without shoes Five feet seven & a half inches high In Testamony &c.   Henry L. **EURE** Clk

(326) 334 State of NCa} County Court Clerks office
        Gates County} September 20th 1856
[No Reg. #.] **JOHN WESLEY** the property of Miss Sarah **COST__** of Gates County N. Ca is hired the present year by Wm.. B **WHITEHEAD** of Nansemond Cy va. and by him registered as one of his hands employed to work in the Great Dismal swamp in the County of Gates aforesaid
    JOHN is about sixteen ye___ of age of black complexion is free of scars has a wide mouth, and stands without shoes five feet one & a half inches high In testamony &C.   H. L.. **EURE** clk

State of NCa} County Court clks office
Gates County} September 20/th/ 1856
[No Reg. #.] **JACKSON** the propert [sic] of Javan R **FRANKLIN** of Nansemond Co va is hired the present year by Wm.. B **WHITEHEAD** of Suffolk Nansemond Co. va. and by him registered as one of his hands imployed to work in the Great Dismal swanp in the County of Gates aforesaid.
    JACKSON is about Twenty five years of age black complexion has a scar near the left corner of the left eye, a good countenance thick lips stands without shoes five feet Eight inches high.   In testamony &C.
                Henry L. **EURE** Clk.

(327) 335 State of NCa} County Court Clerks office
        Gates County} September 20/th/ 1856
[No Reg. #.] Jack **ANDERSON** a free boy of color is hired the present year by Wm.. B. **WHITEHEAD** of Suffolk Nansemond Co. Va & by him registered as one of his hands employed in the Great Dismal swamp in the County of Gates aforesaid
    Jack is about Twenty four years of age of a dark Complexion very low forehead

(327) (Cont.) small eyes wide mouth, bad teeth, and thick lips his hair comes down very near his eyes is free from scars and Stands without shoes five feet Two inches high In testamony &c. HL EURE clk Renewed Septr 24/th/ 1857

State of NCa} County Court Clerks office
Gates County} September 20/th/ 1856
[No Reg. #.] Edmond BOOTH a free man of color is hired the present year by Wm.. B. WHITEHEAD of Nansemond Co Va. & by him registered as one of his hands imployed in the Great Dismal Swamp in the County of Gates aforesaid

   Edmond is about Fifty years of age black complexion is stoutly built, has a scar on his right hand, one on his breast one on the left one one [sic] the left side of his face below the eye & Stands with out shoes five feet eight inches high In testamony &C. H L EURE Clk

(328) 336 State of NCa} County Court clerks office
         Gates County} September 20/th/ 1856
[No Reg. #.] JEFFRY the property of Javan R FRANKLIN of Nansemond Co va is hired the presn [sic] year by Wm. B WHITEHEAD of Suffolk Nansemond Co va. and by him registered as one of his hands employed in the great dismal swamp in the County of Gates aforesaid

   JEFFRY is about nineteen years of age of a copper Color has a good set of teeth and a fierce eye, and stands with out shoes five feet six inches high
In testamony &c. HL. EURE clk

State of NCa} County Court clerks office
Gates County} September 20/th/ 1856.
[No Reg. #.] MILLS the property of Elisha ASHBURM of Nansemond Co Va is hired the present year by Wm. B. WHITEHEAD of Nansemond Co Va and by him registered as one of his hands imployed to work in the Great Dismal swamp in the County of Gates aforesaid

   MILLS is about Twenty Six Seven years of age of a very dark complixion has a scar on the left side of his chin has a scar on the left big toe has a scar on his left hand and stands without shoes full five feet one inch high In testamony &C.
                        H L EURE clk

(329) 337 [Entire page is blank.]

(330) 338 State of NCa} County Court Clerks office
         Gates County} October 7/th/ 1856
[No Reg. #.] Boy MILES the property of Jethro RIDDICK? of Nansemond Co Va and by him registered as one of /his/ hands his? registered as one of his [sic] hands imployed to work in the Great Dismal swamp in the County of Gates aforesaid

   MILES is about thirteen years of age is ofa light complexion has a scar on his forehead has had the smallpox, has a scar on the left shin bone has two small scars on the left kee [sic] bone & stands with out shoes Four feet 7 1/2 inches high
In testamony &C. Henry L.. EURE clk

State of NCa} County Co Clerks office
Gates County} October 7/th/ 1854?6?
[No Reg. #.] Boy MOSES the property of Jethro RIDDICK of Nansemond Co. Va. and by him registered as one of his hands employed to work in the Great Dismal in the County of Gates aforesaid

   Boy MOSES is about Twenty years of age is of rather a dark Complexion has a Small scar on the left little finger, has several small bumps on his face and is free of scars in other respects and stands without shoes Five feet one & a half inches high
In testamony &C. H. L. EURE clk

7 October 1856

(331) 339 State of NCa} County Court Clerks office
　　　　　　Gates County} October 7/th/ 1856
[No Reg. #.]　Boy ISAAC the property of Jethro RIDDICK of Nansemond Co va and by him
registered as one of his hands imployed to work in the Great Dismal swamp in the
County of Gates aforesaid
　　ISAAC is about fifteen yeas of age is very black has a scar upon his left fore-
finger has a scar on his left shin bone & stands without shoes Five feet high
　　　　　　　　　　　　　　In testamony &C. Henry L. EURE clk

State of NCa} County Court Clerks office
Gates County} October 7/th/ 1856.
[No Reg. #.]　Man MOSES the property of Jethro RIDDICK of Nansemond Co. Va. and by
him registered as one of his hands employed to work in the Great Dismal Swamp in the
County of Gates aforesaid MOSES is about Twenty seven years of age is very black has
a scar on the left side of his left leg, has several small scars on each of his hands
has thick lips & a fair countenance with a good sett of teeth & stands without shoes
five feet 3 1/2 inches high
　　　　　　　　　　　　　　In testamony &C.　Henry L EURE clk

(332) 340 State of NCa} County Court Clerks office
　　　　　　Gates County} October 7/th/ /56
[No Reg. #.]　TONEY the property of Jethro RIDDICK of Nansemond Co. Va and by him
registered as one of his hands imployed to work in the Great Dismal swamp, in the
County of Gates aforesaid
　　TONEY is about thirty six years of age is of a dark complexion has a scar just
over his right eye, has two of his fingers deformed on his left hand & has a scar
under neath his left arm　　　　　In Testamony &C　H.. L. EURE clk

State of NCa} County Court Clerks office
Gates County} October 13/th/ 1856
[No Reg. #.]　Man GEORGE the property of James S SEGUINE of Deep Creek va. is
registered the present year by sd. SEGUINE as one of his hands imployed in the Great
Dismal Swamp in the County of Gates aforesaid
　　The said GEORGE is about fifty nine years of age of dark complexion wrinkled face
short teeth full beard and is quite gray the forefinger of his left hand is a little
stiff has a large deep scar upon the left leg just above his knee, two long flat scars
on his right leg has lost the first joint of the little toe of his left foot & stands
with out shoes five feet eight and a half inches high In Testamony &C.
　　　　　　　　　　　　　　Henry L. EURE clk

(333) 341 State of NCa} County Court Clerks office
　　　　　　Gates County} October 13/th/ 1856.
[No Reg. #.]　CHARLES the property of James S SEGUINE of Norfolk County Va and by him
registered as one of his hands imployed to work in the Great Dismal swamp in the
County of Gates aforesaid
　　CHARLES is about Twelve years of age very likely has a large scar on his left hip
a scar under neath his left wrist a scar on the back of his head which was caused by a
burn and stands without shoes about four feet five and a half inches high
In Testamony &C.　　　　　　　　Henry L EURE clk

State of NCa} County Court Clerks office
Gates County} October 13/th/ 1856
[No Reg. #.]　EDWARD the property of James S SEGUINE of Deep creek Norfolk Co va and
by him registered as one of his hands imployed in the Great Dismal swamp in the County
of Gates aforesaid

(333) (Cont.) EDWARD is about fifty years of age of a dark complexion has a good countenance has a full sett of teeth has a scar just below his mouth, a scar on his left hand near the rist joint, a scar on his left foot and stands without shoes five feet seven inches high

In Testamony &C.
Henry L EURE clk

(334) 342 State of NCa} County Court Clerks office
Gates County} October 13/th/ 1856
[No Reg. #.] DRED the property of James S SEGUINE of Deep Creek Norfolk Co va for the present year and by him registered as one of his hand [sic] imployed in the Great Dismal swamp in the County of Gates aforesaid

The said DRED is about sixty two years of age of light complixion has streight hair, thin visage a scar on his left under jaw, a scar on his left thumb a scar on the inside of his right arm about two & a half inches from his hand several bad scars on his right leg and stands without shoes five feet nine inches high In Testamony &C.
Henry L. EURE Clk

State of NCa} County Court Clerks office
Gates County} October 13/th/ 1856- - -
[No Reg. #.] Man ISAAC the property of James S SEGUINE of Deep Creek Norfolk Co. Va for the present year and by him registered as one of his hands imployed in the Great Dismal swamp in the County of Gates aforesaid

ISAAC is about thirty ===== four years of age of dark complexion his face a little disfigured by a burn has a small scar on the middle finger of his wright hand & stands with out shoes five feet 9 1/2 inches high In Testamoy &C.
Henry L. EURE clk

(335) 343 State of NCa} County Court Clerks office
Gates County} October 13/th/ 1856
[No Reg. #.] Man LEWIS the property of James S. SEGUINE of Deep Creek Norfolk Co va for the present year and by him registered as one of his hands imployed in the Great Dismal Swamp in the County of Gates aforesaid

LEWIS is about Forty four years of age of dark complexion has a small scar on his forehead a little above the right eye and a small scar in the face a little under the right eye and is five feet three &3/4 inches high without shoes In Testamoy &Co?
Henry L EURE clk

State of NCa} County Court clk office
Gates County} October 13/th/ 1856
[No Reg. #.] LEWIS the property of James S SEGUIR?E of Deep Creek Norfolk Co Va. for the present year and by him registered as one of his hands imployed in the Great Dismal swamp in the County ofGates aforesaid

LEWIS is about Sixty nine years ofage quite grey has bad teeth has a number of small marks upon booth of his hands has a scar on the left in step and stands with out shoes Five feet six inches high

In Testamoy &C
Henry L. EUREclk

(336) 344 State of NCa} County Court Clerks office
Gates County} October 13/th/ 1856.
[No Reg. #.] JOE the property of James S SEGUINE of Deep Creek Norfolk Co Va. & by him registered as one of his hands imployed in the Great Dismal swamp in the County of Gates aforesaid

JOE is about Forty six years of age of a light brown complexion has sharp features

13 October 1856

(336) (Cont.) with high forehead wide nostrels, has bad teeth tolerable beard a small scar on the back, a scar on the left hand below the thumb &forefinger a scar on the out side of the right knee & a bad scar across the top of the right foot & one on the in step of the left foot & stands without shoes Five feet seven and a half inches high In Testamoy &C.   Henry L. EURE clk

State of NCa} County Court Clerks office
Gates County}   Nov 3rd 1856.
[No Reg. #.]   ROBERT the property of Jethro RIDDICK of Nansemond Co Va and by him registered as one of his hands imployed in the Great Dismal swamp in the County of Gates aforesaid
     ROBERT is about seventeen years of age is of a dark complexion has a full upper lip is free of scars except one between his eyes just above his noes [sic] & stands without shoes Five feet 4 1/4 inches high In Testamoy &C.
                                        Henry L EURE clk

(337) 345 State of N.Ca} County Court Clerk's Office
              Gates County } Decr 8/th/ A D 1856
[No Reg. #.]   Boy ABRAM the property of James S SEGUINE of Deep Creek Norfolk Co. Va for the present year, and by him registered as one of his hands imployed to work in the Great Dismal Swamp in the County of Gates aforesaid.
     ABRAM is about Twenty Two years of age, is of a dark color, has Several small scars on his left hand, has a good set of Teeth, has agood countenance & a full fore Head. And Stands without shoes, five feet six inches high
     In testamony of Which I Henry L. EURE, Clerk of the Court of Pleas & Quarter Sessions in and for the County of Gates, at Office in Gatesville, do hereunto affix my name and seal of Office the day and date first before written [End of entry.]

(338) 346 State of NCa} County Court Clerks office
              Gates County} A. D. 1857. [sic]
[No Reg. #.]   Man LEWIS the property of Mills ROGERS of Nansemond County va. for the present year and by him registered as one of his hands employed to work in the Great Dismal swamp in the County of Gates aforesaid. Man LEWIS is about forty nine years ofage is of a dark complixion has a remarkable high fore head has pointed [sic] on the fore head has two ===== scars on his breast a scar on the right arm just above the elbow a scar on the left arm on the out side at the elbow a scar on the out side of the right leg and Stands without shoes Five feet seven inches high In Testamony &C.
                          Test H. L. EURE Clk

State of NCa} County Court Clk's Office
Gates County} Apl 4/th/ A D 1857
[No Reg. #.]   Man ABRAM the property of James COSTEN hired by Jas. W. HILL for the present year and registered by him as one of his hands employed to work in the Great dismal Swamp in the County of Gates aforesaid
     Man ABRAM is about Twenty five years of age is of a dark complexion and has a good countenance and has Two Scars on his right wrist: /and Stands without shoes 5 feet 7 inches high/ In testamony of which I Henry L EURE Clerk of the Court of Pleas &C
                          H. L. EURE Clk.

(339) 347 State of N.Ca} County Court Clk's Office
              Gates County } Apl 4/th/ 1857
[No Reg. #.]   Man REUBEN the property ofJas. COSTEN's heirs, hired by Jas. W. HILL and by him registered as one of his hands for the present year to work in the great dismal Swamp in the County of Gates aforesaid. Said REUBEN is about Forty years of age, of a Bacon Color, has a scar on his right arm near the elbow and Stands without

(339) (Cont.) shoes Five feet six inches high In Testamony of which I H. L. EURE Clk of the County Court of Pleas &C do affix my name   H. L. EURE Clk.

State of N.Ca} County Court Clk's Office
Gates County } April 4/th/ A. D. 1857
[No Reg. #.]   Man WILLIS the property of Jas. COSTEN's heirs hire [sic] by Jas. W HILL for the present year to work in the Great dismal Swamp in Gates County aforesaid. Man WILLIS is about fifty Two years of age is of a Bacon Color with a good Countenance has a scar on his right arm about the elbow, and Stands without shoes five feet Two inchis high.

In Testamony of which I H. L. EURE Clk. of the Court of Pleas & C do affix my name

H. L. EURE Clk.

(340) 348 State of N.Ca} County Court Clk's Office
Gates County } April 4/th/. A. D 1857
[No Reg. #.] Man ARTHUR the property of the heirs of Henry COSTEN decd. hired by James W HILL for the present year and by him registered to work in the Great Dismal Swamp.   Man ARTHUR is of a dark Bacon Color with agood Countenance has a scar on his forehead and one on his right wrist and is about Thirty one years of age; and Stands without shoes Five feet, five and ahalf inches high.

In testamony of which I. H. L. EURE Clk. of the Court of Pleas &c do affix my name
H. L. EURE Clk

State of N.Ca.} County Court Clk's office
Gates County } April 4/th/ A. D. 1857
[No Reg. #.] Man REUBEN the property of the heirs of Col. Jessee WIGGANS decd - hired by Jas W. HILL for the present year & by him registered to work in the Great Dismal Swamp.

Man REUBEN is about Thirty five years of age, of a dark complexion, good Countenance with no notable scars, and Stands without shoes Five feet, six & a half inches high.

In testamony of which I H. L. EURE Clk. of the Caut of Pleas &C. do affix my name
H. L. EURE Clk

(341) 349 State of N. Carolina} County Court Clerk's Office
Gates County   } April 4/th/ A.D. 1857
[No Reg. #.] Man EDWARD the property of the heirs of Jas COSTEN - hire by Jas. W HILL for the present year and by him registered to work in the Great Dismal Swamp. The said EDWARD is about Forty Seven years of age, of a dark complexion - has several small scars on his left Arm and one on his right elbow, has a good Countenance and stands without shoes Five feet nine inches high.

In testimony of which I H LEURE Clk. of the Court of Pleas &C. do affix my name   H. L. EURE Clk.

State of N.Carolina} County Court Clk's. Office
Gates County   } April 4/th/ A. D. 1857
[No Reg. #.] Man ISAAC the property of John C. GORDON - hired by Robert R. HILL for the present year and by him registered as one of his hands imployed to work in the Great Dismal Swamp.

The said ISAAC is about ==== Thirty Seven years of age, is of a dark Complexion - has a tolerable high forehead with a scar /on it/ just below the hair, and Stands without shoes Five feet six & a half inches high.

In testimony of which I H L EURE Clerkof the Court of Pleas &c do affix my name
H. L. EURE Clk.

4 April 1857

(342) 350 State of N. Carolina} County Court Clerks Office
Gates County   } April 4/th/ A.D. 1857
[No Reg. #.] Man **ALBERT** the property of John C. **GORDON** – hired by R. R. **HILL** for the present year and by him registered as one of his hands to work in the Great Dismal Swamp. Man **ALBERT** is about Thirty seven years of age, of a dark complexion has a scar on his left hand, and Stands without shoes Five feet Six & a fourth inches high.
          In testimony of which I H. L. **EURE** Clk. of the Court of Pleas &c. do affix my name   H L **EURE** Clk

State of N.C.} Court of Pleas & Quarter Sessions
Gates County } June 27/th/ 1857
[No Reg. #.] Man **WILLIAM** the property of Nathaniel **BOOTHE** and hired by Mills **RODGERS** to work in the great dismal Swamp and by him so Registered. Man **WILLIAM** is about Twenty one years of age – of a black complexion – good Countenance and stands without shoes four feet and Eleven & a half inches high.
          In testimony of which I H. L. **EURE** Clerk of the Court of Pleas & Quarter Sessions in and for the County of Gates, at office in Gatesville do hereunto affix my name and seal of Office the day and date first before written
                                        H.L. **EURE**Clk

(343) 351 State of N.Ca} County Court Clerk's Office
Gates County } June 27/th/ 1857
[No Reg. #.] Boy **WILLIAM** the property of Nancy **BROWN** is hired by Mills **RODGERS** and by him Registered to work in the great Dismal Swamp. Boy **WILLIAM** is about sixteen years of age, of a dark Complexion, has a scaron his left arm just above the elbow, and one on his wright foot clost to his little toe – and stands without shoes five feet three and 1/4 inches high. In testimony of which, I H. L. **EURE** Clk of the Court of Pleas & Quarter Sessions in and for the County of Gates, at Office in Gatesville, do hereunto set my name & seal H. L. **EURE** Clk

State of N.Ca} County Court Clerk's Office
Gates County } June 17/th/ [sic] 1857
[No Reg. #.] Man **JACK** the property of Nathl. **BOOTH** is hired by Mills **RODGERS** and Registered by him as one of his hands to work in the great dismal swamp for the present year. Man **JACK** is about Twenty one years of age – dark complexion – good countenance, has a scar on his wright leg just above his Ankle, and stands without shoes five feet four inches high. In testimony of which I H. L. **EURE** Clerk of the Court of Pleas and quarter Sessions, in and for the County of Gates, at Office in Gatesville the day and date first written, do affix my name & seal H L **EURE** Clk.

(344) 352 State of N.Ca} County Court Clerk's Office
Gates County } June 27/th/ 1857
[No Reg. #.] Man Boy **EDGAR** the property of J **FRANKLIN** is hired by Mills **RODGERS** and by him registered as one of his hands emploid [sic] to work in the great Dismal Swamp for the present yea_
          Boy **EDGAR** is about thirteen years of Age – of a Bacon Colour – good countenance – with no notable scars, and stands without shoes five feet high.
          In testimony of which I. H L **EURE** Clk. of the Court of Pleas and Quarter Sessions, in and for the County of Gates at Office in Gatesville do hereunto affix ny name and seal of Office the day and date first before written H. L. **EURE** Clk

State of No .Ca} County Court Clerk's Office
Gates County   } June 27/th/ 1857
[No Reg. #.] Boy **WESLY** the property of Wm. **BEEMAN** is hired by Mills **RODGERS** and by him Registered as one of his hands emploid to work in the great dismal Swamp for the

(344) (Cont.) present year.

Boy **WESLY** is about Sixteen years of Age and of a dark complexion, and has a small scar on his wright leg just above the knee and Stands without shoes five feet three inches high.

In testamony of which, I H. L. **EURE** Clerk of the Court of Pleas & Quarter Sessions in and for the County of Gates, at Office in Gatesville the day and date first before written [sic]   H. L. **EURE** Clk

(345) 353 State of No.Ca} Court of Pleas & Quarter Sessions
              Gates County }   June 27/th/ 1857.
[No Reg. #.]   Boy **JERRY** the property of Thomas **JONES** and hired by Mills **RODGERS** for the present year - is about thirteen years of Age - of a dark complexion good countenance - and stands without shoes four feet nine inches high - has a small   scar on his wright wrist.

In testamony of which I I Henry L. **EURE** Clerk of the Court of Pleas and Quarter Sessions, in and for the County of Gates, at Office in Gatesville the day and date first before written do hereunto fix my hand & seal of Office H. L. **EURE** Clk

State of No. Ca} County Court Clerk's Office
Gates County   }   June 27/th/ 1857
[No Reg. #.]   **RANDAL** the property of Edward **HARRELL** of Nansemond Co. Va., is hire the present year by Mills **RODGERS** and by him Registered as one of his hands employied to work in the great Dismal Swamp

RANDAL is about Thirty? twenty eight years of age, of a dark Complexion, has a large scar on the back of his wright hand, on [sic] on his little finger on the left hand where it joins the hand, and stands without shoes five feet five & three fourths inches high. In testamony of which I H L **EURE** Clerkof the Court of Pleas &C. do hereunto set my hand and affix the seal ofOffice the day and date first before written
                          H. L. **EURE** Clk.

(346) 354 State of North Carolina} Court of Pleas &c
              Gates County   }   Aug. 21/st/ 1857
[No Reg. #.]   Man Watson **FRANKLIN** the property of James B **NORFLEET** for the present year to work in the Great Dismal Swamp in the County of Gates.

Watson is about Sixty years of age, has a scar unde [sic] his wright eye, is of a good countenance, of a dark complexion & has a Stopage in his speech and Stands without shoes five feet & four inches high. In testamony of which I H. L. **EURE** Clerk of the Court of Pleas & Quarter Sessions in and for the County of Gates, do hereunto set my hand and seal   H. L. **EURE** Clk

State of N.Carolina} Court of Pleas &?
  Gates County   }   Aug. 21/st/ 1857
[No Reg. #.]   Boy Henry **FRANKLIN** the property of James B **NORFLEET** for the preasent year and by him registered to work in the great Dismal Swamp in the County of Gates.

Boy Henry is about Eleven years of age, of a bright complexion and has no Scars by which he could be distinguished and Stands without shoes, four feet and Seven & a half inches high. In testamony of which I H. L. **EURE** do set my hand and seal
                          H. L. **EURE** Clk

(347) 355 State of North Carolina} Court of Pleas &c
              Gates County   }   Aug. 29/th/ 1857.
[No Reg. #.]   Boy **MOSES** the property of Jethro **RIDDICK** of Nansemond County Virginia and by him registered as one of his hands employed to work in the great Dismal Swamp in the County of Gates aforesaid. Boy **MOSES** is about Twenty one years of age, of rather dark complexion, has a Small scar on the left little finger, has Several small

(347) (Cont.)   bump [sic] on his face and is free of scars in other respects and
Stands without shoes five feet one & a half inches high. In testamony of which I, H.
L. EURE, Clerk of the Court of Pleas & Quarter Sessions, in and for the County of
Gates, at Office in Gatesville, do hereunto affix my name and seal of Office, the day
and date first before written

Henry L. EURE Clk.

State of N. Carolina} Court of Pleas &C.
Gates County   }   Aug. 29/th/ 1857
[No Reg. #.] Boy POMPEY, the property of Jethro RIDDICK, of Nansemond County,
Virginia and by him registered, as one of his hands employed to work in the great
Dismal Swamp, in the County of Gates aforesaid. Boy POMPEY is about Eighteen sixteen?
years of Age, of dark complexion, has a scar on the backof his wright hand, and has
several small scars on each of his legs, and stands without shoes five feet 2 inches
high

      In testamony of which I H. L. EURE Clerk of the Court of Pleas &c do hereunto
affix my hand and seal of Office   H. L. EURE Clk.

(348) 356 State of North Carolina} Court of Pleas & c
              Gates County   }   Aug. 29/th/ 1857.
[No Reg. #.] Boy TOM the property of Jethro RIDDICK of Nansemond County Virginia,
and by him registered, as one of his hands imployed to work in the great Dismal Swamp,
in the County of Gates aforesaid. Boy TOM is about thirteen years of age, of a dark
complexion has a Small scar on the left knee, is of a good countenance and stands
without shoes four feet seven inches high. In testamony of which I, H. L. EURE, Clerk
of the Court of Pleas & Quarter Sessions, in and for the County of Gates, at Office in
Gatesville, do hereunto affix my name and seal of Office the day & date first before
written   H. L. EURE Clk.

State of North Carolina} County Court Clk's Office
    Gates County   }   Aug. 31/st/ 1857.
[No Reg. #.] Boy ROBERT, the property of James S SEGUNE of Norfolk County, Virginia,
and by him registered as one of his hands employed to work in the great dismal Swamp,
in the County of Gates aforesaid. ROBERT is about Seventeen years ofage, very black,
has a small scar on his upper lip & one on the left knee pan just above the knee and
has lost his little toe on his left foot and Stands without shoes four feet Ten & a
half inches high. In testamony of which I H. L. EURE, Clerk of the Court of Pleas &
Quarter Session, in and for the County of Gates, at Office in Gatesville, do affix my
name and seal of Office the day & date first before written

H.L. EURE Clk.

(349) 357 State of N. Carolina} County Court Clerk's Office
              Gates County   } August 31/st/ 1857.
[No Reg. #.] JOHN, the property of James S SEGUINE of the County of Nansemond, State
of Virginia & by him registered as one of his hands to work in the great Dismal swamp,
in the County of Gates aforesaid. JOHN is about Sixty five years of age, has? of a
black complexion, has bad teeth, flat nose and wide nostrils, a scar on his wright leg
& one on his left leg from a burn, and stands without shoes five feet Seven & a half
inches high. In testamony of which I H L EURE, Clerk of the Court of Pleas & Quarter
Sessions, at Office in Gatesville the day & date first before written

H. L. EURE Clk.

State of N. Carolina} County Court Clerk's
    Gates County   } Office Aug. 31/st/ 1857.
[No Reg. #.] OWEN, a Slave, the property of James S. SEGUINE of Norfolk County

(349) (Cont.) Virginia, and by him registered as one of his hands, employed to work in the Great Dismal Swamp, in the County of Gates aforesaid. OW**I**N is about fifty Three years of age, of a dark copper colour, his middle finger on his right hand is drawn crooked, has a scar on the top of his right foot & one on the top of his right arm & stands without shoes five feet Seven & a half inches high. In testimony of which I H. L. EURE Clerk of the Court of Pleas & Quarter Sessions in and for the County of Gates at Office in Gatesville affix my name H.L.EURE Clk

(350) 358 State of N Carolina} County Court Clerk's
            Gates County   } Office Septr 24/th/ 1857
[No Reg. #.] Boys WALKER, ALBERT, OSBORN, SAM, EDMOND JACKSON, JEFFREY, & CHARLES
The property of Mills ROGERS for the present year, and by him registered as his hands, employed to work in the great Dismal Swamp in the County of Gates aforesaid.
    In testimony of which I H. L. EURE Clerk of the Court of Pleas & Quarter Sessions in and for the County of Gates, at Office in Gatesville, do affix my name and seal of Office, this the 24/th/ day of Septr 1857. H.L. EURE Clk.

State of North Carolina} County Court Clk's office
    Gates County   } September 28/th/ 1857
[No Reg. #.] John NORFLEET the property of James B. NORFLETT of Nansemond County Virginia, and by him Registered as one of his hands employed to work in the great Dismal Swamp in the County of Gates aforesaid
    John is about fifty three years of Age, of a dark complexion, and has a Scar on the left wrist, and stands without shoes five feet, four & a half inches high.
                        In testamony &c
                        HL EUREClk

(351) 359 State of NCarolina} County Court Clerks Office
            Gates County   } September 28/th/ 1857.
[No Reg. #.] John BRINKLEY the property of James B NORFLEET for the present year, of Nansemond Co. virginia, and by him registered as one of his hands, employed to work in the great Dismal Swamp in the County of Gates aforesaid. John is about twenty nine years of age, of a dark complexion, and stand without shoes five feet, Seven & a half inches high   In testimony &c
                        H.L. EURE Clk

State of N Carolina} County Court Clerks Office
    Gates County   } Septr 28/th/ 1857.
[No Reg. #.] Isaac GRIFFIN the property of James B NORFLEET for this year, of Nansemond County Virginia, and by him registered as one of his hands employed to work in the great Dismal Swamp in the County of Gates aforesaid. Isaac is about twenty seven years of age, of a dark complexion, has a scar on the jaw and one on the left hand   In testimony &C.
                        H. L. EURE clk

(352) 360 State of N.Carolina} County Court Clk's Office
            Gates County   } September 28/th/ 1857.
[No Reg. #.] Isaac NORFLEET, the property of James B. NORFLEET, of Nansemond County Virginia and by him registered as one of his hands employed in the great Dismal Swamp, in the County of Gates aforesaid.
    Isaac is about forty years of age, is of a dark complexion, has a scar on the shin bone, and a sunken place on the scull bone, and stands without shoes five feet and four inches high   In testimony &c.
                        H.L. EURE Clk

1 October 1857

(353) [This page is entirely blank and not numbered.]

(354) 361 State of N. Ca} County Court Clerk's
Gates County } Office October 1/st/ 1857
[No Reg. #.] DREAD the property of James S SEGUINE of Norfolk County vrginia and by
him registered as on_ of his hands employed to work in the Great dismal Swamp in the
County of Gates aforesaid. DREAD is about Sixty three years of age, of a light
complexion, has a scar on his left under jaw, one on his left thumb, one on the inside
of his right arm and several bad ones on his right leg, and stands without shoes five
feet, nine inches high   In testamony &c.

State of N. Ca.} County Court Clerk's Office
Gates County   } October 1/st/. 1857.
[No Reg. #.] LEWIS the property of Jas. S. SEGUINE of Norfolk County Virginia and by
him registered as one of his hands employed to work in the great Dismal Swamp in the
County of Gates aforesaid. LEWIS is about Seventy year_ of Age and quite gray, has
bad teeth, a number of ==== Small scars on both of his hands and one on his left
instep and stands without shoes five feet Six inches high
                         In testamony &c.

(355) 362 State of N. Ca.} County Court Clerk's Office
Gates County   } October 1/st/ 1857
[No Reg. #.] LEWIS the property of Jas. S. SEGUINE of Norfolk County Virginia and by
him registered as one of his hands employed to work in the Great d Dismal Swamp.
LEWIS is about forty five years of Age, of a dark complexion, has a small scar on his
forehead a little above the right eye, and a small scar? a little under the right eye
and stands without shoes five feet, three and three fourth inches high.
                         In testamony &c.

State of N. Ca.} County Court Clerk's Office
Gates County   } October 1/st/ 1857.
[No Reg. #.]   Joe WEBB the property of James S. SEGUINE for the present year of
Norfolk County Virginia and by him registered as one of his hands employed to work in
the Great Dismal Swamp.
    Joe WEBB is about forty seven years of age, of a light brown complexion, sharp
features, high forehead, wide nostrils, bad teeth, a small scar on the back, one on
the left hand, one on the outside of the right knee and a bad on [sic] across the
right foot and one on the instep of the left foot and stands without shoes five feet
Seven & 1/2 inches high   In testamony &c.

(356) 363 State of N. Ca} County Court Clerk's Office
Gates County. } October 1/st/. 1857.
[No Reg. #.] ROBERT the property of Jethro RIDDICK of Nansemond County Virginia and
by him registered as one of his hands employed to work in the Great Dismal Swamp, in
the County of Gates aforesaid. ROBERT is about Eighteen years of Age of a dark
complexion, has a full upper lip, is free of scars except one ====== between his eyes
just above his nose, and stands without shoes five feet four & 1/4 inches high
                         In testamony &c.

State of N. Ca.} County Court Clerk's Office
Gates County   } October 1st 1857.
[No Reg. #.] TONY the property of Jethro RIDDICK of Nansemond County Virginia and by
him registered as one of his hands employed to work in the great Dismal Swamp, TONY is
about Thirty seven years of Age, of a dark complexion, has a scar just over his right
eye, has two of his fingers deformed on his left hand and s=== has a scar under his

131

(356) (Cont.) left arm and stands without shoes five feet shix [sic] and 1/4 inches high.
In testamony &c.
H. L. EURE Clk.

(357) 364 State of N. Ca.} County Court Clerk's Office
Gates County. } October 1/st/ 1857.
[No Reg. #.] MOSES the property of Jethro RIDDICK of Nansemond County Virginia, and by him registered as one of his hands employed to work in the great Dismal Swamp in the County of Gates aforesaid.

TONY [sic] is about Twenty eight years of age, very black, has a scar on the left side of his left leg, and several small scars on each of his hands, has thick lips and a fair countenance, with a good set of teeth, and stands without shoes five feet three & 1/2 inches high
HLEURE Clk
In testamony &c

State of N. Ca.} County Court Clerks Office
Gates County } January 1/st/ 1858
[No Reg. #.] Man GILBERT the property of Jethro RIDDICK for this year, and by him registered as one of his hands employed to work in the great dismal swamp, in the County of Gates aforesaid

Man GILBERT is about Seventy years of age, is of a black complexion, has a small scar on his left hand, has no upper teeth in front, and has a large wind between his eyes, & stands without shoes five feet, Seven and a fourth half inches high
In testamony &c
H L EUREClk.

(358) 365 State of North Carolina} C. C. Clerk's Office
Gates County } Feby. 5/th/ 1858.
[No Reg. #.] Man LEWIS the property of Daniel BROTHERS of Nansemond County Virginia, and by him registered as one of his hands employed to work in the great Dismal swamp

LEWIS is about fifty years of age, of a dark complixion, high forehead, has two scars on his breast, one scar on his right arm, and one on his left arm, and one on the out side of his right leg. And stands without shoes Five feet seven inches high
In testamony &c &c
H.L. EURE Clk.

North Carolina,} County Court Clerk's office
Gates County } March 3/rd/ AD 1858.
[No Reg. #.] Man NED the property of Charles J BARNES of the County and state aforesaid, and by him registered as one of his hands to work in the great dismal Swamp. NED is about forty five years of age, of a light Bacon colour, with a bushy head, good countenance and has a small scar on his right thumb, & stands without shoes five feet, six and a half inches high
In testimony of which &c
H. L. EURE Clk

(359) 356 [sic] North Carolina,} County Court Clerk's office
Gates County: } March 3/rd/ A.D. 1858
[No Reg. #.] DREAD, the property of Charles J BARNES of the County and state aforesaid and by him registered as one of his hands employed to work in the great dismal swamp, in the County of Gates aforesaid. DREAD is about sixty four years of age, of a light complexion, has a scar on his left under Jaw, one on his left thumb one on the inside of his /right/ left arm and several bad scars on his right leg, and stands without shoes five feet nine inches high.
In testimony of which &c   Henry L. EURE Clk

(359) (Cont.) North Carolina,} County of Pleas & Quarter Session [sic]
          Gates County. } March 26/th/ 1858.
[No Reg. #.] Boy WILLIAM is the property of Mills ROGERS for the present year of Nansemond County Virginia and by him registered as one of his hand employed to work in the great dismal swamp in the County of Gates aforesaid

    Boy WILLIAM is about four feet nine & 1/2 inches high thirteen years of age, of a dark bacon colour, and has no notable scars by Which he may be distinguished.
                    In testamony &c
                    H.L. EURE Clk.

(360) 367 North Carolina,} County Court Clerk's Office
          Gates County: } March 26/th/ 1858.
[No Reg. #.] Man MILLS, the property of Mills ROGERS for the present year, and by him registered as one of his hands employed to work in the Great dismal Swamp. Man MILLS is about twenty eight years of age, is of a dark complexion, with good countenance; and has a scar on his great toe on the left foot, and one on his left wrist, and stands without shoes Five feet and ahalf inch high.
                    In testamony &c
                    H L EURE Clerk.

North Carolina} C. C. Clerk's Office
Gates County. } April 12/th/ 1858
[No Reg. #.] Man GEORGE the property of Mills ROGERS for this year, of Nansemond County Vrginia, and by him registered as one of his hands, employed to work in the great dismal Swamp, in the County aforesaid.
    Man GEORGE is about fifty eight years of age, of a dark bacon complexion, good countenance, high forehead and has a large scar on the back of his right hand and stands without shoes five feet, seven & 1/4 inch high
        In testamony &c.

                    H. L. EURE Clk

(361) 368 North Carolina} C. C. Clerk's office
          Gates County. } April 12/th/ 1858.
[No Reg. #.] Boy JACK the property of Mills ROGERS for the present year of Nansemond County Virginia, and by him registered as one of his hands, employed to work in the great Dismal Swamp, in the County aforesaid.
    Boy JACK is about Eleven years of age, dark bacon colour, good countenance, and has no visible scars by which he can be distinguished, and stands without shoes four feet, four and 3/4 inches high.
                  In testamony &c
                  H. L. EURE Clerk.

North Carolina} C C Clerk's Office
Gates County } May 8/th/ 1858
[No Reg. #.] Boy Wesly BEEMAN the property of Mills ROGERS of Nansemond Co Va for the present year and by him registered as one of his hands employed to work in the Great Dismal Swamp in the County of Gates aforesaid.
    Wesly is about 17 years of age of a dark, complexion, good countenance, and has one of his under fore teeth broken out, with a samall [sic] scar under his left jaw: and stands without shoes five feet, four inches high
                    In testimony &c
                  H.L.EURE Clk.

(362) 369 North Carolina,} C. C. Clerk's Office
          Gates County. } May 8/th/ 1858.

(362) (Cont.) [No Reg. #.] Boy Jethro **KELLY**, the property of Mills **ROGERS** for the present year - of Nansemond Co. Va. & by him registered as one of his hands employed to work in the Great Dismal Swamp, in the County of Gates aforesaid

Boy Jet is about fourteen years of age, of a bright complexion good countenance and has a scar on his right wrist and one on the inside of his left hand: and stands without shoes five feet & a half inch high.

In testamony &c

Henry L. **EURE**, Clk

State of NCa} County Court Clerks office
Gates County} September 3rd/58
[No Reg. #.] Boy **JOHN** the property of James S **SEGUI__** of Norfolk County Virginia & by him registered as one of his hands employed to work in the Great Dismal Swamp in the County [sic] Gates aforesaid JOHN is a bout Sixty six years of age is a black complex [sic] has bad teeth flat nose & wide nostrils has a scar on his left leg from a burn & one on his right leg & Stands without shoes Five feet Seven & a half inches high In testamy &C   Henry L. **EURE** Clk

(363) 370 State of NCa } County Court Clerks office
Gates County.} September 3rd 1858.
[No Reg. #.] Boy **OWEN** the property of James S. **SEGUINE** of Norfolk County va and by [sic] registered as one of his hands employed to work in the Great Dismal Swamp in the County of Gates aforesaid OWIN is a bout six? Fifty four years of ager? is of a dark copper color his middle finger on his wright hand is drawn crooked has a scar on the top of his right foot & one on the top of his right arm and Stands with out shoes five feet seven & 1/2 inch high In Testamy [sic] &C   Henry L **EURE** Clk

North Carolina} County Court Clerk's office
Gates County. } October 11/th/ 1859
[No Reg. #.] Jethro **KELLEY** the property of O. R. **FLYNN?** of Nansemond County for this year and registered by him as one of his hands employed by him to work in the great dismal Swamp in this County. Jethro is about eighteen years of age, has a scar on his right wrist and one on his left thumb, is of a bright complexion and good countenance, and stands without shoes five feet three inches high

In testimony &c.

H. L. **EURE**, Clk

pr. R.B.G. **COWPER**, D.C.

(364) 371 State of North Carolina,} County Court Clerk's Office
Gates County. } October 11/th/ 1859.
[No Reg. #.] Boy Wm. Henry **JONES**, the property of O. R. **FLYNN** for this year of Nansemond Co. Virginia and by him registered as one of his hands employed to work in the great dismal Swamp in Gates County.

Boy Wm. Henry is about fourteen yeas of age, is of a dark complexion and stands without shoes, four feet 11 1/2 inches high.

In testimony &c.

H. L. **EURE**, Clk.

pr. R.B.G.**COWPER**, D.C.

North Carolina.} County Court Clerk's Office
Gates County: } Novr. 9/th/ A.D. 1859
[No Reg. #.] The following boys, viz. **JOHN, JOE, BILL** and **HENRY** - the property of James B. **NORFLEET** of Nansemond County Virginia, and by him registered as four of his hands employed to work in the great dismal Swamp in the County of Gates aforesaid. **BILL** [sic] is about 18 years old & of dark complexion: **JOE** is about 14 years old &

9 November 1859

(364) (Cont.) light complected: **BILL** is about fourteen years old and of a bright complexion; and **HENRY** is about 12 years old and of a dark complexion
Test. Henry L. **EURE**, Clk.
pr.R.B.G.**COWPER**, D.C.

(365) 372 North Carolina,} County Court Clerk's Office
Gates County: } Novr. 11/th/ A.D. 1859
[No Reg. #.] Jacob **RIDDICK** is registered by James B. **NORFLEET** of Nansemond Co.
Virginia, as one of his hands employed to work in the great dismal swamp in the County of Gates aforesaid.
Jacob is about twenty two years of age, is of a dark bacon color - has a scar over his left eye and one on the end and another on the knuckle bone of his four finger on the right hand, and stands without shoes five feet, six and a half inches high
Test. H. L. **EURE** Clk.
pr.R.B.G.**COWPER**, D.C.

State of N. C.} County Court Clerk's
Gates County: } Office, October 2/nd/ 1860.
[No Reg. #.] Solomon **BROTHERS** the property of Martha **BROTHERS** of Gates County, N.C., is by her registered as one of her hands employed by Jas. B. **NORFLEET** to work in the Great Dismal Swamp, in the County of Gates aforesaid.
Solomon is about fifty years of age, of a dark complexion, and has two notable scars on his person, - one on his right leg just above the ancle, and the other just above his left eye, - and Stands without shoes five feet six & a half inches high.
Test. H. L. **EURE**, Clerk
By R.B.G.**COWPER**, D.C.

(366) 373 North Carolina,} ~~Court of Pleas~~ & County Court Clerk's
Gates County: } Office, Octo 5/th/ 1860.
[No Reg. #.] Man **OWEN**, the property of Jas. S. **SEGUINE** of Norfolk County Virginia, is registered by him as one of his hands employed to work in the Great Dismal Swamp in the County of Gates aforesaid
OWEN is about Fifty seven years of age, of a dark copper color, has his middle == finger on the ~~left~~ right hand drawn crooked, has a scar on his right arm, and stands without shoes five feet seven & a half inches high.
Test H. L. **EURE**, Clk.
By R.B.G.**COWPER**. D.C.

State of NCa} County Court Clks
Gates County} office May 2nd 1861
[No Reg. #.] Boy **CHARLES** the property of Dr Wm. **WHITEE**? of Norfolk County va & by him registered to Work in the Great Dismal swamp in the Couty of Gates
CHARLES is a bout sixteen years of age is of a dark complexion has a scar on his left hip & one on the back of his head Caused by a burn and stands without shoes Four Feet Eigh [sic]
Test Henry L **EURE** C. C.C.

(367) 374 North Carolina} County Court Clks
Gates County. } office May 2.nd 1861
[No Reg. #.] Man **EDWARD** the proper [sic] of Dr Wm.. **WHITE** of Norfolk County Va and by him registered to work in the Great Dismal swamp in the County of Gates, **EDWARD** is a bout sixty six? years of age, is of a dark complexion has a scar just below his mouth and one on the left foot and stands with out shoes Five feet & seven inches high
Test Henry L **EURE** Clk

2 May 1861

(367) (Cont.) North Carolina} County Court Clks
                     Gates County }   office May 2nd/61
[No Reg. #.]   Man **LEWIS** the property of Dr Wm.. **WHITE** of Norfolk County va. and by
him registered to work in the Great Dismal swamp in the County of Gates ======= **LEWIS**
is a bout Forty eight years of age of a dark complexion has a small scar on his fore
head   just a bove his right eye and one on his face a little under his right eye and
stands with out shoes Five feet 3 & 3/4 inches high
                              Tes [sic] Henry L. **EURE** C C C

(368) 375 North Carolina} County Court Clerks
                     Gates County }   office May 2nd/61
[No Reg. #.]   **GEORE** [sic] the property of Dr Wm.. **WHITE** of Norfolk County va & by him
registered to work in the Great Dismal swamp in in [sic] the County of Gates, **GEORE** is
a bout sixty five years of age of a Dark complexion has a good countenance & a large
scar ==== just a bove the left knee joint & stands Five feet Eight inches high
                              Test Henry L **EURE** Clk

North Carolina} County Court Clerks
Gates County }   office May 2nd/61
[No Reg. #.]   **JOE** the property of Dr Wm.. **WHITE** of Norfolk County County [sic] va and
by him registered to work in the Great Dismal swamp in the County of Gates **JOE** is a
bout Fifty years of age is of a light brown complexion has α sharp features has wide
nostrils high fore head bad teeth a small scar on his back one on the left hand & one
on the side of his right knee & stands without shoes Five feet 7 1/2 inches high
                              Test H. L. **EURE** C.CC

END OF BOOK

SEGUIRE (Cont.)
James S. 335
SEGUI__
James S. 362
SEGUNE
James S. 266,
348
SEQUINE
James S. 110,
169,265(2)
SIKES
Jesse D. 266
SKINNER
Abram 132,272,
286
SMALL
____   137,146,
152,232
James A. 82,
85(2)
Janes A. 83(2),
84
SMITH
Albert 24,86
Edwin 77
Elwin 124
Marian 163
R. R. 123,
151(2),152,227
Ro. R. 126
Robert R. 116,
229(2),251
Robt. R. 127
Sarah 212
Washington 91
SPEED
Kufus Kng 50
R. K. 43
Rufus King 50
SPENCE
James B. 110
James R. 110(2)
SPENCER
Thos. 97
STREPSON
Nancy 76
SUMNER
May C. 44

-T-

TAYLOR
James 235,315
TROTMAN
John L. 168

-U-

None

-V-

VANN
Alfred 164
VOIGHT
Andrew 84,
93(2),95,118,167,
193,234(2),235,
245,246(2),247

-W-

WALTERS
Charles 98
WESTON
Mary 55
WHITE
____   208
Andrew 112
Wm. 367(2),
368(2)
WHITEE
Wm. 366
WHITEHEAD
____   47
W. B. 51,81(2),
113,170(2),171(2),
251(2),286(2),
287(2)-291(2),292,
295
Will. B. 3,

WHITEHEAD (Cont.)
Will. B. (Cont.)
5(2)-7(2),8,9(3),
10(4),11(2),12,26,
28(2)
William B. 27,
28,29,41,48,58(2),
60,106,113,114(2),
115(2),116(2),118,
119(2),120,121(2),
122,153(2),154(2),
156,165,166,170,
172(2)-174(2),175,
181,218,219(2),
220,221(2),222(2),
223
Wm. B. 1(3),
2(3),3,4(2),5,6,
8,12,13(2),26,
27(3),29(2),33,37,
44,46(2),47(2),48,
50,51,52(2),53(2),
56,59(2),60,61(2),
69,80,86,94,103,
106,107,108(2),
120,122,123,137,
143,155(2),175,
212(2),213,220,
250(2),252(2),
253(2),254,267,
268,292,293(2),
294(2),322,326(2),
327(2),328(2)
Wn. B. 60
WHITEHED
W. B. 82
Wm. B. 26
WHITHEAD
Wm. B. 53
WHITTHEAD
Wm. B. 11
WHTEHEAD
Wm. B. 37
WIGGANS
Jessee 340
WIGGINS
Jesse 30,32,40,
88,89,91,105,235,
238
Peny* 48
Willis 108(2)
WILKIN
Samuel 82
WILKINS
Saml. 80,169
Samuel 9,224
W. G. 323
WILLIAMS
Francis 35
WILSON
Anisey 96
Ann 169
William 213
WINSLOW
Cate 160
WOODWARD
____   63
WORKERS
ABRAM [] 235
[19] 220
[21] 151,237
[22] 337
[24] 113
[25] 338
[50] 16
[53] 49
[54] 247
ADDER [40] 71
ADMERAL [13] 28
ALBERT [] 350
[18] 290
[30] 27
[37] 342
ALEXANDER [15]
154
[09] 56
ALFRED [14] 209
[20] 62
ALLEN [20] 222
AMOS [15] 102
ARMSTEAD [12] 67

WORKERS (Cont.)
ARMSTEAD (Cont.)
[19] 291
ARMSTED [16]
267
ARTHUR [31] 340
BASSET* [36]
299
[36-37] 324
BEN [16] 53
[18] 142
[20] 178
[24] 269
[25] 193,300
[37] 90
[40] 144
[65] 46
BENJ [20] 17
BENJAMIN [20] 17
BILL [14] 364
BILLY [18] 170
BOB [] 18
[15] 126
[16] 161
[17] 207
[24] 52
[28] 111
[32] 234
[40] 38
BRATT [12] 315
BRISTO [] 203
[55] 202
BUREL [21] 205
BURELL [21] 205
BURWELL [15] 20
[22] 9
[23] 82
[24] 108
CALVEN* [15], of
LAWRENCE* 277
CALVIN [12] 294
CALVIN* [15], of
LAWRENCE* 277
CARY* [17] 100
CHARLES [] 350
[10], of
James S.
SEGUINE 274
[12] 333
[13] 197
[14] 45,226
[16] 366
[17] 242
[26] 152
[30] 227
[41] 95
[50] 7
[51] 122
CHARLES* [16], of
MILLER 267
CHS. [10], of
James S.
SEGUINE 274
CORNELIUS [15]
28
DANIEL [] 24
[16] 102
[24] 104
[30] 239
[37], of COWPER
265
[61] 65
DANZY [14] 243
DAVID [22] 89
[24] 174
[25] 317
[70] 21,30
DAVY [14] 99
[16] 162
[17] 100
[20] 76
[22] 2
[25] 155,199,
221
[50] 90
[70] 38
DEMPSEY [28]
292
[60] 30
DENIS [36] 55
DENNIS [21] 253

WORKERS (Cont.)
DENNIS (Cont.)
[25] 303
DENPSEY [60] 30
DICK [25] 305
[30] 9
[32] 135
[45] 98,178
[49] 133
DREAD [50] 31
[61] 302
[63] 354
[64] 359
DRED [50] 31
[58] 231
[62] 334
EDGAR [12] 323
[13] 344
EDMOND [] 350
[10] 159
[12] 149
[15] 91
[26] 110
[45] 1
[46] 122
EDMOND* [48], of
BOOTH* 272
[49] 286
EDMUND [11] 186
EDOM [23] 150
[25] 190
EDWARD [47] 341
[48], of James
S. SEGUINE
273
[50] 175,333
[66] 367
ELBERT [20] 192
ELI [28] 116
ELISHA [23] 283
EMMOND [65] 59
ENOCH [40] 25
[41] 64
[42] 128
EVERETTE [20]
73
EVERIT [20] 53
EVERITT [20] 53
FLENERY [22] 54
FOSTER [23] 37
FRANK [30], of
SIKES 266
FRANK* [17] 132
GATES [64] 199
GEOGE [23] 86
GEORE [65] 368
GEORGE [13] 324
[14] 229
[23] 86
[25] 54
[27] 153
[28] 119,194
[30] 245
[40] 6
[52] 156
[58] 302,360
[59] 332
GID [47] 265
GILBERT [] 93
[64] 95,181
[65] 228
[68] 312
[70] 357
GLASCOW [60] 40
GRANBURY [33]
241
GRANVIL [12]
260
GRANVILE [12]
260
GRANVILL [36]
31
GRANVILLE [36]
31
[45] 158
[53] 316
GRATT [12] 315
HANCE [50] 70
HARDY [45] 27
HARMAN [30] 104
[35] 214

WORKERS (Cont.)
HARMAN (Cont.)
[42] 244
HARMON [12] 159
[30] 43
HARMUN [30] 104
HARRISON [18]
22
[19] 70
[21] 187
HARRY [12] 262
[19] 198
[21] 270
[23] 45
HARVEY [21] 114
[22] 253
[27] 176
HENDERSON [18]
23
[27] 11
[28] 121
[30] 223
HENRY [10], of
COWPER 266
[11] 313
HENRY [12] 364
[16] 23
[17] 67,170
[18] 130
[19] 186
[20] 53
[24] 105
[25] 8
[29] 235
[65] 319
HENY [20] 53
[32] 80
HIRAM [29] 269
HYRAM [30] 299
ISAAC [10] 25
[15] 21,331
[16] 20
[17] 74,139
[25] 145
[25], of
SKINNER 272
[26] 255
[28] 167
[30] 4,18,200,
204,286
[32] 216
[33] 32,160,
301
[34] 334
[37] 341
[38] 308
[40] 215
[42] 89
[45] 40
[60] 15,78
ISAC [23] 201
[30] 204
ISAH [25] 189
ISAIAH [24] 234
ISIAH [] 235
[25] 189
ISOM [35] 41
ISRAEL [16] 161
[21] 311
ISREAL [21] 311
JACIT [30] 74
JACK [] 8,201
[11] 361
[20] 33
[21] 116,343
[23] 231
[24] 151
[26] 112,178,
229
[35] 2,277
[37] 135
[40] 50,131,
143,202,209
[41] 238
[45] 5,23
[46] 68
[47] 129
[48] 187
[48], of
RIDDICK 263
[63] 157

WORKERS (Cont.)   WORKERS (Cont.)

DIXON	RIDDICK (Cont.)
Mallory* [17]	Jacob [22] 365
307	Stephen [56]
EDWARDS	172
Peter [50] 58	SAUNDERS
[51] 121	Isaac [15] 36
FAULK	Peter [21] 59
Lorenzo* [35]	SAWYEAR
165	Jim* [16] 171
FAULKS	SAWYER
Henry* [20]	Dick* [12] 261
164	SEGUINE
FOLK	Charles [12]
Justin* [16]	300
56	Edward [49]
FRANKLIN	313
Henry [11] 346	SKEETER
Warich [34] 58	Frank* [21]
Watson [60]	233
346	Jacob* [22]
GRIFFIN	282
Isaac [27] 351	Kinsey* [15]
GRIMES	282
George [50] 34	Kinsy* [15]
[53] 162	282
[56] 245	SMITH
HOPPER	Davy* [12] 163
Owin [42] 34	Watson* [12]
JONES	254
Charles* [36]	SOWERY
63	Lemus [22] 47
Dempay* [] 198	Lomus [22] 47
Dempcy* [] 198	WEBB
Dick* [21] 50	Jo [37] 35
[25] 200	Joe [37] 35
Peter [37] 255	[45] 308
Wm. Henry [14]	[47] 355
364	WHITE
KELLEY	Emanuel [9]
Jethro [18]	208
363	WIGGINS
KELLY	Ben* [18] 48
Jet [14] 362	WILLIAMS
Jethro [14]	Robert [32] 35
362	WINSLOW
MACKEY	William Henry*
Basset* [35]	[10] 160
278	YOUNG
MATTHEWS	Jacob* [66] 37
John* [21] 232	
MELTEER	-X-
Arkey* [25]	
305	None
MILTEAR	
Arkey [24] 187	-Y-
MILTEER	
Arkey* [25]	None
228	
NORFLEET	-Z-
Isaac [40] 352	
John [53] 350	None
PEARCE	
Davey* [14]	INCOMPLETE NAMES
295	
Davy* [14] 295	BOOTH* 272
John* [13] 294	BOOTHE* 286
Siah* [16] 293	COWPER 265,266,
PERKINS	313
William* [13]	LAWRENCE* 277
213	MILLER* 267
REED	RIDDICK 263
Dempsey* [20]	SIKES 266
39	SKINNER 272
Hardy* [30]	____LEY
208	____ 4
Mills* [10]	
156	
Richard* [18]	
184	
REID	
Allen* [25]	
247	
Hardy* [21]	
107	
Henry* [15] 28	
Juston* [19]	
306	
Mills* [17] 29	
RIDDICK	
Jack [27] 298	

DISMAL SWAMP CANAL

CONNECTING CHESAPEAKE AND
ALBEMARLE-CURRITUCK AND PAMLICO SOUNDS
AND THEIR TRIBUTARY STREAMS

D. S. WALTON, CIVIL ENGINEER

1867